The Magic Lotus Lantern and Other Tales from the Han Chinese

World Folklore Advisory Board

The Magic Lotus Lantern and Other Tales from the Han Chinese

Haiwang Yuan

World Folklore Series

Foreword by Michael Ann Williams

A Member of the Greenwood Publishing Group

Westport, Connecticut • London

Library of Congress Cataloging-in-Publication Data

Yuan, Haiwang.
  The magic lotus lantern and other tales from the Han Chinese / By Haiwang Yuan ;
  Foreword by Michael Ann Williams.
      p. cm. — (World folklore series)
  Includes bibliographical references and index.
  ISBN 1-59158-294-6 (alk. paper)
  1. Tales—China. I. Title. II. Series.
  GR335.Y72   2006
  398.20951—dc22   2006011702

British Library Cataloguing in Publication Data is available.

Library of Congress Catalog Card Number: 2006011702
ISBN: 1-59158-294-6

First published in 2006

Libraries Unlimited, 88 Post Road West, Westport, CT 06881
A Member of the Greenwood Publishing Group, Inc.
www.lu.com

Printed in the United States of America

∞™

The paper used in this book complies with the
Permanent Paper Standard issued by the National
Information Standards Organization (Z39.48–1984).

10 9 8 7 6 5 4 3 2 1

The publisher has done its best to make sure the instructions and/or recipes in this book are correct. However, users should apply judgment and experience when preparing recipes, especially parents and teachers working with young people. The publisher accepts no responsibility for the outcome of any recipe included in this volume.

For my mother and father

CONTENTS

FOREWORD

For many Americans, China is a mystery, due to the vast differences between Chinese and American cultures. This book intends to lead American readers into that unfamiliar territory through a doorway painted with fascinating tales from Chinese tradition.

China has produced countless tales of various genres in its 5,000-year history. The tales transmitted from generation to generation, by mouth and in print, have gone through a long process of transformation, changing with the growth of Chinese culture. The narratives are expressions of the Chinese people's wisdom, records of their lives, and reflections of their thinking. This book includes fifty-four tales of the Han Chinese, who constitute the largest ethnic group of China, totaling 91.5 percent of its entire population. Of these tales, seven were collected from oral sources in China by the author. Although the majority of the tales contain materials based on either written sources or performing arts, this is the first time they have been retold and published together in English in a World Folklore Series book, along with notes about folklore motif numbers and descriptions. Conscientiously selected and divided into the categories of animal; magic, love and romance; myth, legend, and immortals; moral; how things came to be. and proverbial tales, they are good representations of the Han Chinese folk narrative tradition.

Preceding the tales, Part 1 familiarizes American readers with the Chinese land, people, languages, history, religion, customs, literature, and performing and fine arts, as well as providing an account of Chinese storytelling. Part 2 highlights traditional Chinese food, spiced with a dozen recipes; Chinese pastimes with instructions for popular children's games; and a brief introduction to Chinese crafts, with examples that offer easy-to-follow directions. Rather than being a simple storybook, this collection offers a rich context in which to understand Chinese folktales.

This book is notable for its flowing text, enchanting stories, and captivating photos and pictures. Readers of all ages and walks of life will find the volume useful, including students, school teachers and librarians, instructors of Chinese, folklorists, travelers and businesspeople who plan to visit China, and everyone who has an interest in Chinese culture.

Cultures of the world may differ in many ways, but human desires and aspirations are the same; peace, justice, love, and happiness are the themes of many of the tales included in this book. These tales, which have already moved Chinese people for generations, are bound to touch the heart of American readers as well. Retold and interpreted by the author, who has a deep understanding of both Chinese and American cultures, the tales in this book, annotated with insightful background information, will engage American readers who wish to comprehend the ancient and rich tales of the Han Chinese.

Michael Ann Williams, Ph.D.
Head, Department of Folk Studies and Anthropology
Western Kentucky University

ACKNOWLEDGMENTS

With deep gratitude, I proclaim that this book would not have been possible without help from many people. First, I want to thank Barbara Ittner, my excellent editor, for her trust in my writing and for being so readily accessible for consultation. I am also indebted to Sharon DeJohn, who worked on the manuscript of the book. At the same time, I want to give thanks to Western Kentucky University's Faculty Summer Scholarship Committee for funding my fieldwork in China. I am grateful to Dr. Mike Binder, Dean of WKU Libraries, and his office staff for giving me all the support I needed. My appreciation goes to WKU professors Dr. Brian Coutts, Connie Foster, Dawn Hall, and Roxanne Spencer, as well as student Nicole Whitescarver and Kaylee Holloway, who kindly proofread my manuscript. I want to thank Dr. Michael Ann Williams, Dr. Christopher Antonsen, and Dr. Erika Brady from the WKU Department of Folk Studies and Anthropology for sharing their knowledge with me. I am indebted to Wang Kai, Sun Dongyan, and Tu Shupo for introducing me to the storytellers in China. Su Chuanzhi and the Quanyechang Elementary School in Tianjin, China, provided me with the opportunity to photograph their schoolchildren playing traditional games. Members of my extended family in China—my niece Ding Ling in particular—have been wonderfully supportive and provided many of the needed materials that I could not easily access from America. My colleagues Bryan Carson and Gayle Novick graciously looked after our house while I took my family on my research trip to China. I am grateful to my Web site team members, who helped maintain the University Libraries' Web sites during my absence. I am obliged to the Copyright Department of Baihua Wenyi Chubanshe, Tianjin, China, for allowing me to use some of the illustrations in the book. My gratitude also goes to my English professors at Nankai University and Nankai Teachers' School, Tianjin, China, particularly my late father-in-law, Professor Gao Diansen, and two other of my English mentors, Professors Chang Yaoxin and Wu Yanquan. My fellow Nankai University 1977 classmates offered continual encouragement and moral support. Finally, my thanks go to my wife Shizhen and our son Hao, who have shared every one of the bitter and sweet moments while I was writing this book.

INTRODUCTION

When I was a child, I was never tired of listening to my mother tell how two little sisters outsmarted a treacherous big wolf and to my father recount the Herculean deed of a greenwood hero who subdued a man-eating tiger single-handedly. My mother's story had been retold to her by my grandmother. My father's story was one he had read in an ancient classic. That is roughly how Chinese folktales came to be: from oral as well as written traditions. That is also how my interest in folktales originated. In a word, my parents sowed the seed of interest in me at an early age.

The emergence of Web publication gave me a venue in which I can bring this interest in Chinese folktales into full play. After I came to the United States from China and became a professor and librarian, I began to turn my interest into a self-assigned duty: I wanted to play the role of a cultural bridge, sharing the stories I had heard, read, and watched (performing art, like opera, is another way of preserving and telling stories in China) with an American audience. Extensive research made it possible for me to retell the stories of more than thirty prominent women found in Chinese folktales, legends, and ancient literature. I published these tales on my personal Web site. When I learned about the World Folklore Series produced by Libraries Unlimited, I proposed to write this book.

China has fifty-six ethnic groups. A single story from each would be more than a 200-page book can hold. The largest of the ethnic groups is the Han, so I felt that retelling a fine assortment of tales from the Han Chinese would be a good start. This was easier said than done, for, like all the other ethnic groups, the Han Chinese boast a reservoir of countless tales. I made sure that tales included in the book are well-known to the Chinese, such as the four classic folktales "Butterfly Lovers," "Xu Xuan and His White-snake Wife," "Meng Jiang Wails at the Great Wall," and "Cowherd and Weaving Girl." I have also included tales from renowned classic Chinese fiction, such as the two Monkey King stories and those authored by a Qing writer from his "Make-do Studio." I also selected tales made famous by the performing arts, such as "The Magic Lotus Lantern" and "A Forsaken Wife and Her Unfaithful Husband." Legendary demigods, heroes, and heroines, such as Nezha, Mulan, Mu Guiying, Bao Zheng, and Ji Gong, who have become household names, are of course covered here as well. I made a research trip to China to collect half a dozen tales from Chinese storytellers. While making sure that the stories retold in the book are popular among the Chinese, I tried to cover a broad range of story types and group them into several categories. I aimed to give the American reader a better perspective on Chinese tales, and thereby also on the multiple facets of Chinese culture. "The Origin of the *Duanwu* Festival" is the only exception to this rule, because it is a rarely heard version of a story very well known to the average Chinese. Its regional flavor, however, has its own merit, and it is therefore collectible.

This book of tales, aided by a brief introduction to many aspects of China—its land and people, its art and food, and its crafts and games—and background information about specific stories, is intended for readers of all ages and for all purposes. Schoolchildren can read the tales just for fun; librarians and teachers can use them for read-aloud and story time; older children can use the book to do research on China and Chinese storytelling; adoptive parents may find the book useful to bring them closer to their adopted children from China; college instructors of elementary Chinese may use the book as a cultural supplement; and businesspeople and travelers will find the book helpful in preparing them for a land in which they may never have set their foot. However you use the book, it is hoped that these stories bring you enjoyment and a deeper understanding of traditional Chinese culture.

Locations of provinces, autonomous regions and municipalities

Xingjiang

Gansu

Inner Mongolia

Beijing

Heilongjiang

Jilin

Liaoning

Tianjin

Ningxia

Hebei

Qinghai

Shanxi

Shandong

Shannxi

Henan

Jiangsu

Tibet

Sichuan

Hubei

Anhui

Shanghai

Chongqinge

Zhejiang

Jiangxi

Hunan

Guizhou

Fujian

Yunnan

Guangxi

Guangdong

Taiwan

Macao

Hong Kong

Hainan

Islands of South China Sea

Map of China. Courtesy of *People's Daily Online,* available at
http://english1.people.com.cn/china/19990923A101.html.

Part 1

A General Introduction to China

Yangtze, China's longest river.

LAND

Located on the west coast of the Pacific Ocean in East Asia, China has an area of 9.6 million square kilometers (3.7 million square miles), about the same area as the United States. The total length of its border is over 22,000 kilometers (13,671 miles). To the east lies North Korea; to the north, Mongolia; to the northeast and northwest, Russia; to the west and northwest, Afghanistan and several Central Asian countries; to the southwest, Pakistan, India, and other South Asian countries. Directly to the south lie Vietnam, Laos, and Myanmar. Across the seas to the east and southeast lie South Korea, Japan, the Philippines, Brunei, Malaysia, and Indonesia. To China's east and south are the Bohai, Yellow, East China, and South China Seas. They form a 14,500-kilometer (9,010-mile) coastline and embrace about 5,400 islands, the largest being Hainan and Taiwan.

More than 1,500 rivers run through China. The Yangtze, Yellow, Heilongjiang, Pearl, Liaohe, Haihe, Huaihe, Lancang, and Yarlungzangbo are among the longest. Most flow from west to east into the Pacific Ocean. The Yangtze, 6,300 kilometers (3,915 miles) long, is a few dozen miles short of the distance from Los Angeles, California, to Washington, D.C. It is the third longest river in the world, after the Nile (4,160 miles) in northeast Africa and the Amazon (4,000 miles) in South America.

Mountains abound in China. Only 15.4 percent of its land is fit for farming (CIA 2004). A bird's-eye view of the land surface shows that China descends in four steps from west to east. The first step is the Qinghai-Tibet Plateau. Averaging 4,000 meters (about 13,123 feet) above sea level, it is known as "the roof of the world." The tallest part of the plateau, the Himalayas, is famous for the 8,844.43-meter (about 29,017-foot)-high Mt. Qomolangma. The second step includes the Yunnan-Guizhou plateaus and the Sichuan basins, with an average elevation of 1,000 to 2,000 meters (3,281 to 6,562 feet). The third step rises about 500 to 1,000 meters (1,640 to 3,281 feet) above sea level. It covers a series of mountain ranges and plains in Northeast, North, and South China, reaching all the way to the east coast. The fourth step is the continental shelf, spreading out into the ocean floor to a depth of about 200 meters (656 feet) (Permanent ' Mission of China to the United Nations 2004).

China extends 5,500 kilometers (3,417.6 miles) from north to south, mostly in the temperate zone. As a result, the majority of Chinese experience four distinct seasons and varied climate conditions. The cold and dry winds from Siberia and Mongolia in the north are in a

---

constant tug-of-war with the warm and moist monsoonal winds from the south, resulting in cold, dry winters and hot, rainy summers.

China spans four time zones from east to west in the Eastern Hemisphere. When the Chinese in the far west are still asleep, those on the Pacific Ocean are already bathed in sunshine. Nevertheless, the Chinese are accustomed to a single Beijing Standard Time. That is, they do not observe the four distinct time zones, and even when it is dark at 8:00 A.M. in the west and bright and sunny in the east, it is still considered 8:00 A.M. in both places.

Additional Reading

Field, Catherine. *China*. Oxford: Raintree, 2004. 128pp. $37.07. ISBN 0817257810.

Population

China is by far the most populous country in the world. Two minutes after midnight on January 6, 2005, China's official news agency, Xinhua, announced that the country's 1.3 billionth baby had been born in the Beijing Gynecology and Obstetrics Hospital ("China Welcomes 1.3 Billionth Citizen in Mixed Mood" 2005). China's population is about 4.4 times that of the United States, which, according to the 2000 U.S. census, has 281,421,906 people. To use another frame of reference, one out of every five people in the world is Chinese. This number includes the 6,882,600 residents in Hong Kong ("Hong Kong in Figures" 2005), 448, 500 in Macao ("2004 Macao in Figures" 2005), and 22,703,295 in Taiwan ("Registered Population" 2005).

Historically, China has been an agrarian country. Since its economic reform in 1978, however, the pace of its urbanization has accelerated. The 2000 census revealed that China's urban population had reached about 456 million, accounting for slightly more than 36 percent of the total population. That number did not include another 100 million *liudong renkou* (floating population), who are mostly farmers seeking job opportunities in cities.

During the early 1950s, China followed the then Soviet Union's example and encouraged larger families, despite some experts' warning of imminent overpopulation. Then, starting in the late 1960s, China began to enforce a stringent, unpopular family-planning policy among the Han Chinese, which encourages mostly city residents to have only one child, excepting families with handicapped children. Economic and administrative penalties have never been effective, while overzealous local administrators and social workers sometimes go beyond the law to fulfill self-imposed quotas. With the growth of China's economy, however, there have been more voices calling for the reexamination of this policy and its social impact on the country.

Ethnicity

China is a multi-ethnic nation. Officially, it has fifty-six ethnic groups. Each has a distinct culture of its own, ranging from languages, customs, and artifacts to clothing, architecture, and food. The Han nationality is the largest, accounting for 91.5 percent of the country's total population. Therefore, the rest of the ethnic groups are referred to as *shaoshu minzu*, meaning "national minority" or "minority nationality."

Most of the *shaoshu minzu* live in the border regions of China. There are twenty-five minority ethnic groups in the remote southern province of Yunnan alone. Some of the *shaoshu minzu* in China, like the Hui and Manchu, have largely merged with the Han Chinese. Seven of the *shaoshu minzu* each have a population of over five million. Zhuang, with its 15,489,630 people, is the largest minority group. Loba is the smallest; the 1990 census showed that it has only 2,312 people. Large or small, *shaoshu minzu* in China have generally enjoyed a peaceful and harmonious relationship among themselves and with the Han Chinese.

Definition of Han Chinese

All Chinese, despite their citizenship, claim a common ancestry known as Huaxia. The word *Huaxia* represents the ancient Hua and Xia tribes, who cohabited throughout their histories. Hence, Huaren (people of Hua) has become a general term for people of Chinese origin all over the world. A Chinese citizen is specifically referred to as Zhongguoren (a person of China or Chinese). Chinese citizens refer to their compatriots residing in foreign countries as Huaqiao and those who became American citizens as Meiji Huaren.

The Chinese call their country *Zhongguo* (Middle Kingdom) while the English-speaking world refers to it as "China." The origin of the term "China" for "*Zhongguo*" is somewhat of a mystery. Some argue that it stems from the name of the Qin dynasty (221 B.C.–206 B.C.), because it is pronounced as "chin." Another argument, however, attributes the term "China" to *cha* (tea), a favorite Chinese beverage exported to the West via the Silk Road. Still others view it as a derivative of the word "Cina," a name that ancient India gave to its northern neighbor.

The term "Hanren" came into use much later in Chinese history. In 1644, the Manchus from Northeast China conquered the rest of the country and ruled over it for more than two and a half centuries. In the nineteenth century, the Chinese, bent on overthrowing the rule of a minority nationality that they considered to be barbarous, began to call themselves Hanren (Han Chinese). The word "Han" was borrowed from the Han dynasty (206 B.C.–200 B.C.), which was a successor of the Qin Empire.

Additional Reading

Ferroa, Peggy Grace, and Elaine Chan. *China*. New York: Benchmark Books/Marshall Cavendish, 2005. 144pp. ISBN: 0761414746.

**A rubbing of a painted stone from the Han dynasty (206 B.C.–A.D. 220).
Courtesy of Baihua Literature and Art Publishing House.**

LANGUAGES

Putonghua (Common Speech of the Chinese Language), known to Westerners as Mandarin, is the official language of China. It is taught in most Chinese schools; in ethnic regions like Tibet, *Putonghua* and local ethnic languages are taught concurrently. Chinese students start to learn a foreign language, usually English, from an early age—some in kindergarten, some in elementary school, and most in middle school. Although spoken Chinese has many dialects with varied pronunciations, the written system is the standard *hanzi* (Chinese characters), hieroglyphics rather than an alphabet to represent words or syllables. Unlike other Romanized languages (such as French and Italian), which have several hundred pronunciations, *Putonghua* has slightly more than 400. There could have been a tremendous number of homophones (words with the same pronunciations) but for a system of four distinct tones for each syllable—level, rising, falling-rising, and falling—marked respectively by the symbols "–," "/," "v," and "\". A different tone given to the same syllable may produce an entirely different meaning, represented by a different *hanzi* or Chinese character. For instance, the syllable "fei" means "fly" in the level tone, but "fat" in the rising tone. The ideas of "machine" and "chicken" share a homophone, "ji." Combining these two syllables while changing the tones of "fei" results in very different meanings. A level-toned "fei" plus "ji" means "flying machine," which is "an airplane," but a rising-toned "fei" combined with "ji" (a different word with the same tone) refers to "a heavy chicken." There are more examples of these subtle variations in language in the "Customs" chapter.

While the second edition of the *Oxford English Dictionary* contains full entries for 171,476 English words in current use ("How Many Words Are There in the English Language?" 2004), the *Zhonghua zi hai* (*China's Sea of Words*), the largest Chinese dictionary, registers only 85,000 characters, and most of them have become outdated. In 1998, the Chinese government issued a table of 2,500 most frequently used Chinese characters plus an additional 1,000 less frequently used characters. Armed with a vocabulary of about 8,000 words formed by these 3,500 characters, one can conduct fluent conversations with native Chinese and read Chinese newspapers and magazines with the help of a collegiate Chinese-English dictionary.

A language with its written system and spoken tongue independent of each other is very difficult to learn. For that reason, the Chinese have created an auxiliary phonetic system called *Hanyu Pinyin* (Chinese Phonetic Alphabet) to help the Chinese as well as foreigners learn *hanzi* and to facilitate printing Chinese in foreign publications such as this book.

Computers initially presented a great challenge to inputting and displaying Chinese characters and thereby gave rise to sporadic calls for alphabetizing the Chinese language. In 1983, however, Wang Yongmin, a computer science professor from Beijing University, resolved the crisis by inventing *wubi shuma* (five-stroke *hanzi* input and display method), making it possible for the oldest writing system in the world to marry with the latest information technology.

Additional Reading

DeFrancis, John. *The Chinese Language: Fact and Fantasy*. Reprint ed. Honolulu: University of Hawaii Press, 1986. 330pp. $21pa. ISBN 0824810686.

DeFrancis, John, ed. *ABC Chinese-English Comprehensive Dictionary*. Honolulu: University of Hawaii Press, 2003. 1439pp. $59. ISBN 082482766X.

HISTORY

Like Egypt, Greece, and India, China has a very ancient history. Archeological finds from the cultural sites of Cishan and Peiligang in the Yellow River Basin reveal 7,900-year-old early Neolithic civilizations (An 1984). However, before Chinese historians knew better, they could only trace a documented history of 2,800 years. Between 1996 and 2000, the government-sponsored Xia-shang-zhou Chronology Project added another 1,200 years (from 2100 B.C. to 771 B.C.) to China's recorded history, making it a total of 4,000 years.

The Chinese believe that they all came from the common ancestors *Sanhuang Wudi* (three primordial sovereigns and five legendary emperors), namely, Taihao (Fuxishi); Yandi (Shennongshi); Huangdi (Yellow Emperor); and Shaohao, Zhuanxu (Gaoyangshi), Diku (Gaoxinshi), Yao, and Shun, referring to themselves as *Yanhuang zisun* (descendants of Yandi and Huangdi).

According to Chinese legends, before *Sanhuang wudi* there lived another two mythical leaders named Youchaoshi (The Nest Builder) and Suirenshi (The Fire Builder). Prior to them were the alleged creators of the universe and mankind, Pangu and Nüwa, whose stories are retold in this book.

From the first Xia monarch to the last Qing emperor in a span of 4,018 years, numerous dynasties and a total of 419 kings and emperors came and went in China. Notable in history were the following dynasties, under which China was largely unified:

Xia (2200 B.C.–1750 B.C.)

Shang (1750 B.C.–1040 B.C.)

Zhou (1100 B.C.–256 B.C.)

Qin (221 B.C.–206 B.C.)

Han (206 B.C.–A.D. 220)

Sui (A.D. 581–618)

Tang (A.D. 618–907)

Song (A.D. 960–1279)

Yuan (A.D. 1279–1368)

Ming (A.D. 1368–1644)

Qing (A.D. 1644–1911)

The Zhou dynasty was particularly important to the development of China. During its middle phase (772 B.C.–481 B.C.), known as the Spring and Autumn Period, Confucius and a multitude of other thinkers were free to express themselves. Laozi, also known as Lao Tzu, whose legend is recounted in this book, also lived during this period.

Eventually the state of Qin established China's first centralized imperial government, in 221 B.C. Its monarch, Ying Zheng, gave himself the name *Shihuangdi* (The First Emperor). Although he was deemed cruel, he left such monumental legacies as the Great Wall, a unified system of currency and measurement, and a standardized writing system that is still in use today.

The next prominent empire in Chinese history was the Tang dynasty (A.D. 618–907). Its influence is still visible today, for example, in the name of overseas Chinese communities known as *Tangrenjie* (Chinatown), meaning "Streets of the Tang People."

Emperors Kangxi (1662–1723), Yongzheng (1723–1736), and Qianlong (1736–1796) are remembered as the best of the Qing monarchs; they oversaw a unified and prosperous China. Beginning in the nineteenth century, however, Qing began to spiral into decline and experienced invasions from a coalition of foreign powers, including Britain, France, Germany, Austria, Italy, Japan, Russia, and the United States. As a result of the Opium War in 1840, China ceded Hong Kong to Britain (reclaimed in 1997). Threatened with wars, China also ceded Macao to Portugal in 1887 (reclaimed in 1998), large pieces of land to Russia in 1858, and the island of Taiwan to Japan in 1895 (reclaimed in 1945).

In 1911, Dr. Sun Yat-sen's Nationalist Revolution overthrew the Qing government and founded the Republic of China. At the time, warlords rampant in north China posed a serious threat to the new republic. As its first president, Dr. Sun led a coalition of Nationalists and Communists in a military campaign against the warlords, known as the North Expedition. Unfortunately, Sun's untimely death in 1925 brought the expedition to an abrupt end. The First Civil War broke out between the Nationalists, now led by Chiang Kai-shek (or Jiang Jieshi), and the Communists, eventually led by Mao Zedong (or Mao Tse-tung). Japan's all-out invasion of China in 1939 led to a temporary Nationalist–Communist united front to fight the aggressors. In the wake of Japan's surrender in 1945, however, the Second Civil War ensued. Defeated in 1949, the Nationalists retreated to Taiwan, where they continued to claim the Republic of China, established by Dr. Sun Yat-sen. In the meantime, the Communists on the mainland renamed China the People's Republic of China and claimed Taiwan as a renegade province.

During its first three decades, the People's Republic of China made great achievements. Land reform ended the feudal land system, water conservation efforts helped build thousands of reservoirs, a call to serve the people brought basic health care to millions in rural areas, and scientific and technological research sent China's first satellite into orbit around the earth. At the same time, however, China suffered a great deal from Mao Zedong's obsession with mass movements and class struggles. For example, the irrational Great Leap Forward from 1958 to 1960 was a mad dash toward socialist industrialization, aimed at catching up with, if not surpassing, capitalist Great Britain and United States, through collective labor in communes and state-owned enterprises. The Great Leap Forward was notorious for such absurdities as killing off pest-eating sparrows, which were mistakenly thought to deprive farmers of their crops; producing tons of useless iron from shoddy furnaces that melted household utensils as raw materials; and inflating agricultural output figures by transplanting harvested crops to designated fields. China suffered grave consequences, and a protracted drought was the straw that broke the camel's back, for it caused a famine that soon killed tens of millions of Chinese. In 1966, before China had fully recovered from the catastrophe, Mao led the country into another disaster by initiating the "Great Cultural Revolution." Intended to cleanse China of "capitalist evils" and their "king-pin" Liu Shaoqi, then president of the country, the revolution got out of hand when it was placed under the leadership of Lin Biao, Mao's hand-picked successor, who later betrayed him, and "the Gang of Four," namely Mao's wife Jiang Qing and three political associates. The Cultural Revolution further isolated China from the rest of the world and played havoc with every aspect of the Chinese people's lives. By 1976, when the Cultural Revolution was brought to an end with the death of Mao and the arrest of the Gang of Four, China had experienced horrendous human rights violations: Tens of thousands of its people, particularly intellectuals and entrepreneurs, perished due to persecution, as did President Liu Shaoqi. The country was literally on the brink of bankruptcy, with every daily necessity—from salt and eggs to matches and bicycles—rationed. China's legal system had been shattered, its social order disrupted, and its cultural legacies nearly destroyed.

Beginning in 1978, China, under the leadership of Deng Xiaoping, took on the monumental task of reforming its economy and opening it to the outside world. He first abolished the "communes," a Soviet system of farming that collectivized all modes of production and consequently smothered individual initiative. He then allowed private ownership of property and capital and invited foreign investment into the country. The reform was not without its difficulties. High inflation and complaints about government corruption culminated in students' and urban residents' protests in 1989; these were suppressed by the government for fear of another period of chaos such as that of the "Cultural Revolution. The apparent harsh treatment of the protesters at Tiananmen Square brought international condemnation and temporary economic sanctions.

Nevertheless, Deng Xiaoping did not stop the pace of reform, but instead accelerated it. As a result, remarkable changes have taken place over the past two decades. Today, China's economy has become one of the largest in the world. Only a quarter of a century ago, the dream of average Chinese was to own "three machines with wheels and one with sound," namely, a bicycle, watch, sewing machine, and radio. Today, however, their goal has become the possession of an automobile, a furnished house, and high-yielding stocks. Awed spectators of foreign tourists have become tourists themselves in almost all the Asian and European countries. Over ten million privately owned cars travel on some 41,000 kilometers (25,477 miles) of superhighways, a road system second in length only to that of the United States. China may still have a long way to go before it becomes a democratic, prosperous, and powerful nation like those in Europe and North America, but its people are definitely enjoying more political, social, and financial freedom than ever before.

Additional Reading

Jiang, Ji-li. *Red Scarf Girl: A Memoir of the Cultural Revolution.* New York: HarperCollins, 1997. 285pp. $6.99pa. ISBN 0060275855.

Khanduri, Kamini. *Great History Search.* London: Usborne Publishing, 2003. 48pp. $9.95. ISBN 0794504272.

Roberts, J. A. *Concise History of China.* Cambridge, Mass.: Harvard University Press, 2000. 368pp. $18.98. ISBN 0674000757.

RELIGION

Religious belief is a constitutional right in China, although separation of religious activities from political life and independence of churches from foreign decrees have been the official position since the establishment of New China in 1949. Today, there are an estimated 17 to 75 million professed Protestants and Catholics, around 25 million Muslims, and countless followers of Buddhism and Taoism in China (Ji 2003, 123). In addition, many more Chinese are, to a lesser or greater degree, believers in the Chinese popular religion, explained below.

Confucianism and Taoism are indigenous Chinese beliefs. More a code of ethical, social, and political behaviors than a religious denomination, Confucianism originated from a collection of sayings and works allegedly compiled by Confucius, who advocated the individual's self-cultivation and the government's benevolent rule. Contributing to Confucianism were Mencius (372 B.C.–287 B.C.), Zhu Xi (1130–1200), and several other Confucian scholars. Mencius taught that men were all originally good but subject to the environment in which they lived. Zhu Xi promoted *Sangang wuchang* (Three Cardinal Guides and Five Constant Virtues). *Sangang* means "a ruler guides his subjects; a father, his children; and a husband, his wife"; *wuchang* indicates *ren* (benevolence), *yi* (righteousness), *li* (propriety), *zhi* (wisdom), and *xin* (fidelity).

Confucian temples are called *wenmiao* (temple of literati), and they look very much like Buddhist temples. The Confucian Festival takes place annually from September 26 through October 10 in Qufu, Shangdong province, Confucius's birthplace. Elaborate rituals of paying homage to the sage are part of the event.

The original philosophy of Taoism owed its existence to a book, *Tao Te Ching* (*The Book of Tao*), attributed to Laozi (or Lao Tzu), a deified Chinese thinker of the sixth century B.C. Laozi believed that everything in the universe consisted of two opposite elements, the *yin* and the *yang*. The *Tao* was the invisible hand that held the *yin* and *yang* together as an organic whole. If *yin* and *yang* were unbalanced, all troubles would follow. Therefore, the pursuit of a Taoist was to seek harmony with the universe. However, this obsession with a quest for integrating humanity with nature eventually gave rise to the belief in immortality and the establishment of the Church of Tao by a Taoist named Zhang Daoling (A.D. 34–156). He promised his followers they could become immortals by doing good deeds. Various superstitious sects and secret societies under the guise of the Taoist church ran rampant until 1949, when the new communist government suppressed them. Taoist priests wear quiet costumes and do not shave their heads as the Buddhist monks do. They call their temples *guan,* while Buddhists and Confucians call theirs *miao.*

Buddhism entered China around the first century A.D. and became popular two centuries later, when protracted warfare among rival states inflicted great misery upon the people. Buddhism became a source of comfort by preaching that desires were the cause of all pains, and that meditation could help a person reach nirvana, or the end of sufferings. Today, Han Chinese generally subscribe to the *Xiaocheng* (Hinayana) sect of Buddhism, while Tibetans and Inner Mongolians believe in Lamaism, a branch of Buddhism mingled with elements of indigenous religions.

Catholicism and Islam came to China around the seventh century A.D., and Protestantism arrived in the early nineteenth century along with foreign missionaries and business interests. While numerous Hui (Muslim) people mingle with the Han Chinese in other parts of the country, there are still two enclaves of Muslims in Northwest China: the Ningxia Huizu Autonomous Region and the Xinjiang Uigur Autonomous Region.

Chinese popular religion is a catchall term for a medley of inherent Chinese beliefs bordering on religion and superstition. The influence of these beliefs on the Chinese is particularly apparent in their observance of traditional festivals and occasions such as weddings and funerals. For example, before and during the Chinese New Year season, the Chinese observe a series of rituals and conventions. One in particular is to bribe Zao Wangye (Kitchen God) so that he can put in a favorable word for the family when he pays his annual visit to the Jade Emperor of Heaven. "The Origin of Kitchen God and the *Jizao* Festival" is included in Part 3 of this book.

Popular religion permeates Chinese legends and folktales, which you may notice in many tales retold here. Classical fantasies—such as *Shan hai jing* (*The Book of Mountains and Seas*), *Fengshen yanyi* (*A Historical Romance of Apotheosization*), *Liaozhai zhiyi* (*Strange Stories from a Make-do Studio*), *Xi you ji* (*Journey to the West*)—and a myriad of oral traditions have helped establish a polytheistic hierarchy. This hierarchy, in many ways, copies that of the mundane world: There are kings, ministers, generals, and maids of honor in both Heaven and the Netherworld. Gods and goddesses are omnipresent. Like the deities in the Greek mythology, they have human desires and weaknesses. Some marry earthlings, as does *Qixiannü* (the seventh fairy) in "Cowherd and Weaving Girl"; some are deified human beings, like the immortal Lü Dongbin in "A Dancing Crane"; some are exiles to Earth from heaven, like the couple in "The Origin of Mid-Autumn Festival"; and others are reborn to different beings, such as Piggy in "Monkey King Strikes at the White-bone Demon Three Times." The concept of immortality is taken from Taoism and the idea of reincarnation from Buddhism.

Additional Reading

Houghton, Gillian. *China: A Primary Source Cultural Guide.* New York: Rosen Publishing Group, 2005. 128pp. ISBN 1404229086.

Quinn, Daniel P. *I Am a Buddhist.* New York: Rosen Publishing Group, 2003. 24pp. ISBN 0823923797.

帝大皇玉

Yuhuang Dadi, the supreme deity of the Chinese popular religion.
Courtesy of Baihua Literature and Art Publishing House.

CUSTOMS

As mentioned in the "Languages" chapter, Chinese characters are first created as hieroglyphs, or pictorial symbols that represent meanings. A great number of *hanzi*, or Chinese characters, are homophones, having different meanings but sharing the same pronunciations and intonations. For these reasons, the Chinese are expert in playing on words and symbols. Following are a few examples.

Unlike cultures that associate bats with darkness and evil, the Chinese use the symbol of bats for decoration because the Chinese word for bat, pronounced "fu," sounds the same as the word for "happiness"! Another example is a very popular Chinese New Year painting motif, which involves a combination of sounds and symbols: a chubby boy riding on a fish in a pond full of lotus leaves and flowers. Every Chinese knows that this mosaic means "*liannian youyu*" (more than sufficiently provided for years running) because the pronunciation of lotus, "lian," sounds like "for years running," and the fish, "yu," sounds the same as "more than sufficient."

The most popular words on which to play are *fu* (happiness), *xi* (good marriage), *lu* (official salary), *shou* (longevity), and *ning* (peace). One of the symbols for *xi* is a coined double-character word representing a happily married couple, who can also be embodied by a pair of butterflies or mandarin ducks. The symbol of *lu* is often a figure in traditional official costume. The symbols for longevity include peaches, pines, cranes, and *laoshouxing* (a gray-haired old saint with a bulging forehead).

When you see a motorcade parading along a city street in China, do not mistake it for a funeral. In fact, it is a wedding procession! Chinese brides prefer being chauffeured to the bridegroom's home, as their grandmothers were in a sedan chair in the old days. Traditionally, the costume of the bride must be red, as this is the color of celebration and happiness. Young brides today, however, are fond of white wedding gowns, a custom they have learned from the West. Their grandmothers would never have worn white wedding clothes, because white and black were, and still are, the colors of a funeral. Attending upon a dying senior relative and handling his or her funeral affairs are acts of *songzhong*. Unfortunately, *songzhong* sounds the same as the act of giving a clock to someone as a present. So *never* choose a clock as a present for Chinese people, no matter where they live in the world. Watches are fine because the Chinese word for them is "*biao*," which is an entirely different pronunciation.

There are so many customs and taboos in Chinese culture that it would take an entire book to discuss them all. Here we just cover how to be a host and guest in China. The Chinese often find Americans rather direct upon first meeting them. That is because the Chinese themselves often say things in a roundabout way. For example, even though the great poet Li Bai (A.D. 701–762) knew he was very famous, he said humbly to a governor, "I have assembled some scrolls with which I would wish to soil your sight and sully your hearing, though I fear my minuscule talent of writing poetry is unworthy of attention from such a great man as yourself" (Birch 1967, 234). A modern counterpart of this story is a cultural misunderstanding between a visiting Chinese professor and his American students. The professor opened his first lecture with a traditionally modest statement that he had used in front of his Chinese audience, something like, "I don't know much about the topic. Please put up with my ignorance," although in fact he was an expert in the field. The American students, however, took what he said at face value. One exasperated student stood up and said bluntly, "If you don't know much, why do you have to waste our time?" The moral is, you cannot take what the Chinese say literally, as they tend to be over-modest and courteous, a way to show their respect. If you ask a Chinese person to stay for dinner, he or she will say "no" the first, second, or even third time you ask, even if he or she wishes to accept the invitation.

You may notice how some of your Chinese friends respond when they are served a cup of tea. Instead of expressing their gratitude verbally, some may choose to make a low-profile gesture with their fingers. Hooking up their middle and forefingers, they gently and quietly tap their knuckles on the table a few times. The gesture used to be a custom of the Cantonese but has spread all over China in recent decades. This custom stems from a legend about Emperor Qianlong of the Qing dynasty, who liked to tour South China to get firsthand knowledge of his people's living conditions. To avoid being detected, he and his small group of accompanying servants were dressed like ordinary folks. One day Qianlong took his servants by surprise when he served them tea at dinner instead of asking them to serve him, as he had always done in the imperial palace. Stunned, the servants were at a loss what to do. At court in the capital, they would have wasted no time kneeling down and kowtowing to him in gratitude. If they had done so in this situation, they would have betrayed the emperor's identity. Finally, a smart servant came up with the idea of using his knuckles to serve as his knees. Try this with your Chinese friends and see how they react.

Additional Reading

Flower, Kathy. *Culture Smart! China: Quick Guide to Customs and Etiquette.* (Culture Smart Series). Portland, Ore.: Graphic Arts Center Publishing Company, 2003. 160pp. $9.95pa. ISBN 1558687025pa.

Hu Wenzhong and Cornelius Grove. *Encountering the Chinese: A Guide for Americans.* Yarmouth, Maine: Intercultural Press, 1999. 208pp. $22.95pa. ISBN 1877864587pa.

MUSIC AND PERFORMING ARTS

The magazine *Nature* reported in 1999 that Chinese archeologists had excavated a 9,000-year-old musical instrument, a playable flute carved out of a large bird's wing bone (Zhang et al. 1999). The ancient Chinese used music as part of their rituals to enforce the political and social order. Some 3,000 years ago, Confucius worked hard to persuade rulers of his time to restore the rituals practiced by their ancestors, thus unwittingly contributing to the development of a complete musical theory and a set of sophisticated musical instruments.

Ancient Chinese music used a five-scale system, corresponding to the black keys on a modern keyboard. Musical instruments were largely made of *jin* (metal), *shi* (stone), *si* (string), *zhu* (bamboo), *pao* (gourd), *tu* (earth), *ge* (leather), and *mu* (wood). During the Tang dynasty (A.D. 618–907), as commercial contact with Central Asia increased, musical instruments such as *pipa*, a guitarlike plucking instrument, and *erhu*, a violinlike string instrument, were introduced to China. Chinese today have not only adopted the seven-scale system but have also invented a numerical musical note system based on the Western staff, so that beginners of music will find it easier to learn. They call this numbered system *jianpu* (simplified notation).

In contemporary Chinese music, *xiyang yueqi* (Western musical instruments) and *min yueqi* (traditional Chinese musical instruments) complement each other. Vocals fall roughly into three categories: *meisheng changfa* (Western singing), *minzu changfa* (Chinese singing, with regional and ethnic varieties), and *tongsu changfa* (popular singing). The younger generation is particularly receptive to new trends, such as rap, hip-hop, and street dances. Foreign and domestic record companies find China a booming market. China's increasingly relaxed social control and intensified commercialization have encouraged idolization of singing stars. The long-standing *Tong yi shou ge* (*Sing Together*), a Central TV–sponsored concert that takes place regularly in different places in China and around the world, provides a second chance for pop singers who have passed the prime of their singing careers, and the extremely popular *Chao ji nüsheng* (*Super Girl*) singing contest churns out new stars through fan voting using mobile phone short text messages, as the *American Idol* show does.

Chinese performing arts largely took the form of singing and dancing until about A.D. 960, when *xiqu* (operas) and *shuochang* (talking and singing) became increasingly popular.

Today, China boasts more than 300 types of operas with different regional flavors, of which Beijing Opera is of national significance, and Kunqu Opera is on the United Nations' list of "oral masterpiece[s] and intangible heritage of humanity."

All Chinese operas have several things in common. Their stylized performance consists of *chang* (singing), *nian* (speaking), *zuo* (acting), and *da* (fighting), assisted by the techniques of acrobatics, martial arts, and pantomimes. The majority of the opera performers use painted faces instead of masks. The colors of the paint are symbolic. Generally, white suggests treacherousness, but red indicates devotion, courage, and loyalty. Chinese operas have fixed roles, namely *sheng* (men), *dan* (women), *jing* (men with painted faces), and *chou* (clowns) and their relative subsets. Unlike their Western counterparts, confined to the concept of "three unities," namely "one plot, one location, and one time," Chinese operas engage the audience's imagination to create infinite time and space. For instance, if an actor or actress walks a few steps on the stage and tells the audience that he or she has covered a hundred miles, then, by tacit agreement, the audience will accept that distance in their mind's eye. Chinese operas use symbolic, rather than realistic, props. For example, a tasseled whip is understood to be a horse. An oar and a well-choreographed dance make a rocking boat on wavy waters come to life, as in the famed opera *Qiu jiang* (*Autumn on the River*). Finally, there are different schools in each of the Chinese operas. The *dan* (women) role of the Beijing Opera alone boasts the schools of Mei Lanfang, Cheng Yanqiu, Shang Xiaoyun, and Xun Huisheng.

With *caizijiaren* (gifted scholars and pretty women) as their main characters, and legends and historical events as their themes, Chinese operas have been an important means of preserving and disseminating folklore and folktales, some of which are retold in this book, such as the story of Qin Xianglian, retold here in "A Forsaken Wife and Her Unfaithful Husband" and of Mu Guiying, retold in "The Women Generals of the Yang Family and Commander-in-Chief Mu Guiying."

Huaju (plays) came to China in the early twentieth century. Some famous Chinese playwrights are Tian Han (1898–1968), Xia Yan (1900–1995), and Cao Yu (1910–1996). *Leiyu* (*Thunderstorm*) and *Chaguan* (*Teahouse*) are two of the most famous *huaju*.

Chinese movies emerged in Shanghai in the early 1930s and enjoyed their heyday in the 1930s, 1950s, and early 1960s. Many, such as *Yi jiang chun shui xiang dong liu* (*Spring River Flows East*), *Liu sanjie* (*Sister Liu*), *Wu-duo jinhua* (*Five Golden Flowers*), and the animated film *Sun wukong da nao tiankong* (*Monkey King Plays Havoc in Heaven*), have become classics. Zhang Yimou, Chen Kaige, and Feng Xiaogang are some of the most prominent contemporary directors. Chen Kaige is known for his experimental movies, like *Huangtudi* (*Yellow Earth*) and *Bawang bie ji* (*Farewell My Concubine*). Feng Xiaogang is good at using comedy to tackle serious social issues, and his recent *Shou ji* (*Cell Phone*) lashes out at unfaithful husbands. Zhang Yimou first exposed the rustic nature of China in a series of international award winners, including *Lao jing* (*Old Well*) and *Yi-ge dou bushao* (*Not One Less*). He also directed one of the first Chinese movies to be distributed in the United States, *Hong gaoliang* (*Red Sorghum),* and the critically acclaimed *Da hong denglong gao gao gua* (*Raise the Red Lantern*). More recently he has produced martial arts movies like the big box-office hits *Yingxiong* (*Hero*) and *Shi-mian maifu* (*House of Flying*

Daggers), apparently encouraged by Western audiences' reception of *Crouching Tiger Hidden Dragon,* a masterpiece by the famed Taiwanese director Ang Lee .

China's television industry is much younger. It began with a nine-episode TV play series, *Di ying shiba nian* (*A Secret Agent of Eighteen Years*), on February 5, 1980. Soap operas, imported mainly from Brazil, captivated Chinese audiences in subsequent years, before China began producing its own soap in 1990, called *Ke wang* (*Yearnings*). Production of Chinese TV plays reached its climax in the last years of the twentieth century with such great hits as *Si shi tong tang* (*Four Generations Under One Roof*), based on a modern classic by the renowned writer Lao She, and *Huanzhu gege* (*A Defiant Fake Princess*), adapted from a romantic novel by the famous Taiwanese writer Qiong Yao. Two trends dominate current Chinese TV production: plays that recast "revolutionary" movies or novels authored in the 1950s–1960s and plays that recount the romances and secret lives of monarchs. Among the latter, *Yong zheng wangchao* (*The Reign of Yongzheng Emperor*) and the multi-sequeled *Kangxi weifu sifang ji* (*Kangxi Emperor Tours the Country in Plain Clothes*) excel in content and presentation.

Chinese traditional dances vary among regions and peoples. Well-known traditional dances of the Han Chinese include those using red ribbons and lotus blooms. *Baoliandeng* (*The Magic Lotus Lantern*), based on a tale retold in this book, is China's first attempt to present an opera using traditional Chinese dances. The ballet called *Hongse niangzi jun* (*The Red Women Army Regiment*) has been a successful initiative to present a Chinese theme in a Western art form. Various kinds of folk dances are performed in the streets during festival celebrations, such as the dragon dance, lion dance, *yangge* dance (rural folk dance), *hanchuan* (folk dance with model boat and other props), *gaoqiao* (stilt), and various types of drum dances.

**An amateur folk drum dance troupe performs to celebrate
the grand opening of a business in Tianjin.**

Today, China embraces all genres of music and performing arts. There are also efforts to bring the West and the East together, such as the famed *Nüzi Shi-er Yuefang* (Twelve Girls Band), who have won fame worldwide, and sporadic experiments in marrying the art form of Beijing Opera with Shakespearean themes.

Additional Reading

Lynch, Emma Lynch. *We Are from China*. Chicago: Heinemann Library, 2005. 32pp. $25.36. ISBN 1403458030.

Sun Ming-Ju. *Chinese Opera Costumes Paper Dolls*. Mineola, N.Y.: Dover Publications, 1998. 32pp. $5.95pa. ISBN 048640367X.

FINE ARTS AND ARCHITECTURE

The history of Chinese fine arts can be traced back to cliff paintings 20,000 years ago (Chang 2004). Chinese pictographic characters are artworks in and of themselves. It is no wonder that calligraphy has been an important part of Chinese art. In fact, a typical Chinese painting scroll must have three indispensable elements: a picture, a complementary script, and a seal that usually serves as the signature of the artist. A Chinese painter must be both a good calligrapher and a good seal cutter.

The spread of Buddhism starting in the second century A.D. had a tremendous impact on Chinese artistic creation, evident in the Buddhist murals and statues in the Mogao Grotto (A.D. 366) and the stone carvings in Yungang (A.D. 450) and Longmen Grottos (A.D. 494). Around the same period, artists began to flee the Central Plains to escape pillaging by nomadic invaders. Awed by the natural beauty of South China, these exiled artists began to paint what they saw, creating what is known as the *shanshuihua* (paintings of mountains and waters). For the first time in Chinese history, paintings were created for esthetic instead of moral purposes.

Traditional Chinese artists do not portray models, instead painting from memory. Their works are supposed to catch the spirit, rather than the exact form, of an object, as in the image of *feitian* (flying angels or fairies) found in the murals of the Mogao Grotto. Unlike their counterparts in Western paintings, *feitian* do not have wings. Instead, their flying posture is hinted at by long, flowing ribbons, which are part of their beautiful costumes.

Courtesy of Baihua Literature and
Art Publishing House.

It does not follow, however, that Chinese artists did not pay attention to forms. The lifelike *Terra Cotta Soldiers and Horses* guarding the tomb of the First Emperor of Qin, for example, are as vividly detailed as Michelangelo's *David*.

Traditional Chinese artists paint on *xuanzhi* (rice paper), or silk, with brushes, ink, and pigments. There are two basic painting techniques: *xieyi* (a freehand style that highlights contrasts of colors and bold outlines with simple brush strokes) and *gongbi* (a precise style that emphasizes minute details).

Some of the modern masters of Chinese painting are Zhang Daqian, Qi Baishi, Xu Beihong, Fu Baoshi, Pan Tianshou, Guan Shanyue, Li Keran, Fan Zeng, and Luo Zhongli. New generations of Chinese artists tend to be overwhelmed by the various postmodern Western concepts and are faced with many choices. Nevertheless, the tradition of Chinese painting is far from being in danger. On the one hand, Chen Yifei, an American Chinese, has made a bold attempt to mingle Western oil painting techniques with Chinese themes. On the other hand, some native Chinese painters are using Western concepts such as perspective and shades of colors to complement traditional Chinese techniques. Some young Chinese artists are creating cutting-edge contemporary art in the Western style, as evidenced at the Chinese Biennale in Beijing in 2003. At the same time, numerous farmers are using their untrained talents to paint their rich and colorful country lives, creating a new genre known as the *nongminhua* (peasant paintings), the most famous of which are from Huxian County, Shaanxi Province (Chinese Folk Art 2003). Folk art in various regions is still going strong. The famed *Niren Zhang* (*Clay Figures of the Zhang Family*) and *Yangliuqing nianhua* (*Yangliuqing New Year Paintings*) in the author's hometown, Tianjin, are only two of innumerable examples.

The Chinese *yuanlin* (garden) is a Chinese *shanshuihua* in real life. With careful, artistic layout of *jiashan* (rockery), woods, buildings, and artificial bodies of water, a garden of this nature is an embodiment of the Chinese ideal that people and nature are an organic whole.

Traditional Chinese architecture is also an art. A raised foundation of stone, a body frame of wood, and a roof of pottery tiles are the basic elements of a traditional Chinese building. The frame, formed by columns and beams, carries the weight of the roof. Built like the wings of a big bird, the roof extends its curving ridges as far as it can in the four directions. Supporting this super-heavy roof are brackets called *dougong*, which don't use any nails and are peculiar to ancient Chinese architecture. Sculptured mythical figures and animals line up on the tip of the ridges. They act as nails as well as ornaments, serving the dual purposes of holding the tiles onto the ridges and protecting the house from artificial and natural disasters, as talismans. Traditional Chinese buildings always have elaborate *louhua* (ornamental engravings) on the windows and doors. Sculptured bricks and colored drawings are also integral parts of the building facade.

Additional Reading

Barnhart, Richard M., et al. *Three Thousand Years of Chinese Painting*, New Haven, Conn.: Yale University Press, 2002. 416pp. $39.5. ISBN 0300094477.

Keswick, Maggie, Charles Jencks, and Alison Hardie. *The Chinese Garden: History, Art and Architecture*, Harvard University Press, 2003. 240pp. $39.95. ISBN 0674010868.

LITERATURE

China has a wealth of literary collections, "from the four-syllable epigram to the hundred-chapter novel and the hundred-volume history. In between lie folk ballads and metaphysical odes, epitaphs and commemorations of the siting [sic] of pavilions, love lyrics and shamanistic hymns, travel diaries and sermons, memorials to the emperor and letters to friends" (Birch 1967).

Shijing (*Book of Songs*), a collection of 305 lyrics created 3,000 years ago, is the first Chinese anthology of poetry. Qu Yuan (339 B.C.–277 B.C.) wrote the first full-length poem, *Lisao* (*The Lament*). The *Yuefu* (Royal Conservatory) of the Eastern Han dynasty (A.D. 25–220) collected and preserved a great number of lyrics created largely by common people in the vernacular. About 50,000 poems written by over 2,200 poets during the Tang dynasty (A.D. 618–906) have survived. Li Bai (Li Po), Du Fu, and Bai Juyi were the greatest of the Tang poets. A new type of poetry called *ci* thrived during the Song era (960–1279). Su Shi, Xin Qiji, and Li Qingzhao were among the most famous *ci* poets.

The tradition of prose dates back to the Spring and Autumn Period (770 B.C.–476 B.C.), when various schools of thought flourished. Representative works are *The Analects*, a collection of Confucius's sayings, and *Tao Te Ching* (*The Book of Tao*). Legendary stories began to develop in the Tang dynasty, paving the way for full-blown fiction in the Ming (1368–1644) and Qing (1645–1911) dynasties. Outstanding among the Ming-Qing novels are the four great classics: *Shuihu zhuan* (*Water Margin*), *Sanguo yanyi* (*Romance of Three Kingdoms*), *Xi you ji* (*Journey to the West,* known to Westerners as *Monkey King*), and *Honglou meng* (*The Dream of the Red Mansion*).

Water Margin (or *Outlaws of the Marsh*) is a saga of 108 rebel heroes. Wu Song, in particular, has become a household name in China due to his single-handed fight with a man-eating tiger and his vengeance against his adulterous sister-in-law, who had killed his brother. *The Romance of Three Kingdoms* is based on the history of the three rival states at the end of the Han dynasty (A.D. 220–265). The blood brothers Liu Bei, Guan Yu, and Zhang Fei, founders of the state of Shu, have set an example of true fraternity. Their chief of staff, Zhuge Liang, has become a synonym for wisdom and devotion. Today, people all over the country still worship Guan Yu and Zhuge Liang as gods. *The Dream of the Red Mansion* depicts over 400 named characters from all walks of life. Using allegory, it tells of a tragic platonic love between two rebellious youths: the boy Baoyu, the family heir, and the girl Daiyu, his orphaned cousin. As a backdrop, the novel documents the rise and fall of the traditional families that raised and ruined these innocent young people.

Journey to the West is the most popular of the four classics. The fantasy is based on the true story of a monk in the Tang dynasty, who went to India to seek copies of original Buddhist scriptures. Bringing them back to China, he translated them into Chinese and helped spread the religion. *Journey to the West* is an allegorical account of the monk's adventures, set in a land of fantasy full of demons and monsters threatening his life and mission. Every step of the way, the monk's disciple, Monkey King, led three fellow disciples in subduing their adversaries and helped the monk come closer to the holy destination. Born from a rock, the Monkey King had learned magic tricks and martial arts from a Taoist. He could transform himself into seventy-two forms and could travel 108,000 *li* at a single somersault. The story is packed with action and adventures that fascinate both children and adults. Monkey King is as well known to the Chinese as Mickey Mouse is to Americans. Readers of this book will find two of the best-known monkey escapades, "Monkey King Strikes the White-bone Demon Three Times" and "Monkey King and the Iron Fan Princess."

The Chinese have a long tradition of documenting their history. The most famous Chinese historian, Sima Qian, compiled the first official history of China, *Shiji* (*Historical Records*), which covers from the prehistoric *Huangdi* (Yellow Emperor) to his own time (135 B.C.–86 B.C.). Sima Qian set an example for later historians.

In modern China, literary creation is often tied closely to political and social upheavals, producing such prominent writers as Lin Yutang, renowned for his *Wuguo yu wumin* (*We Chinese*); Ba Jin, known for his trilogy <u>Jia</u> (*Family*), *Chun* (*Spring*), and *Qiu* (*Fall*); Lao She, famous for his *Si shi tong tang* (*Four Generations Under One Roof*); Mao Dun, celebrated for his *Ziye* (*Midnight*); and Lu Xun, noted for his pungent essays, such as *Nahan* (*A Call for Help*). With the establishment of New China in 1949, a number of novels depicting the Anti-Japanese War and the Civil Wars were produced, including *Dihou wugongdui* (*Armed Working Team Behind the Enemy Line*), *Pingyuan qiangsheng* (*Gun Shots on the Plain*), *Yehuo chunfeng dou gucheng* (*Fight in an Ancient Town Amidst Wild Fire and Spring Wind*), and *Hongyan* (*Red Crag*).

Well-known contemporary poets include He Jingzhi, Zang Kejia, Ai Qing, and Bei Dao. Yu Qiuyu, Wei Minglun, and Yu Guangzhong (Taiwan) are among the most favored prose writers. The martial arts novels of Jin Yong (Hong Kong), such as *Tianlongbabu* (*Eight Heavenly Gods*), and the love stories of Qiong Yao (Taiwan), such as *Huanzhu gege* (*The Defiant Fake Princess*), have been adapted into hit movies and TV series.

The Cultural Revolution (1966–1976)—an anarchic campaign initiated by Mao Zedong to rid the country of anything he deemed capitalist and bourgeois—effectively ended almost all genuine literary creations on the mainland of China. Only a few writings survived, because of their political correctness, such as Hao Ran's *Jinguang dadao* (*The Golden Path*), an account of a struggle between socialist farmers and capitalist landowners, and Yao Xueyin's historical novel *Li Zicheng*, a saga of a peasant rebel leader. Immediately after the Cultural Revolution ended, a *shanghen wenxue* (Scar Literature) movement appeared, led by Liu Xinwu and Zhang Kangkang; it was a movement of literary creation that recalled and castigated the brutality of the catastrophic revolution.

In the past three decades, however, Chinese literature has thrived as the country has experienced tremendous changes due to its economic reform and opening to the outside world. At the same time, it has had to meet the challenge of preserving its own tradition while embracing mushrooming popular cultures, both indigenous and foreign.

Additional Reading

Lau, Joseph S. M., and Howard Goldblatt. *The Columbia Anthology of Modern Chinese Literature*. New York: Columbia University Press, 1996. 726pp. $29.50. ISBN 0231080034.

McDougall, Bonnie S., ed. *Popular Chinese Literature and Performing Arts in the People's Republic of China, 1949–1979.* (Studies on China). Berkeley: University of California Press, 1984. 341pp. $59.93. ISBN 0520048520.

STORYTELLING IN CHINA

There is no doubt that storytelling in China, as elsewhere, is as old as its civilization. People have been telling stories for millennia to educate and entertain. Chinese parents and grandparents have been using storytelling to make their children and grandchildren aware of the importance of academic advancement and filial piety (Pearson and Rao 2003, 131–146). A Qing author, Pu Songling (1640–1715), collected 431 stories about ghosts, phantoms, spirits, and fairies from storytellers on the roadside and in teahouses and compiled *Liaozhai zhiyi* (*Strange Tales from the Make-do Studio*).

The profession of storytelling, known as *shuochang* (talking and singing), did not appear until the Tang (A.D. 618–906) and Song (960–1275) periods. During the Qing dynasty (1644–1911), forms of *shuochang* diversified, and the term *quyi* (literally, art of melodies), a generic term for all forms of storytelling, came to encompass them. *Quyi* fell into four major categories: *xiangsheng* (comic dialogues), *kuaiban* (clapper talk) and *kuaishu* (Shandong clappers), *guqu* (drum storytelling), and *pingshu* (storytelling with commentary). Each had a great number of variants. A 1982 survey showed that there were 341 of them throughout the country (Børdahl 1999).

Storytelling in China has evolved over centuries, and it lives on to this day in many forms. *Quyi* storytelling is characteristic of minimal theatrical performance. The Han Chinese generally are reserved and sophisticated and therefore can be difficult to amuse. To entertain them, storytellers cannot rely on witty jokes alone. They have to be expert in facial expressions and ventriloquism or mimicking sounds and voices. This is particularly true for the *pingshu* storyteller, who has no device other than his or her mouth to galvanize the audience. Of the contemporary *pingshu* storytellers, Yuan Kuocheng, Shan Tianfang, Liu Jinglin, and Liu Lanfang are the most prominent.

Famous *xiangsheng* performers of the older generation include Hou Baolin, Guo Qiru, Guo Quanbao, Ma Sanli, and Yu Baolin, as well as Chang Baohua, Chang Baoting, Gao Yingpei, Li Jindou, Fan Zhenyu, Tang Jiezhong, and Ma Ji. Among the younger generation are Jiang Kun, Feng Gong, Shi Shengjie, Niu Qun, Qi Zhi, and Da Bing.

Some regional variants of *quyi* are still popular today: *erren zhuan* (two-performer storytelling with singing and dancing) in Northeast China and Yangzhou *pingtan* (storytelling accompanied with comments and plucking instruments) in South China. Zhao Benshan, Gao Xiumin, Fan Wei, and Pan Changjiang are some of the best known *erren zhuan* performers; they also have made a name initiating a new form of entertainment known as *xiaopin* (comic skits), along with Chen Peisi, Gong Hanlin, and many others. There are at present five prominent Yangzhou *pingtan* performers: Wang Xiatang, Li Xintang, Fei Zhengliang, Hui Zhaolong, and Dai Buzhang.

Quyi did not enjoy a status equal to the various Chinese operas and therefore has had a hard time getting into formal venues like theaters. The *shuchang* (place of storytelling), often a temporary space in a market or a teahouse, used to be the only place where *quyi* could be performed. The irony today is that theaters are open to *quyi*, but many types of *quyi* are close to extinction, losing their battle with such media as movies, TV shows, concerts, cartoons, and computer and video games. At present, only *xiangsheng* and *pingshu* are still holding their ground, but their audiences are getting increasingly older.

Traditional storytelling is trying its best to survive by making use of multimedia technology. Television has brought *xiangsheng* and *xiaopin* to millions of households; a record company in Guangdong has produced a video CD series with a collection of about 200 Chinese tales. In fact, media storytelling has a longer history. Chinese people growing up in the 1960 and 1970s will never forget the name of Sun Jingxiu, the beloved radio storyteller for children, and those growing up in the 1980s cherish his successor, Ju Ping, who was one of the first to tell stories on television.

Particular forms of *quyi* may decline and disappear, but storytelling among the people continues. It takes place at school and at home every day. There are even communities where almost everyone, man and woman, old and young, is a good storyteller. The Geng Village of Gaocheng City, Hebei Province—300 miles from Beijing—has earned national fame for its storytelling tradition. A villager, Jin Zhengxin, is able to tell more than 500 tales. Fifty-five of his fellow villagers can each tell at least a hundred. Six of the tales in this book were collected from two of the Geng Village storytellers.

Additional Reading

Børdahl, Vibeke, ed. *Eternal Storyteller: Oral Literature in Modern China*. London: Taylor & Francis, 1998. 405pp. $49.95. ISBN 0887273564.

Part 2

Food, Games, and Crafts

A design pattern on *you*, a wine vessel of the Western Zhou dynasty
(1046 B.C.–771 B.C.). Courtesy of Baihua Literature and Art Publishing House.

FOOD

Because of the country's variety of climatic conditions, food sources, and the cultural backgrounds of its ethnic peoples, Chinese food is amazingly diverse. Chinese restaurants in America serve only a small sample of assorted Chinese food, adapted to the taste and pace of life of American customers.

The Han Chinese alone claim eight major cuisines, or different styles of food preparation, each further divided into several local variants. These major cuisines bear nicknames from the regions where they originated: *lu* from Shangdong, *chuan* from Sichuan, *yue* from Guangdong, *min* from Fujian, *su* from Jiangsu, *zhe* from Zhejiang, *xiang* from Hunan, and *hui* from Anhui. The cuisine *lu* specializes in savory seafood, *chuan* is marked by its spicy and peppery flavor, *su* is particularly good for poultry, *zhe* emphasizes freshness of ingredients, *yue* is renowned for its deep-fried foods, *xiang* is famed for its hot and sour taste, *min* is eminent for its sweet and sour dishes, and *hui* is distinguished for its skillful use of temperature in the preparation of gourmet stews.

Like Americans, the Chinese usually cook most of their meals at home, although an increasing number are choosing to dine out to socialize, celebrate, or simply for a change. What they prepare at home is called *jiachangcai* (home-cooked dishes), which are simple, casual, and often impromptu. Chinese food prepared either at home or in restaurants is characteristically a balanced composition of meat and vegetables. On average, the Chinese consume more vegetables and carbohydrates than Americans do.

Besides food for regular meals, there is also a great variety of *xiaochi* (things eaten in small quantity), or snacks. Each region offers a few nationally known *xiaochi*, such as the *goubuli baozi* (steamed dumplings) of Tianjin, the *yangrou paomo* (mutton soup with bread) of Xi'an, the *jianbing* (thin pancakes made of millet flour) of Shandong, the *dandanmian* (spicy noodles) of Sichuan, and the exotic *shegeng* (snake soup) of Guangdong.

Just as Americans traditionally eat turkey for Thanksgiving and ham for Christmas, the Chinese also have customary foods for special occasions. On the eve of the Chinese New Year, every family north of the Yangtze River will eat *jiaozi* (boiled dumplings wrapped in wheat dough), and families in the south will eat *niangao* (steamed rice cakes). This difference has developed because wheat is a major crop in North China, whereas rice is

---

cultivated heavily in the south. Today, however, this distinction among eating habits is increasingly blurred as geographical barriers are giving way to improved transportation of goods and eased migration of people throughout the country.

The Chinese also have their particular breakfast favorites, which vary greatly from region to region. For example, the Tianjinese prefer *jianbing guozi* (battered cakes cooked with eggs and served with plum sauce, green onions, and deep-fried dough), the Beijingese like *douzhi* (soybean milk) and *youtiao* (deep-fried twisted dough sticks), and the Shanghainese favor *paofan* (soup of cooked rice) and *shengjian* (fried dumplings).

A long history has taught the Chinese to prepare their food in a great many ways, *jian* (dry-fry), *chao* (stir-fry), *peng* (instant-fry), *zha* (deep-fry), *zheng* (steam), *shao* (roast), *zhu* (boil), and *dun* (stew) being only a few of them. Traditionally, rural Chinese cook their meals in a huge iron pot sitting on a clay stove, with bellows to boost the combustion of plant fuel like dried corn and wheat stalks. City residents first used coal stoves and now use gas ranges to prepare their meals. Neither the clay stove nor the gas range has an oven. The Chinese seldom roast and bake their food at home. Instead, they boil and steam the food that they want well cooked.

Chinese food differs from that of America in many ways. When asked about these differences, an observant American friend, whom I once entertained at my home in China, said, "We cut the food as we eat, but you cut it up before you cook!"

Following are recipes for some traditional Chinese food and snacks, along with a few home-cooked dishes. Nearly all the ingredients required in the recipes are available in Asian groceries.

Jiaozi (Dumplings)

Introduction

Historically, the Chinese used *tiangan* (ten heavenly stems) in combination with *dizhi* (twelve earthly branches) to designate years, months, days, and hours. The time of *zi*, the first of the twelve-branched *dizhi*, corresponds to a time between eleven o'clock in the evening and one o'clock in the morning. The Chinese *jiao* means "join." Hence, the two-syllable word *jiaozi* refers to midnight—the hour that connects the two hours across a new day. The term has become the name of the food eaten to celebrate the arrival of the Chinese New Year.

Jiaozi (Dumplings)

Ingredients:

>1 lb all-purpose flour
>
>10 oz ground pork

Wet ingredients: ½ tbsp cooking wine, 3 tbsp soy sauce, 3 tbsp salad oil, and ½ tbsp sesame oil

Spices and flavorings: 2 oz minced green onion, 1 oz minced ginger root, ½ tsp salt, ¼ tsp white pepper, ½ tsp sugar, and ½ tsp powdered chicken bouillon

>½ lb Chinese cabbage, finely chopped, mixed with 1 tbsp salad oil to coat
>
>3 cups cold water

Instructions:

To make the dough:

1. Mix flour with cold water in a food processor until it forms tiny, moist pieces.
2. Place the flour mixture in a bowl and knead until dough forms. Cover bowl with plastic wrap to prevent drying.

To make the stuffing:

1. Mix ground pork with wet ingredients and stir in one direction until sticky.
2. Add spices and flavorings, and stir again in the same direction until blended.
3. Add cabbage and stir in the same direction until mixed evenly.

To make the dumplings:

1. Knead and roll a piece of dough into a log shape, about half an inch in diameter.
2. Cut the log-shaped dough into pieces about a square inch or smaller. Flatten the pieces with a rolling pin to form a thin circle 1½ inches in diameter.
3. Place ⅔ tsp stuffing (add more as you perfect your skills) in the center of each circle, fold in half, and press the edges together with your fingers until they are tightly sealed.

To cook the dumplings:

1. Bring water to a boil and drop in the dumplings one at a time. Stir gently to separate them.

2. Return to a boil and add 1 cup cold water. Do this twice more, then remove the dumplings from the water and drain.

To serve: Some Chinese use rice or wine vinegar as a sauce, while others prefer a concoction of vinegar, soy sauce, sugar, garlic juice, chili sauce, and sesame oil. Serves 4 or 5.

Hongzao niangao (New Year's Cake with Dates)

Introduction

While Northerners eat *jiaozi* to celebrate the Chinese New Year, people in the South cannot do without *niangao,* because its pronunciation can be interpreted as "Life improves with each passing year." They believe that eating *niangao* on the eve of the Chinese New Year will bring them good fortune in the year to come. This recipe introduces one of the many *niangao* cakes.

Hongzao niangao (New Year's Cake with Dates)

Ingredients:

> 10 oz glutinous rice flour (available in Asian groceries)
>
> 1 cup water plus a little extra
>
> 2 oz sugar
>
> 2 single-serving size packets (1¼ tbsp) artificial sweetener
>
> 15 seeded jujubes (Chinese dates) or other dates

Instructions:

1. Mix rice flour, water, sugar, and sweetener thoroughly.

2. Add dates and stir until paste forms.

3. Spread the paste on a lightly greased, heatproof plate.

4. Set the plate on a steamer tray and steam on high heat for two hours.

The cake is done when a chopstick (or cake tester) inserted in the center comes out clean. Serves 2 or 3.

Laba zhou (The Twelfth Month Congee)

Introduction

Zhou (congee, porridge made from rice) is an important part of traditional Chinese food, and there are numerous kinds in various regions of China. *Laba zhou* is known to every Chinese, as it marks a particular day, namely, the eighth day of the twelfth Chinese lunar month, which is usually at the beginning of January. Most Chinese treat it as a reminder of the approaching Chinese New Year, hardly aware of its Buddhist origin. In fact, *laba zhou* was originally used to celebrate the day when Sakyamuni, the founder of Buddhism, experienced his first revelation after six years of practicing asceticism, surviving on one meal of rice congee every day.

Laba zhou (The Twelfth Month Congee)

Ingredients:

Dry ingredients: ½ lb glutinous rice; total of ½ lb red bean, mung bean, jujubes, peanuts, lotus seeds (available in Asian groceries), or other beans or seeds

Flavorings: 6 oz brown sugar; 2 packets (1¼ tbsp) artificial sweetener

Instructions:

1. Rinse the dry ingredients, then add them to a pot half filled with water.

2. Bring to a boil and turn the heat down to medium-high.

3. Simmer covered for 1½ hours, until ingredients are softened.

4. Add flavorings, stir until blended, and serve. Serves 4 or 5.

Zongzi (Dumplings in Bamboo or Reed Leaves)

Introduction

Zongzi is a traditional Chinese food similar to tamales. It is a special treat for the *Duanwu* or Dragon Boat Festival. A tale about it is retold in Part 3.

Zongzi (Dumplings in Bamboo or Reed Leaves)

Ingredients:

> 1 lb glutinous rice
>
> ½ lb red bean paste
>
> 20 pieces dried bamboo leaves (available in Asian groceries)
>
> length of cotton twine or strong white thread

Instructions:

1. Rinse glutinous rice, soak for 4 hours, then drain.

2. Divide red bean paste into 10 portions.

3. Overlap two bamboo leaves lengthwise to make a sheet one-and-a-half leaves wide.

4. Fold the bamboo sheet to form a cone.

5. Add 1 tbsp glutinous rice to the cone, then $\frac{1}{10}$ of the red bean paste. Top with 1 tbsp rice.

6. Fold the edges over to cover the top of the cone. Fasten securely with twine or thread so that no contents leak out.

7. Boil the *zongzi* for three hours. Drain, then arrange on a platter and serve hot. Serves 5.

Zhima shaobing (Sesame Cake)

Introduction

Sesame cake is one of the numerous cake snacks eaten for breakfast. Sesame cake is as popular as American muffins or biscuits.

Zhima shaobing (Sesame Cake)

Ingredients:

> 1 lb self-rising flour
>
> 1 cup lukewarm water
>
> 2 oz peanut butter
>
> 1 oz sesame seeds
>
> dash of salt and Sichuan pepper powder, mixed
>
> 2 tbsp water mixed with equal amount sugar to make 4 tbp sugar syrup

Instructions:

1. Mix flour with water and knead until soft dough forms (make sure dough is not sticky).
2. Roll dough out on slightly floured surface into circle about $\frac{1}{3}$-inch thick.
3. Spread peanut butter on circle, sprinkle salt and pepper powder mixture on top evenly, and roll circle up into a log.
4. Slice log into 1½-inch-thick pieces. Flatten pieces into about $\frac{2}{3}$-inch-thick cakes
5. Brush sugar tops of cakes with syrup and sprinkle sesame seeds on top.
6. Bake the cakes at 375°F (190°C) until lightly browned. Serves 4 or 5.

Yuanxiao (Rice Dumplings)

Introduction

Yuanxiao, also known as *tangyuan*, is a traditional food for the Lantern Festival on the fifteenth day of the first Chinese lunar month, which is generally considered the end of the Chinese New Year season. The word *yuanxiao* means "eve of the first day," and its round shape is symbolic of family reunion, a major theme of the Chinese New Year.

Yuanxiao (Rice Dumplings)

Ingredients:

> 1 package glutinous rice powder (about 1 lb)
>
> 1 cup hot water
>
> 4 oz Chinese date or red bean paste
>
> ½ oz white sesame seeds
>
> 2 or 3 cups shortening or cooking oil

Instructions:

1. Mix rice powder and water to form dough.
2. Shape date or bean paste into 20 portions.
3. Knead dough gently and roll into a log about 1 inch in diameter; divide into 20 slices.
4. Press each piece of dough at the center to make a hollow and place a portion of paste in it.
5. Gently press the dough to close it and shape it into a ball (the *yuanxiao*).
6. Roll balls in sesame seeds until coated.
7. Heat oil to 350°F (177°C), then turn heat down to medium high.
8. Deep-fry the *yuanxiao* until golden brown. (Option: boil *yuanxiao* without sesame seeds. See recipe for *jiaozi* for boiling method.) Serve warm. Serves 5.

Dandanmian (Sichuan Noodle)

Introduction

The name *dandanmian* derives from the traditional way of peddling noodles in the streets. Peddlers carried the cookware and ingredients on their *dandan* (shoulder poles). *Dandanmian* is a specialty of Sichuan and is becoming increasingly popular throughout the country.

Dandanmian (Sichuan Noodle)

Ingredients:

3½ oz ground pork

½ oz hoisin sauce (available in Asian groceries)

⅓ tsp cooking wine

2 tsp soy sauce

1 tbsp cooking oil

½ oz pea sprout or spinach

dash of salt

¼ tsp chili oil

⅓ oz chicken bouillon

⅓ tsp rice vinegar

¾ oz chopped green onion

½ lb Chinese noodles (available in supermarkets)

Instructions:

1. Stir-fry pork with hoisin sauce, cooking wine, and ½ tsp soy sauce until mixture becomes aromatic. Add pea sprout or spinach and stir for about a minute. Set aside.

2. Divide remaining soy sauce, chili oil, bouillon, vinegar, and green onion among 5 or 6 bowls.

3. Boil noodles until slightly soft. Drain. Divide among the bowls.

4. Add pork mixture, toss, and serve warm. Serves 5 or 6.

Yuebing (Moon Cake)

Introduction

Moon cakes, shaped like the full moon, are traditional Chinese snacks for the Mid-autumn Festival, which takes place on the fifteenth day of the eighth Chinese lunar month (near the beginning of October), when the moon looks the brightest. On that evening, Chinese families will customarily get together and eat moon cakes, along with fruit and wine. As they enjoy the beauty of the full moon, they commemorate the Moon Goddess, Chang'e, whose tale is retold in Part 3 of this book. The significance of this festival is comparable to the American Thanksgiving.

Yuebing (Moon Cake)

Ingredients:

> 1½ lb all-purpose flour
>
> 6½ oz butter
>
> ½ cup water
>
> ¾ cup sugar
>
> 2 single-serving size packets (1¼ tbsp) artificial sweetener
>
> 6½ tbsp peanut oil
>
> 5 oz sesame seeds
>
> 2 oz minced green onion
>
> 1 egg, beaten
>
> 1 oz salt and Sichuan pepper powder mixture

Instructions:

Dough:

1. Cut 6 oz butter into ½ lb flour to make "buttered dough." Divide into 10 portions.

2. Melt ½ oz butter and add ½ cup water. Stir in another ½ lb flour to make "water-oil dough." Divide into 10 portions.

Stuffing:

1. Steam last ½ lb flour 15 minutes and let cool in a bowl. It should look slightly darker, with a rough texture, and be slightly hardened, but the lumps should be easy to break.

2. Add sugar, artificial sweetener, peanut oil, sesame seeds, minced green onion, salt, and pepper powder to the steamed flour and mix evenly. Divide the stuffing into 10 portions.

To make the moon cakes:

1. Flatten each piece of water-oil dough into a circle, forming a "wrapper".

2. Wrap a piece of buttered dough in each water-oil dough circle and then flatten again into a new circle (wrapper).

3. Distribute the stuffing among the wrappers and press each into a floured pattern mold, 3 or 4 inches in diameter, to make a cake.

4. Brush the cakes with the beaten egg. Bake at 355°F (180°C) for 20 to 25 minutes or until lightly browned. Halfway through baking, turn the cakes over and brush the other side with the egg.

Let cool before serving. Serves 10.

Ban douya (Bean Sprout Salad)

Introduction

A formal Chinese dinner has three courses: first cold dishes, including salads, usually served with alcohol; then hot dishes (also known as the main course), along with *zhushi* (main food)—rice and wheat products comparable to the bread and potato products in a Western dinner; and finally soup and fruit. Cold dishes, usually smaller in quantity than hot dishes, fall into three categories: meat, vegetarian, and mixed. *Ban douya* is a cold vegetarian dish. A homemade dish, it is rarely found in fancy restaurants.

Ban douya (Bean Sprout Salad)

Ingredients:

> 1 lb fresh mung bean (green bean) sprouts (available in supermarkets)
>
> cold water
>
> Wet ingredients: ⅓ tsp soy sauce and 1 tsp rice vinegar
>
> Flavorings: dash each of salt, sugar, and powdered chicken bouillon; few drops of sesame oil; and ½ oz *suanrong lajiang* (chili paste with garlic, available in Asian groceries)

Instructions:

1. Boil sprouts for 2 minutes (do not overcook).
2. Strain, soak in cold water for about a minute, strain again, and squeeze out any remaining liquid.
3. Place the sprouts in a salad bowl and add wet ingredients and flavorings.
4. Mix, then serve at room temperature.

Suanlatang (Hot and Sour Soup)

Introduction

Tang (soup) is an indispensable part of a Chinese dinner, but when it is served varies in different regions of China. Generally, people in the north prefer having *tang* after the main course. Southerners, particularly those in Guangdong (Canton) and Hong Kong, prefer having *tang* prior to the main course, as done in some American Chinese restaurants. There are numerous kinds of *tang* in Chinese cuisines. *Suanlatang* (hot and sour soup) is a Sichuan specialty and a favorite of many Chinese. Two recipes are listed here to give you an idea of how Chinese food changes after its migration to America.

Original Sichuan Hot and Sour Soup

Ingredients:

Wet ingredients: 1 cup chicken stock, 2 cups water, 1 tsp soy sauce, and ½ tsp vinegar

Flavorings: pinch each salt, white pepper, and powdered chicken bouillon

Dry ingredients: 1 oz sliced tofu, ½ oz cooked chicken or ham, sliced; ½ oz fresh mushrooms, sliced; ½ oz cooked lean pork, sliced; ½ oz presoaked sea cucumber, and ½ oz presoaked squid

⅔ oz cornstarch mixed with water to form a paste

1 egg, beaten well

⅛ oz chopped green onion

Instructions

1. Combine flavorings and wet ingredients in a saucepan and bring to a boil on high heat.
2. Add dry ingredients.
3. Add cornstarch paste, turn heat down to medium high, and add beaten egg.
4. When egg floats, turn up heat until shredded pork rises to the surface.
5. Put chopped green onion in large serving bowl.
6. Add contents of saucepan. Serve hot. Serves 4.

American Chinese Hot and Sour Soup

Ingredients:

Wet ingredients: 1 can chicken broth, 2 cups water, 1 tsp soy sauce, and ½ tsp rice vinegar

Spices and flavorings: 1 tsp sugar, ½ tsp white pepper, ½ tsp chili sauce, pinch each salt and powdered chicken bouillon

Dry ingredients: 1 oz sliced tofu, ½ oz bamboo shoots, ½ oz mushrooms, ½ oz barbecued pork, all shredded

⅔ oz cornstarch, dissolved in water

1 egg, beaten well

⅛ oz chopped green onion

few drops sesame oil

Instructions:

1. Combine wet and dry ingredients and spices and flavorings in a saucepan. Bring to a boil until barbecued pork rises to the surface.
2. Add cornstarch, turn heat down to medium high, and add beaten egg.
3. When egg floats, add chopped green onion and sesame oil.
4. Pour into a bowl and serve. Serves 4.

Jiang niurou (Multiflavored Beef)

Introduction

Pork is the major meat source of the Chinese, followed by fish, chicken, mutton, and beef, in that order. Chinese stew, fry, and roast their meats, as Americans do. The beef-cooking technique described in this recipe is peculiar to the Chinese, and the cooked beef, cooled and sliced, is a favorite Chinese cold dish.

Jiang niurou (Multiflavored Beef)

Ingredients:

1 lb steak, trimmed and rinsed

Wet ingredients: ¼ cup soy sauce, 1 tbsp cooking wine, ½ can beer

Spices and flavorings: 2 pieces Chinese cinnamon, 5 anise seeds, ½ oz green onion, and ½ oz squashed ginger root

pinch powdered chicken bouillon

few drops of sesame oil

Instructions:

1. Submerge steak in water in saucepan. Bring to boil; boil until meat turns gray and water becomes foamy.
2. Drain steak. Submerge in a fresh pot of water.
3. Add wet ingredients and spices and flavorings and bring to a boil again.
4. Skim off any foam, reduce heat, and simmer, covered, for 2 hours.

5. When steak is tender (can be easily pierced with a chopstick), increase heat to thicken the sauce. Add powdered chicken bouillon and sesame oil to flavor.

6. Cool (optional), slice, and serve. Serves 2 or 3.

Fanqie chao jidan (Stir-Fried Tomato and Egg)

Introduction

People of different cultures treat fruits, vegetables, and staple foods differently. The Chinese, for instance, approach tomatoes and potatoes largely as vegetables. They stir-fry them as they do cabbages. This recipe shows how the Chinese fry tomatoes and present them beautifully in a mosaic of red, yellow, and green. This dish is a favorite Chinese *jiachangcai* (home-cooked dish).

Fanqie chao jidan (Stir-Fried Tomato and Egg)

Ingredients:

3 tomatoes

3 eggs

1½ tbsp cooking oil

½ oz green onion, chopped

Spices and flavorings: pinch salt, sugar, powdered and chicken bouillon, and dash sesame oil

Instructions:

1. Cut the skin of each tomato once lengthwise. Boil for a few seconds, drain, then dip in cold water. Peel and slice.

2. Beat eggs well with salt and powdered chicken bouillon. Heat nonstick cooking spray in a frying pan and stir-fry eggs until firm. Set aside;

3. Heat cooking oil in frying pan or wok and add green onion. Sauté until mixture becomes aromatic. (Do not brown green onions.)

4. Add tomatoes and stir-fry on high heat until tomatoes are soft.

5. Add fried eggs and spices and flavorings.

6. Stir well, then serve. Serves 2 or 3.

Additional Readings

Halvorsen, Francine. *Food and Cooking of China: An Exploration of Chinese Cuisine in the Provinces and Cities of China, Hong Kong, and Taiwan.* Hoboken, N.J.: John Wiley, 1995. 226pp. $26.95. ISBN 0471110558.

Lin, Lee Hwa. *Rice, Traditional Chinese Cooking.* Taipei: Wei-Chuan Publishing, 1995. 96pp. $17.95. ISBN 0941676439.

Simonds, Nina, and Leslie Swartz. *Moonbeams, Dumplings & Dragon Boats: A Treasury of Chinese Holiday Tales, Activities and Recipes.* Orlando, Fla.: Harcourt, 2002.

Wright, Jeni. *Chinese Food & Folklore.* (Food & Folklore). San Diego: Laurel Glen Publishing, 1999. 80pp. $13.60. ISBN 0152019839.

GAMES

Like people in other cultures, the Han Chinese have a long tradition of entertaining themselves with games. For instance, a painting that dates from the Tang dynasty (A.D. 618–906) depicts people playing with a ball on horseback—a game similar to today's polo.

The Chinese know a great variety of games. There are games that test strength, like *bahe* (tug-of-war) and *shuaijiao* (wrestling); those that test skills, like *tijianzi* (kicking shuttlecocks) and *doukongzhu* (spinning bamboo yo-yo); and games to prove one's intelligence, like *caimiyu* (solving riddles) and the board games *weiqi* (Go) and *xiangqi* (a Chinese chess). Games are played for fun, monetary gains, or both, such as the famous *majiang* (Mah Jong).

The author and his sister's family playing *majiang*. The table can shuffle and roll dice at the push of a button. This "innovation" shows how popular the game is in China.

Chinese children can entertain themselves simply with their bare hands by playing the *shitou-jianzi-bu* (stone-scissors-cloth) game. Sound familiar? It is popularly known as "paper-rock-scissors" in America. In fact, it may be popular among children of many cultures in the world. While numerous Chinese children's games require no props or toys, others use materials of bamboo, wood, bricks, rubber bands, pencils, stones, ropes, metal, clay, paper, handkerchiefs, bones, cloth, marbles, sand, and cans. Even apricot pits can be used for a very demanding hand game.

Before they are old enough to take on the more difficult *weiqi* and *xiangqi*, Chinese children play quite a few board games. The most popular are the chess games *feixingqi* (aerial battles), *luzhanqi* (infantry battles), and *doushouqi* (animal fight). The board game *tiaoqi* (marble-jumping chess) is a favorite among Chinese children because they can play with their parents. Indeed, children and adults share a great number of games. One in particular is worth mentioning because it is very Chinese. While bullfights, dog fights, and cock fights are very popular in many cultures, Chinese, old and young, enjoy the sport of cricket fighting. Cricket fighting is hundreds of years old. Emperors even indulged in the sport. Players catch or purchase a male cricket and keep it in a jar alone for a few days. Then they find someone who has another male cricket kept under the same circumstances. One of the crickets is placed in the other's jar. Almost immediately the two crickets lock in a fierce fight. Eventually one wins and starts chirping to celebrate its victory. The defeated cricket tries to jump out of the jar to flee. A tale about cricket fighting is retold in the "Magical Tales" section in Part 3.

Today, however, the popularity of arcades, playstations, computers, and Internet gaming threatens a great number of traditional children's games. Most of them, such as cricket fighting, *daga* (hitting a diamond-shaped twig tossed in the air), *tuitiehuan* (pushing a metal ring with a hooked poke), *danziqiu* (playing marbles), *tiaopijin* (dancing over rubber band chains), *tiaofangzi* (different versions of hopscotch), and *maopian* (printed paper cards and chips) are extinct. There has been a call to revive traditional games as parents and teachers come to realize that they are good for children's physical and mental health and better at teaching them social skills. The Quanyechang Elementary School in Tianjin, for example, is making conscientious efforts to revive traditional children's games by incorporating them into physical education classes. Following are a few traditional Chinese games that require almost nothing but children's participation.

Laoying zhuo xiaoji (Eagle and Chicks)

Laoying zhuo xiaoji is one of the most popular outdoor recess games for schoolchildren, because it requires about a dozen players. One child plays the preying eagle; another, the protective hen; and the rest, the chicks. The eagle tries to catch one of the chicks, who dodge behind the mother hen. The mother hen extends her arms and moves about in response to the eagle's attack, trying to protect her chicks.

To start, the eagle stands alone, facing the mother hen, who has her chicks lined up behind her. The first chick holds on to the mother hen's clothing or shoulder, the second chick holds on to the first, and so on. The game starts with a countdown. If the eagle catches a chick, the game is over, and another round will start. The chick that was caught plays the eagle in the new round.

Two teams can compete with each other. Each chick in a team that gets caught drops out. When five minutes are up, the team that has the most chicks left wins.

Schoolchildren playing the "Eagle and Chicks" game in the playground. The hen is trying to protect her chicks from the attacking eagle.

Tiaoma (Horse Jumping)

This is another popular outdoor game for children all over China. It is similar to the Western game of leapfrog. One of the players crouches low to play the pommel horse, while the others line up a few yards away. One by one, the children jump over the pommel horse by pushing down on its back to give themselves a lift up and over. When all the players have succeeded in jumping over, the "horse" rises an inch higher. This process continues until one player fails. The one who fails becomes the pommel horse, and a second round of the game starts.

NOTE: This game is not suitable for very young children. Adult chaperons should be present to monitor the players to prevent possible injury.

Zhuangguai (Leg Bumping)

Zhuangguai is a simple children's outdoor game from North China, particularly popular in rural areas. It is better played in winter when children are in heavier clothing that can provide more protection. It can be played one-on-one or in competing groups. To play one-on-one, each of two children lifts a foot up with his or her hand to form a "bumper." Hopping on the other leg, the players bump each other with their "bumpers." Whoever gets his or her bumper dislodged first loses the game.

A variant of the game is to have two players bump in a designated circle. Whoever bumps the opponent out of the circle wins the game.

Jiguchuanhua (Drum and Flower)

This is a popular indoor and outdoor game that children play in all parts of China. It requires a drum and a paper flower big enough to be passed around with ease. A portable boombox can replace the drum. A group of at least a dozen players sits in a circle, facing the center. A drummer or boombox operator sits near the circle. When the drum or boombox sounds, the players start to pass the flower, either clockwise or counterclockwise (but the direction must be consistent in each game). When the drum or music stops without warning, the player who currently has the flower in his or her hands has to step to the center of the circle and perform a song or dance, tell a story or joke, or recite a poem. This game engenders in the players a sense of community and is a lot of fun.

Diushoupa (Drop the Handkerchief)

Diushoupa or *diushoujuan* was supposedly a pioneer game of the Oregon Trail in America ("Oregon Trail" 2004). As an American invented a simplified version of the Chinese *majiang* known as Mah Jonng, so the Chinese created a more complicated version of *diushoupa* as an indoor or outdoor game. To play, a dozen or so players sit in a circle, facing the center. One player runs around outside the circle with a handkerchief, as the players in the circle chant:

> *Drop, drop, and drop the handkerchief,*
>
> *Drop quietly behind your friend,*
>
> *And no one will tell.*
>
> *Hurry, hurry, and catch him/her.*
>
> *Hurry, hurry, and catch him/her.*

While running around the circle, the player with the handkerchief can drop it behind anyone without being detected. After running another round, the player will signal the unknowing victim by tapping lightly on his or her back. The victim will have to pick up the handkerchief at the signal and spring up to run after the first player, before the first player runs completely around the circle again and sits in the victim's spot. If the victim fails to catch the first player, she or he must accept defeat, step into the center of the circle, and perform a talent show. If the victim catches the first player on the way around the circle, the first player will have to come to the center of the circle to perform, and then start the game over again.

Additional Readings

Lau, H. T. *Chinese Chess*. Boston: Charles E. Tuttle, 2003. 248pp. $10.36. ISBN 080483508X.

Ma Guojun and Ma Shuyun. *Zhonghua chuantong youxi da quan (Anthology of Chinese Games)*. Beijing: Nongcun duwu chubanshe, 1990. pages unknown. $4.00. ISBN 7504810169.

Shotwell, Peter, Huiren Yang, and Sangit Chatterjee, *Go!: More Than a Game*. Boston: Charles E. Tuttle, 2003. 192pp. $14.95. ISBN 080483475X.

CRAFTS

Chinese *shougongyi* (handicrafts) have a history that spans 4,000 years, as evidenced by the excavated relics on display in museums throughout the country. Chinese *shougongyi* falls into two categories: *tezhong gongyi* (special handicrafts) and *minjian gongyi* (folk handicrafts). *Tezhong gongyi*, mostly made from rare and costly materials, require more sophisticated workmanship and therefore possess higher artistic value. These handicrafts include works of *jingtailan* (cloisonné enamel); *daqi* (lacquer ware); carpets of wool and silk; and carvings of ivory (now its artificial substitute), jade, and other precious stones. Chinaware is also a special type of handicraft, although most are made of inexpensive china earth. *Jingdezhen, Tangshan, Longquan, Jun,* and *Ru* are brand-name ancient kilns that are still in full production.

Minjian gongyi has distinct ethnic and regional flavors. *Minjin gongyi* of the Han Chinese falls into the following categories:

- *jian* (cutting), which includes the cutting, folding, and sculpting of paper;

- *zha* (tying), which includes crafts made of bamboo or metal frames covered by paper and silk, such as kites and lanterns;

- *bian* (plaiting), which includes crafts plaited with straw and threads of cotton or silk, such as tiger dolls, fragrant pouches, and *caiqiu* (a pom-pom-like ball);

- *zhi* (weaving), which includes crafts woven and dyed with special techniques, such as *laran* (batik) and *zharan* (bandhnu);

- *xiu* (embroidery), which includes the famed *shuangmianxiu* (an embroidery with the same image on both sides);

- *su* (sculpting), including crafts sculptured with clay, wood, ghee (Tibetan butter), dough, and pottery, such as the famed pottery kettles of Yixing; and

- *hui* (painting), including crafts painted, countermarked, pieced, and burnt. Painted fans, silk scarves, and snuff bottles (with pictures painted on the inside surface of the glass) fall into this category.

Many *minjian gongyi* crafts, like the paper cuts that illustrate some of the tales in this book, allude to Chinese folktales. Although largely made of inexpensive materials, *minjian gongyi* demands a tremendous amount of experience and training. The few examples given here are merely illustrative of the rudimentary skills required to create Chinese folk handicrafts.

Cutting a Chinese Knot

Introduction

For centuries Chinese women in the rural north have been natural paper cutting artists, creating their works of art with scissors and sheets of red paper. They use paper cuttings to decorate their residences, particularly the windows of their houses, on festivals and occasions of celebration. The themes and patterns of paper cuttings may be endless, but all are designed to extend good wishes. The Chinese knot described here has seemingly infinite loops, are symbolic of a blessing for endless happiness.

Instructions

1. Take a 5-inch square piece of thin red paper and fold it in half diagonally to form a triangle with two equal sides (see a).

2. Fold it in half diagonally three more times, into a very small triangle (see b).

3. Fold it once more, into an even smaller triangle, leaving an exposed edge slightly more than $\frac{1}{8}$ inch wide at the baseline (see c).

4. Fold the triangle back to form an even smaller triangle, leaving the uneven exposed edge outside (see d).

5. Cut the tip of the 90 degree angle as shown in the diagram (see e).

6. Open the folded triangle four times until it looks like a mask, with two square eyes, a nose pointing up (or down, depending on how you hold it), and two ears pointing horizontally (see f).

7. Slit the section of the baseline directly beneath the left "eye" where the "nose" points up (see f).

8. Remove the section along the baseline that forms the right "ear" (see f).

9. Carefully unfold the paper. You now have a paper-cut Chinese knot (see g).

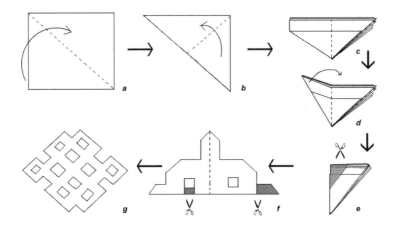

Tying a Chinese Knot

Introduction

Real Chinese knots are tied and plaited instead of being cut. Tying a Chinese knot demands a lot of patience, but with practice, you will eventually learn how to make one of your own. The following example of a simple knot is a good start.

Instructions

1. Stretch out a 20-inch long and ⅛-inch thick red, braided ribbon or string on a level surface, such as a desk.

2. Pick up one end and bring it down and across to the right to form a large loop.

3. Pick up and move the right end of the ribbon or string all the way to the left, beneath the other end of the ribbon or string that is lying in the middle, and take it back beneath that end to the right to form a smaller loop under the bigger one (see a).

4. Take the end of the ribbon or string that is in the middle up across the entire smaller loop under it and feed it into the bigger loop beneath it (see b).

5. Take the same end and bring it down to feed into the smaller loop on top of it (see b).

6. Carefully pull both ends (see c). You have created a Chinese knot!

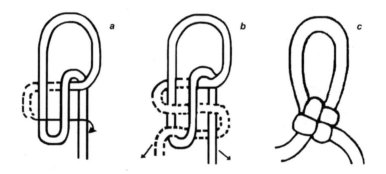

Making a Lantern

Introduction

Lanterns are a big part of Chinese holiday celebrations. This is particularly true of the Lantern Festival, which takes place on the eve of the fifteenth day of the first Chinese lunar month, usually in early February. On that evening, all types of lanterns are on display everywhere in the country. Here you will learn how to make a simple one of your own. All you need is a rectangular piece of construction paper, a pair of scissors, and a glue stick or Scotch tape.

Instructions

1. Fold the construction paper in half lengthwise (see a).

2. Make a dozen cuts along the fold, without cutting all the way to the other edge, because the area left uncut will serve as the top and bottom of the lantern (see b).

3. Unfold the paper and match up the ends (see c).

4. Glue or tape the ends together, and there is your Chinese lantern (see d)!

5. You may glue or tape a paper strip across the top of the lantern to make a handle.

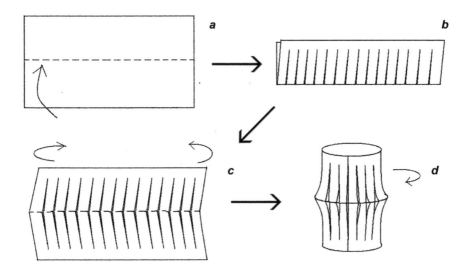

Folding a Chinese Boat

Introduction

Chinese *zhezhi* (paper folding) may have a longer history than Japanese origami, but it is not as popular as its foreign cousin. Nevertheless, Chinese children love *zhezhi* and enjoy making many objects with this intricate craft. This Chinese *shanban* (a flat-bottomed boat, known to Westerners as a "junk") is the first *zhezhi* that I learned to make as a child.

Instructions

1. Fold a rectangular piece of paper lengthwise in thirds, accordion style (see a).

2. Flip up one of the four ends to make a right-angled fold, with the top edge flush with the unfolded edge (see b).

3. Fold up the folded edge of this angle halfway, to form an acute angle on top of the right angle (see c).

4. Do the same with the other three ends to form a trapezoid.

5. Fold the baseline of the trapezoid up ⅕ inch on both sides (see c).

6. Carefully open the paper from inside out (see d), and you will have a Chinese *shanban* (see e).

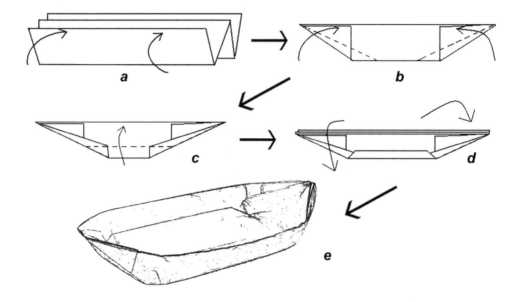

Additional Reading

Bledsoe, Karen E. *Chinese New Year Crafts*. Berkeley Heights, N.J.: Enslow Elementary, 2005. 32pp. $22.60. ISBN 0766023478.

Borja, Robert, and Corinne Borja. *Making Chinese Papercuts*. Edited by Kathleen Tucker. Morton Grove, Ill.: Albert Whitman, 1980. $14.98. ISBN 0807549487.

Chen, Lydia. *Chinese Knotting*. Boston, Mass.: Charles E. Tuttle, 2003. 116pp. $16.47. ISBN 0804833990.

Soong, Maying. *Chinese Paper Folding for Beginners*. Mineola, N.Y.: Dover Publications, 2002. 144pp. $4.95. ISBN 0486418065.

Temko, Florence. *Traditional Crafts from China*. Minneapolis, Minn.: Lerner Publishing Group, 2000. 64pp. $48.89. ISBN 0822529394.

Part 3

The Tales

The author collecting folktales from two villagers at the Geng Village of
Gaocheng City, Hebei Province, China. Courtesy of Hao Yuan.

Animal Tales

Animal tales are not just tales about animals. The animal characters usually act and speak like human beings so that they can make a point, either to educate or to advise. In this sense, animal tales are primarily fables. Chinese animal tales are no exception. "Monkeys Fishing the Moon" tells us to think before acting, "A Frog in a Well" demonstrates the embarrassment of bragging, "A Fox and a Tiger—Who Is the Real King of the Jungle" warns us not to be gullible, "A Tiger That First Sees a Donkey" says not to be scared by appearances, "Wolf 'Mother' " shows us how to face up to danger, and "A Monkey and a Tiger" demonstrates the consequences of dishonesty. Animal tales are often humorous, and for this reason they are loved by adults and children alike.

MONKEYS FISHING THE MOON

Courtesy of Baihua Literature and Art Publishing House.

A long, long time ago, there lived in a forest a kingdom of monkeys. There were several hundred of them altogether. They lived a harmonious and uneventful life for generations.

At the edge of the forest there was a pond. It was neither deep nor shallow. The trees that stretched their limbs far over the pond above the water served as perfect jumping boards for the over-active monkeys, for diving was their most favorite sport. Under the summer sun, they would climb up to the extended branches and inch out as far over the pond as they dared. Then they would splash into the water one after another, in various styles. This pastime not only helped them cool off in the summer heat, but also provided them with an opportunity to display their courage and their acrobatic talents. When night fell, the monkeys would shun the pond and hide themselves in the trees in the forest. They all knew that the pond was also a source of drinking water for many nocturnal animals, including beasts of preys.

Moonlit evenings were the exception, especially when the moon was big, round, and bright. Beasts of prey, fearing human hunters, would seldom linger at the pond after they quickly quenched their thirst. Unfortunately, the moon became this big and bright only once a year. Nonetheless, the young monkeys, particularly those who were extremely hyper and daring, claimed the moonlit pond as a paradise. They ventured out of the forest to continue their diving contest.

Normally the monkeys would turn a blind eye to the surface of the water while they were playing. Their only concern was whether it was safe around them. One time, however, a young monkey, who had been out in the brightest moonlit night for the first time, found something that startled everybody.

"Look!" shrieked the young monkey as the party reached the pond, "The moon has fallen into the water!" The sight of a big, round, bright moon lying on the surface of the pond stunned all the monkeys, as if it were the first time they had seen this phenomenon.

"What shall we do?" asked another young monkey.

The news that the moon had fallen into the pond quickly spread to the monkey king and other elders who were ready to go to bed in the forest. They rushed to the scene and were also astounded to see the moon lounging on the surface of the water. They had come out to play in the brightest moonlight many, many times when they were young, but they had never paid any attention to where the moon was, taking for granted that it was high above in the evening sky. They scratched their heads and buttocks, not knowing what to do. A moment later, one of the elders, who thought of himself as the smartest of all creatures, had an idea and suggested it to the king, "Let's fish the moon out of the pond."

"But how?" the king asked.

After a brief silence, one of the hyper young monkeys jumped over to the king, "I got it! I got it!"

When he told the king the idea, the king broke into a smile and patted him on the back in appreciation, saying, "You are really the smartest of all monkeys!" He then made the young monkey leader to put his idea into practice. The young leader asked a robust, young monkey to climb up to a limb of the tree that reached the farthest over the pond and told him, "Grasp the limb tight with your feet. You are the key link to a chain we are going to form. If you fail, all will. Do you think you are up to the task?"

"Yes, sir!" the young monkey answered with resolution. He climbed nimbly up the tree, maneuvered cautiously closer to the tip of its limb, and hung himself upside down, his feet grasping the limb firmly.

The young leader then ordered another young monkey to join the monkey hanging from the limb and asked him to hold the first monkey's hands with his feet. The first monkey gripped the new arrival's feet securely, remembering what the leader had said about his key role in the monkey link they were forming.

The leader ordered other monkeys to do the same, one by one, until the last monkey's hands almost reached the water. He then mounted the tree himself and carefully clambered down the chain to reach the last monkey at its end. His feet locked steadfastly in the hands of the monkey above him, the monkey leader could stretch his hands into the water. He tried to fish the moon out, but each time he did, the moon would break into pieces. He waited until the moon came together before he made another attempt. As he struggled, amid the cheers of the monkeys on the bank, the chain of monkeys swayed and swung with each of his movements.

The monkey chain was swinging and swaying when all of a sudden the limb of the tree cracked. All the monkeys splashed into the pond. As the bedraggled monkeys clambered to shore, one of them happened to raise his head and could not help shouting, "Look! The moon is still up in the sky!"

A FROG IN A WELL

A frog lived in an abandoned well all his life. Little bugs, small fish, and tiny shrimps were his only companions. Everything in the well—the water, the mud, the cylindrical brick wall, and the moss on it—were all he knew about the world. He had no idea what the real world looked like.

One day, a big sea turtle wandered near the well and caught the attention of the frog, who happened to look up to enjoy the little, circular, blue sky. The frog would not let this opportunity to brag about his knowledge of the world pass.

"Look! How happy I am! I know everything about the world: the bugs that can walk on the surface of the water in the well, the little fish that swim beneath them, and the tiny shrimps that eat dirt at the bottom," the frog rumbled along, not giving the turtle a chance to speak. He continued, "I am living the happiest life in the world. When I am in a good mood, I jump up and down in the well shaft; when I am tired, I lie down on that brick sticking out from the wall; and when I'm hungry, I catch the little fish, shrimps, and bugs. The thing I enjoy the most, you know, is to swim beneath the water, raising my mouth out of the water to breathe from time to time. Sometimes, I even take a deep breath and dive to the bottom to take a walk on the soft sand . . . ."

"Hey, listen! Have you ever been to the sea?" The sea turtle had had enough of the frog's babble and stopped him short.

"What? What do you mean by the 'C'?"

"No, it has nothing to do with the alphabet. It is S-E-A, a large body of water," the turtle raised his voice and explained patiently.

"But why do I have to bother since I have a large body of water here in the well?" asked the frog.

"Let me tell you what a large body of water is," replied the turtle. "You can never imagine how vast the sea is. It is I don't know how many times larger than the body of water in your well. Let me put it this way, ten years of flood and another eight years of drought would have little impact on the level of the sea waters. Living in a body of water like that will give you a real sense of happiness."

" . . . ?!" His big mouth wide open, the frog was at a loss for words. Knowing that there was a much larger world outside his well, the frog never bragged again. His descendants simply moved out of the well. However, unable to find the big sea they had been told about, they settled in farmers' rice fields, above which the sky was as extensive as their big, raised eyes could see.

A FOX AND A TIGER—WHO IS THE REAL KING OF THE JUNGLE?

Once upon a time, a hungry tiger was prowling in a forest looking for food, that is, other animals. He could eat them because he was their king. The tiger had not eaten anything for the past two days, because animals like deer, boars, wolves, rabbits, and, certainly foxes all seemed to have become smarter than ever before. Each time he came out hunting, they would scatter in all directions and disappear before he could reach them. How ironic it was to be a king! Tiger was the supreme leader of the jungle, but his subjects feared him so much that they all shunned his presence, and their fear of him almost deprived him of his food source. "I would give up my throne for a bunny," he would sometimes say to himself sullenly. However, if an animal should challenge his authority, that would be the end of it. He never really wanted to give up his throne.

At the same time, a conceited fox, taking advantage of the hubbub and commotion of the fleeing animals, caught a big bunny and gobbled it up. Smart as she was, the fox hadn't anticipated that her bulging belly would weigh her down so much that she could not run as fast as she usually did. She became the hungry tiger's easy prey. This fox, however, was no ordinary beast. She thought she was the smartest animal in the entire animal kingdom, and she would prove it.

"Hold it," the fox blurted out at the top of her voice, as the tiger snarled, arched his hips, and opened his watering mouth. "You think you are still the King of the Jungle?" the fox asked, pressing her forefinger on the wet nose of the tiger. If the tiger had concentrated his sense of feeling on that part of his body at the moment, he could have felt the fox's slender finger quivering. The strange question, however, simply bewildered him. Besides, he had never known a fox to talk to him in such a bold and arrogant manner. He asked, "What do you mean?"

"I mean you are not the King of the Jungle anymore!" responded the fox categorically.

The tiger dropped his big jaw at the fox's shocking remark. Completely baffled, he asked, his tone still carrying some contempt, "How do you know?"

"Haven't you heard that the Jade Emperor of Heaven has made me the new King of the Jungle?" the fox cocked up her head and said, "His Majesty ruled that all animals, including you, should submit to me. He said that if you disobey, he will punish you without mercy!"

The tiger sized up the fox with mixed feelings of disbelief and dread. The fox's entire body was no bigger than the tiger's foreleg. A mere flap of his paw would smash her skull and break her backbone. Emboldened by these thoughts, the tiger demanded that the fox show him proof.

The fox was relieved to find that the tiger might be taken in. She had to act before the tiger saw through her trick. The tiger's demand prompted her to come up with an idea quickly: She was going to challenge him to a test. She said to the tiger with great confidence, "The Heavenly Emperor's decree is on its way, but I can show you who the king really is if you can't wait."

"Sure, show me," the tiger roared with impatience, because he was too hungry to wait. He was ready to pounce on the little fox as soon as she failed to produce the evidence. The fox invited the tiger to inspect the jungle with her, and see whether the animals ran for their lives at the sight of her. "Follow me and watch," the fox commanded.

While the tiger and the fox were in the heat of this test of intellect, the other animals had resumed their daily routine, thinking that the tiger had eaten the fox and would call it a day. They had never expected to see the tiger come their way again, chasing the fox in an unhurried manner. No matter what, a tiger was a tiger. The animals took to their heels at the very sight of him.

The tiger's astonishment was beyond description. He could not figure out why in the world all the animals, big or small, ran for their lives at the mere sight of the fox. The thought of being dethroned and the prospect of submitting to the fox and, what was worse, becoming her food, struck the deepest fear into him. He shuddered. When the strutting fox ahead of him paused and turned, he leapt back a few steps, startled.

"What do you think?" asked the fox proudly.

The tiger was speechless, shivering all over. He wanted to run from this small but fierce animal as soon as his shaky legs could carry him.

"Let me tell you what more the Heavenly Emperor told me before I returned to rule this jungle: he wanted me to tear you into pieces before I gobble you up!"

At this, the already terrified tiger ran for dear life, leaving the fox chuckling at the success of her deception. But knowing that lies can't last forever, the fox wasted no time and scampered away to safety.

A TIGER THAT FIRST SEES A DONKEY

Courtesy of Baihua Literature and Art Publishing House.

Long, long ago, in a remote place called Qian, there were no donkeys. A merchant who had seen donkeys elsewhere wanted to import one. One day he bought a donkey a few hundred miles away and shipped it back to Qian. However, after he returned to Qian he found that he had no use for the beast, so he set it free in the wilderness.

A tiger prowling in the wilderness spotted the donkey. The sudden appearance of a strange beast in the territory puzzled the animal king. Deer and hogs were the biggest animals he had ever tackled, but this one was much bigger than anything he had seen before. He said to himself under his breath, "It must be a supernatural being that has landed here to prey on us." Terrified at the thought, the tiger sped away without looking back.

The tiger stopped after scampering a few hundred yards. "Whom am I running from?" He asked himself. "I am the king of the wilderness, and being a king, I should fear nobody. I need to know for sure what that creature is before I show it respect." So thinking, the tiger returned. He stalked toward the donkey with great caution. Then he hid behind a big tree and peeked around it. Seeing the beast doing nothing unusual, the tiger gained some confidence. He even began to feel the urge of his hunting instincts. He leaped out from behind the tree and crept toward the donkey. The strange beast seemed to have heard something stir, for it stiffened its long ears, blew its white nose, and stomped its black hooves on the grass. Startled, the tiger scurried away, uncertain what the donkey would do.

The next day the tiger went to look at the donkey again and was about to approach it when, all of a sudden, the donkey brayed, "Heehaw, heehaw, heehaw . . . ." The previously unheard bellow frightened the tiger out of his wits. He wished that his legs could be longer as he dashed into the thickness of the woods.

A few days passed. Curiosity took hold of the tiger once again. He went to watch the donkey, but there seemed to be nothing out of the ordinary about it. The strange animal was grazing peacefully, swiveling its long ears and wagging its tail from time to time. The tiger became bold enough to move closer. He tried teasing the donkey, but the donkey responded merely with a few brays and kicks. The tiger leaped back a few yards to dodge the attack. Eager to know what else the donkey could do, the tiger decided not to run. Instead, he tried provoking it a second time. Again, the donkey responded with the same braying and kicking.

"Hah, hah! That's all the donkey can do!" the tiger chuckled. With that happy realization, he pounced on the donkey and ate it up. If the donkey had not exposed its weakness so soon, its fate might have been different.

WOLF "MOTHER"

A long, long time ago, two sisters lived with their mother on the edge of a village. The older sister was ten, and the younger was six. They were both smart and courageous. Knowing that, their mother went to visit their grandmother early one morning, leaving them at home. She told them to lock the door and not to open it until they heard her say when she got back,

"Tap the bolt staple; tap the hasp.

Big and small sisters open the door."

Promising to return that evening, their mother departed, taking with her a basket of *momo* (steamed bread) and *guozi* (deep-fried dough), which were their grandmother's favorite foods. The two sisters and their mother did not know that a big, grey wolf had been outside the door and over-heard their conversation, particularly the password. It had sneaked into the woods nearby as the mother opened the door to leave. The two sisters said good-bye to their mother and locked the door behind her.

As the mother passed a graveyard on her way, the big, grey wolf intercepted her. Before the wolf pounced on her, the mother emptied her basket of *momo* and *guozi*, hoping that the wolf would eat them instead of her. In no time the beast gobbled the food up, but it still would not let the mother go. She promised to bring more food when she returned from her visit to her parents. The wolf re-lented because it had a plan.

When she reached her parents' home, the mother of the two sisters wept. Her parents and broth-ers asked her what had happened, and she told them of the wolf and its intention to eat her. At sunset, the mother asked to leave. Her father and brothers insisted on seeing her back to her home. They armed themselves with axes, hoes, and clay bricks in order to fight the beast should it show up.

When they had escorted the mother past the graveyard and found no wolf, the mother let them go, saying that it was safe for her to return to her daughters. However, the cunning wolf had con-cealed itself in the woods close to the two sisters' house. When the mother entered the woods, it at-tacked her. Then it put on her clothes, took her basket, went straight to the house, and knocked at the door, cupping its mouth to mimic the mother's voice:

"Tap the bolt staple; tap the hasp.

Big and small sisters open the door."

The two sisters, who had been anxiously waiting for their mother's return, opened the door and let the wolf in without hesitation. The older sister was about to light the oil lamp when the wolf stopped her, saying, "I am having an eye problem and can't stand the light and the smoke. They would hurt my eyes." The two sisters obeyed, for they loved their mother too much to cause her dis-comfort.

"I'm tired," the wolf said, "Let's go to bed now." In fact, it feared that the sisters would see through its disguise if they stayed up. Besides, it was anxious to eat them in their sleep, when they would be defenseless. In bed, the two sisters happened to feel their "mother's" furry body. (Chinese parents used to share their bed with their young children.) Surprised, the sisters asked why.

"Your grandma gave me a fur coat."

"Why don't you take it off when you sleep?"

"I have a fever."

When the sisters touched their "mother's" hands, they could not help asking, "Why are your hands furry, too?"

"I'm wearing the fur gloves your grandma has just given me."

After a moment, the sisters heard their "mother" eating something crispy. They asked, "What are you eating that's making that crackling noise?"

"I'm having some snacks that your grandma gave me." In fact, the wolf was chewing the fin-gers of the mother that it had left over.

The sisters became suspicious. They realized that this was the big, grey wolf that their mother had often told them about. Although grieved, frightened, and angry, they did not make a stir. Instead, they pretended to go to sleep and waited for the right moment to act. The wolf pretended to fall asleep also, but while doing so, it actually dozed off. Seizing their chance, the two sisters climbed out of the window leading to the backyard, where there was a big date tree. They dashed for the tree and climbed nimbly to the top, as they had often done as child's play.

Their action roused the wolf, which went after them, but it was a few seconds too late. The closing window caught its big tail when it tried to crawl out to catch the two sisters. The wolf wriggled itself free despite the pain. However, when it rushed to the tree, the sisters already sat safely among the foliage. As you know, wolves have never learned how to climb trees. The animal had to conceal its anger and put on a forced smile. It wanted to coax the children to come down, saying, "What's wrong with you girls? Don't you see it's still midnight? Come down and go back to sleep."

The two sisters knew the wolf's intentions. They had an idea and answered, "Mother, come up and see for yourself. We are here to watch a show going on in the neighboring village." The wolf knew they were not telling the truth, but it concealed its resentment. Bent on getting at the sisters, it asked, "I want to watch it, too. How can I come up?"

The two sisters were happy that their plan was working. They replied, "It's easy. We'll tie our belts together and let one end down. Then you tie it around your waist, and we'll lift you up."

"That's so smart of you!" As the wolf flattered them, its mouth could not help watering. Quickly it tied the end of the belts around its waist and asked the sisters to pull it up, which they did. However, when the wolf was halfway up, the two sisters let go, and the wolf crashed to the ground.

Making certain that the wolf was motionless, the two sisters climbed down the tree. They skinned the dead beast and cooked its meat. By now, it was already daybreak. They called in all their neighbors and shared the meat with them. They then poured the meat soup into a vegetable plot in their backyard. After things were calmed down, they began to miss and mourn their lost mother.

A few days later, a cabbage shoot grew where the sisters had poured the meat soup. The sisters took heart to attend to the plant. Their care of the cabbage brought them some solace. To their amazement, the plant grew into a full cabbage in a couple of days. One morning when they went to water the cabbage as usual, they were stunned: The cabbage was transforming into a human figure right before their eyes. As they rubbed their eyes and looked closely, they saw it was none other than their beloved mother. The sisters threw themselves into the open arms of their mother, who had been revived in such a strange manner. They did not care because they were reunited with her.

A MONKEY AND A TIGER

There were once two rulers on a mountain, a smart Monkey and a fierce Tiger. They were blood brothers. One day, Tiger said to Monkey, "It's true that you and I are the kings of the mountain, and we are living a leisurely life, you on wild fruits and I on wild animals. But I begin to find them boring. So what's your take?"

"I think they are boring, too" Monkey answered, "but what else can we find that is interesting?"

"How about going to the villages down the mountain and seeing what food humans eat?" suggested Tiger.

"A great idea!" Monkey jumped with joy.

Evening came, and it began to snow. Tiger and Monkey waited until it was pitch-dark. Then they went down the mountain and arrived in a village at its foot. It was the New Year season, and the entire village was permeated with delicious, meaty aromas. It was customary for Chinese villagers to slaughter their pigs and goats at this time of year and prepare big feasts to celebrate the New Year.

"It smells so good," said Tiger, sniffing with its big nose, "Domestic animals must taste good, too." They began to search for pigs and goats in the village, but all they could find were cattle. Chinese farmers did not kill their best helpers in their farm work unless they became useless.

"Let's steal a cow. Beef must taste better than pork and mutton!" said Monkey.

"Yes, let's get a cow for our supper tonight," Tiger said, smacking its watering mouth.

As they slipped into a courtyard in the darkness, a human thief had just sneaked into it and was lurking on the roof of the house. They did not hear each other because both parties tried to be very quiet. In the house there lived an old couple. They had built a big fire to warm themselves. However, they did not realize that the heat would melt the snow on the thin roof above them, and the roof began to leak. The old couple could not go to sleep and started chatting. Their conversation was loud enough for the animal and human thieves to hear.

"We've had a good year and are looking forward to another. We have nothing to worry about but the leak," said the old woman to her husband.

"Sure, I really fear what the leak would do to us on a dark night like this," responded the husband.

Tiger and Monkey pondered, "We are the most fearful creatures in the world as kings of the mountain. Why does the old couple fear 'Leak'? Who in the world is this 'Leak'?" Monkey pressed its mouth to the big ear of Tiger and whispered, "We'd better leave here and find another residence. Or we'll be losing our lives when Leak knows we are here."

The human thief was also asking himself the same question on the roof and decided to leave. He jumped off the roof and, as it happened, fell on the back of Tiger. Believing that Leak was on the offensive, Tiger began to run like mad, followed blindly by Monkey. When Tiger reached the mountain, it was almost daybreak. Tiger was so tired that it could not even pull itself up.

The human thief was terrified when he realized what he was riding on. As if he had a guardian angel, a branch of a tree happened to brush him as the tiger hobbled beneath it and stopped to rest. Wasting no time, the human thief jumped onto the tree and climbed to the top. When they found out what had been riding on Tiger's back and had ruined their "night out," both Tiger and Monkey were exasperated. They wanted to tear the human thief to pieces. However, Tiger had never learned to climb trees. Its teacher, a cat, had stopped short of teaching Tiger the skill when it found the beast of prey starting to threaten its life. Therefore, Tiger turned to its nimble partner Monkey for help. It asked Monkey to go up and drive the human thief down so that it could catch him. Then, we'll share his flesh!" Tiger said with clenched teeth.

"That's easy!" said Monkey. However, halfway up the tree it balked, thinking, "What if I fail to get the man, but instead, he gets me?"

Monkey came down and said to Tiger, Find us a rope. Tie one end to my waist and the other to your tail. Start running when I wave my hand."

"That's a marvelous idea," said Tiger. It then found a rope and did as Monkey suggested. Monkey began to approach the human thief. The thief was so nervous and scared that he sweated profusely. His sweat fell like rain on the face of Monkey, approaching from below. Monkey had to rub his face and shake the perspiration off its hand. When Tiger saw Monkey shaking its hand, it thought that Monkey was signaling it to run. Tiger scampered off wildly, thinking that the human thief was even more frightening than Leak! Tiger ran and ran until it reached its den, totally forgetting its primate friend, which had been dragged to its death.

Magic Tales

Magic tales tell of supernatural beings, gods, demigods, and fairies, with magic powers—of their selfless heroism, as in "Nezha Fights Sea Dragons"; of their devotion to their parents, as in "The Magic Lotus Lantern"; of their forgiveness of past grievances, as in "Monkey King and the Iron Fan Princess"; and of their compassion for human beings, as in "The Field-snail Fairy" and "A Beauty on the Painting Scroll." Sometimes humans also help supernatural beings, as in "Dragon Princess," and humans help other humans with powers from unexpected sources, as in "A Cricket Boy." Fantasies may not be real, but each of these fantasy stories makes real sense. It is up to you to figure it out.

Courtesy of Baihua Literature and Art Publishing House.

NEZHA FIGHTS SEA DRAGONS

Nezha was originally a Buddhist fire god named Nalakuvara. Thanks to Xu Zhonglin and Wu Cheng'en, two famous Chinese fantasy novelists of the Ming dynasty (1368–1644), Nezha has be-

come a popular young Chinese god. He is popular for his bravery, intelligence, sense of justice and self-sacrifice. The tale of Nezha appears in textbooks, cartoons, and movie series.

Stationed at the Chentown Pass on the coast of Northeast China were General Li Jing and his family. His wife had been expecting their third child for three and a half years. With each passing day, their worries grew deeper. In the sixth month of the third year, the general's wife finally went into labor. When Li Jing heard no crying from her chamber, he thought the baby had been stillborn. That would not have been a surprise at all, for what child could survive such a protracted pregnancy!

The reality was even worse. Instead of a baby, dead or alive, the newborn was a living ball of flesh! General Li Jing thought of it as a demon and decided to destroy it. He was about to halve it with his sword when his wife stopped him. She told him about a dream she had had the night before she gave birth to the fleshy ball.

"I dreamed of an elderly Taoist," she began. "The Taoist came to me, swept his magic whisk across my belly, and told me to accept the baby and name him Nezha," she said in a single breath. She begged her husband to spare the life of their son, even though it was an ugly ball of flesh.

The general, however, would not listen. With a swoop of his blade, he sliced the ball open. To everyone's surprise, when the ball split, a little boy sprang out, with a dazzling red light in his wake. No sooner had he landed on the floor than he grew into a boy of six. When he saw the general and his wife, he immediately held out his hands and called out, "Mom! Dad!" The father accepted the boy as his son, although he resented the strange manner of his birth. As requested by the Taoist that the mother had met in her dream, they named the boy Nezha.

Suddenly there was a commotion outside the house. Before General Li could rush out to see what was happening, a servant dashed in and reported, "An elderly man suddenly appeared in our courtyard on the back of a crane. He said he wanted to see his disciple, Nezha."

When she followed her husband into the courtyard, the mother immediately recognized the elderly man. It was the Taoist from her dream. The Taoist told them that his name was Taiyi Zhenren, or the True Primordial Taoist Master. He had come to see Nezha, who had dashed out into the yard ahead of his parents and stood beside the Taoist master. With the parents' consent, Taiyi Zhenren placed a large ring around Nezha's neck and a long damask silk ribbon over his shoulders. The ring and the ribbon would become his magic weapons to protect him from possible dangers.

"Son, use them sparingly and only to the good of your fellow people," Taiyi Zhenren told Nezha as he sailed away on the back of the big bird.

That year, a serious drought hit the Chentown region. For months and months, not a single drop of rain fell. People were close to starvation. Nezha asked his mother what had happened. His mother told him that the culprit was the vicious Dragon King of the East Sea, who demanded that each day the people of Chentown sacrifice a little boy and girl at his altar in the temple dedicated to him. The children would be his special meal. When people refused to surrender their children, the Dragon King stopped raining. He also asked other dragon kings to hold their rainwater. As people would rather suffer a natural disaster than give up their babies, the Dragon King sent a *yecha* (a man-eating monster) to roam the region and snatch them for him.

One afternoon the blazing sun was scorching the earth as usual. Nezha went to the seashore to swim, a way to fend off the summer heat. When he arrived, a boy and a girl were looking for seashells on the beach. Suddenly the *yecha* emerged from the sea. He had seen the two children playing from beneath the water. His sudden appearance terrified and paralyzed the children. Before the *yecha* could get hold of them, Nezha stopped him.

"Who do you think you are?" said the monster in disdain. "I'll take the three of you together to the Dragon King."

"Stop blustering! I'm not going to hurt you if you leave the children alone," said Nezha.

"But I want to hurt you, you little rascal!" roared the *yecha* as he charged Nezha, his pair of bronze hammers held high and ready to fall upon Nezha's head. Nezha fended off the attack with his ring. This was the first time he had tried his magic weapon. He really did not mean to use it, for he remembered what his master Taiyi Zhenren had told him. The power of the ring amazed him: a mere touch on the poor *yecha*'s head broke it into pieces.

Enraged at the loss of his henchman at the hands of a boy, the Dragon King dispatched his third and favorite son to capture Nezha. The Dragon King wanted to see what kind of a child Nezha was and to mete out the severest punishment against him

The dragon prince did not take Nezha seriously at all, thinking that he could easily cut the boy in half with his sword. He challenged Nezha to a fight. Nezha, however, trying to avoid a bloody fight, was unwilling to engage his opponent.

"Go tell your father to give up his evildoing and mend his ways, or I'll break his neck as I smashed the head of the *yecha* monster!" warned Nezha. Humiliated, the dragon prince was eager to destroy the little boy. Brandishing his sword, he swooped down on Nezha.

To meet the dragon prince's attack, Nezha let loose one end of the red damask silk and, holding the other end tight, he flung it again and again. The silk extended and swirled until it enwrapped the body of the dragon prince. With a gentle jerk, Nezha brought him down to the beach, his dragon head plunging into the sand. When Nezha pulled the dragon prince out, he was already dead of a broken neck. Once again, Nezha learned the unexpected lethality of his magic weapons. As a warning to the Dragon King of the East Sea, Nezha pulled a tendon out of the dragon prince's body and tossed it into the sea.

Nezha slaying the dragon prince.

Part 3: The Tales

The death of the dragon prince shocked and grieved the Dragon King. To avenge his son, he called in all his brothers, the Dragon Kings of the South, North, and West Seas. Together they poured torrential rain down on Chentown and its surrounding areas. The incessant downpour caused a big flood, which threatened to decimate the people already devastated by many months' drought.

Flying above the house of General Li, the Dragon King of the East Sea demanded that he give up his son, Nezha, and said that in return he would call off both the flood and the drought. Caught between the plight of his people and the fate of his son, the general did not know what to do. Finally, he made up his mind and agreed to kill Nezha, only to be stopped by his wife.

"How can you trust the vicious dragon? What if he won't keep his promise even after you kill our son?"

"But if we don't give him up, our people will all be drowned. At least we will have a chance by getting rid of him," General Li responded.

Nezha could not bear seeing his parents mentally and emotionally tormented by the difficult position in which he thought he had placed them. Neither could he stand the people perishing because of his action or inaction. Knowing the limitations of his power in front of the formidable dragon alliance, Nezha had only one option: suicide.

"Listen, you dirty dragons! Do as you promise or I'll go after you in my death," said Nezha, standing firmly in the rain beside his father. As he finished, he snatched the sword from the trembling hand of his father and slit his throat.

As Nezha's body fell to the ground, the Taoist master Taiyi Zhenren sent for his spirit. The Taoist's assistants brought Nezha's spirit to his Golden Light Cave on Qianyuan Mountain, where Taiyi Zhenren reconstructed Nezha's body with lotus leaves and blossoms. Then he merged Nezha's spirit with his new body. This time, in addition to the ring and the silk ribbon, he armed Nezha with a spear as his new weapon and a *fenghuolun* (a pair of wind-and-fire wheeled shoes) as his means of transportation. The Taoist master also enabled him to transform into a giant with three heads and six arms when necessary. The newborn Nezha was much more powerful. He sought out the Dragon King.

The Dragon King of the East Sea had never expected to see Nezha alive again, and more formidable. With his new powers, Nezha had no problem overcoming the Dragon King. Subdued, the dragon vowed not to do any more harm to the people of Chentown.

A BEAUTY ON A PAINTING SCROLL

According to one of the greatest Tang poets, Bai Juyi, a Chinese emperor could have as many as 3,000 concubines residing in his sangong liuyuan (nine harems). Such extravagance reflected the dissipation of the emperors, and at the same time caused great pain to those women and their families. Another great Tang poet, Du Mu, tells about a concubine living in a harem for thirty-six years who did not even know what the emperor looked like. Suicide and mutual assault were common

occurrences in the royal household. Under this evil system, people outside the palace fared no better, as is evident in the tale I retell here.

A long time ago, there was a vicious emperor in China, who cared for nothing except treasures and women. He dispatched his men to the four corners of the country to find him valuables and beauties.

In a far-off province, Sister Qiao, a very pretty young woman, lived in the depths of a mountain with her grandfather, the only family member she had. As she did the housework, her grandfather supported the family by carving stones. Sister Qiao's grandfather often went out to hunt for stones needed for his carving projects. One day he spotted a rock embedded in a cliff. His trained eyes told him that it could be a perfect material for a carving project he had on hand. Despite the danger of climbing the cliff, he tried to get to it, but he lost his balance and fell into the valley below. A young stonecutter, who happened to be quarrying beneath him, extended his arms and caught him, saving his life.

The young man was Brother Zhuang, known for his bravery, honesty, and kindness. He saw the old stonecutter home, carrying the stone for him. Sister Qiao and Brother Zhuang fell in love with each other at first sight. Knowing that they could make a happy couple, the old stonecutter picked a *jiri* for their wedding.

At the same time, however, the emperor's prime minister had learned of Sister Qiao's beauty and whereabouts. The emperor's men came to take her to the emperor. In a fight to protect his granddaughter, the old stonecutter lost his life. Sister Qiao was so grieved that she threw herself off a nearby cliff, but a fairy passing by rescued her. The fairy cast a blank painting scroll down to catch Sister Qiao as she fell. As soon as she touched the unfolded scroll, Sister Qiao became an image in the painting. The fairy then retrieved the scroll and left the scene, unnoticed.

The next day, when Brother Zhuang came to see Sister Qiao, he found out what had happened. After burying the old stonecutter with great sorrow, he set out to look for Sister Qiao's body, but no matter how hard he looked, he could not find it. How could he, as she was now with the guarding fairy? The fairy wanted Sister Qiao to "hide" in the painting and would return her to Brother Zhuang when it was safe to do so. While she was looking for a chance to reunite the young couple, the fairy gave Sister Qiao a magic sewing kit as a gift for their future wedding.

The Chinese New Year was approaching, and this gave the fairy a chance to reunite the couple. Dressed as a haggish old woman, she wandered in a crowded market carrying the painting scroll under her arm. When she spotted Brother Zhuang, she caught up with him and begged him to purchase the scroll. The kind-hearted Brother Zhuang bought it with the little money he had. He might have to celebrate the New Year without the necessary provisions, but he felt happy that he had given joy to someone else.

Back home, Brother Zhuang hung the painting scroll on the wall. Only then did he have a chance to take a good look at the painted beauty. The closer he looked at her, the more she appeared to be Sister Qiao. As Brother Zhuang puzzled over the image, Sister Qiao weighed the possibility of getting back to her fiancée. She would have quit the painting immediately, but feared that the emperor's soldiers might show up at any time. Unwilling to get Brother Zhuang in trouble, she decided to keep him company the way she was for the time being.

Soon strange things began to happen to Brother Zhuang. Each day he would come back home from work to see the bed made, the floor cleaned, and the dinner table laden with piping-hot dishes. Brother Zhuang wanted to find out what was going on. One day he hid himself in the courtyard.

When he heard something stirring in the house, he dashed into it, catching Sister Qiao cooking his meal. Sister Qiao told him the whole story and begged him to let her return to the painting.

"The emperor's men are everywhere," she said, "They will come after you once they know I am alive."

"They don't scare me a bit," replied Brother Zhuang, "Besides, you may always return to the scroll when we sense any danger. So long as you don't go out, no one will know you're here with me."

Sister Qiao consented to Brother Zhuang's plea, and they lived a modest but happy life. A year later, the young couple had become less vigilant. Thinking that the emperor might have forgotten her, Sister Qiao asked Brother Zhuang to sell her needlecrafts to supplement his meager income. As it happened, Sister Qiao was very good at needlework, and the fairy's magic sewing kit bettered her skills and made her more productive. However, the lustful emperor and his treacherous prime minister had never given up on Sister Qiao. Their men were like bloodhounds, and in time they traced the needlecrafts to Sister Qiao. They came, fought Brother Zhuang and killed him, and took Sister Qiao to the emperor.

At the palace, the emperor forced Sister Qiao to marry him, but before he could get hold of her, she produced the painting scroll, which she had hidden in her clothes, and returned to it as an image. The frustrated emperor ordered that she be restored by every possible means.

In the meantime, the fairy brought Brother Zhuang back to life with her magic spell and encouraged him to rescue Sister Qiao. Brother Zhuang sneaked into the palace, searching for his fiancée. Unfortunately his movements caught the attention of the emperor's prime minister, who took the painting scroll and ordered every gate closed. Brother Zhuang, who didn't have a weapon, fought the guards with whatever he could lay his hands on. As he stormed into the palace, he saw a tripod cauldron with charcoal burning red in it. The cauldron was used as a heating device to keep the emperor warm. Brother Zhuang lifted it and threw it at the emperor, who ducked just in time. His royal dragon robe, however, was not so lucky. A flying piece of charcoal burned a hole in it. Frightened and furious, the emperor sentenced the captured Brother Zhuang to death.

"Stop!" cried Sister Qiao. To save Brother Zhuang's life, she could no longer remain in the painting scroll. Coming out of the scroll, held in the hands of the prime minister, Sister Qiao demanded, "Release Brother Zhuang, and I will mend your robe." Seeing the emperor stumped, the prime minister whispered something to him. The emperor nodded understandingly. Putting on a sinister smile, the emperor turned to Sister Qiao, "I'll stay his execution. If you can mend my robe, I'll set you both free, but if you can't, you know what the consequence will be."

The prime minister ordered Sister Qiao to complete the mending before sunrise. To make the job impossible, he asked that she add to the robe an embroidered pattern of a red sun above surging waves. Despite the great difficulty, Sister Qiao complied. With the help of the magic sewing kit, she finished the robe in no time. Instead of presenting it to the emperor, the prime minister messed up the embroidery and ordered Sister Qiao to mend the robe again. Now she began to worry whether she could finish the task and save her beloved husband, Brother Zhuang. She worked hard and incessantly. Before the first ray of sunlight appeared on the horizon, the fairy appeared and helped her finish the embroidery.

When the emperor put on the robe, he told Sister Qiao that he would award her with something precious. He had Brother Zhuang brought into his presence. "His heart will be the prize I am going to award you, hah, hah, hah," chuckled the vicious emperor.

A Beauty on a Painting Scroll

"You blatant liar! You brute!" Sister Qiao yelled. She felt so betrayed and indignant that she did not know what else she could say. She would have charged at the emperor, but the guards held her back.

Before an executioner could approach Brother Zhuang, the fairy freed him from his shackles. Brother Zhuang seized the knife from the executioner, turned around, and went straight at the emperor. The knife missed the emperor, who leapt aside in desperation, but it left a cut on his robe where the surging sea was embroidered. Instantly a torrent gushed out and flooded the entire palace.

The emperor, the prime minister, and all their men were drowned. Brother Zhuang and Sister Qiao, however, found themselves in a boat prepared by the fairy. Saying good-bye to the villagers on the mountain, they sailed away to where they could find a peaceful and happy life.

THE FIELD-SNAIL FAIRY

The tale first appeared in A.D. 977. Originally, the field-snail fairy was one of the Jade Emperor's maidservants. At his request, she descended to the world to help, instead of marrying, a wretched bachelor. She returned to Heaven after the bachelor unwittingly revealed her identity. In time, the tale spread everywhere, mostly by word of mouth, and eventually the field-snail fairy lost her celestial connection.

Long, long ago, in a village in South China, there lived a young man named Xie Duan. He had lost his parents when he was very young. The kindhearted villagers had adopted and raised him. He was diligent and respectful, but was too poor to start a family. When his fellow villagers tried to talk him into thinking of marriage, he would always say, "Thanks, but I don't think I can afford to feed one more person under my roof."

One day, working in the paddy fields, he stepped on something hard in the mud. He stooped, scooped up a handful of mud, and found something glistening in it. It was a big field snail. Its greenish shell with spiraling lines looked fascinating. Xie Duan decided to keep it in a big jar in front of the thatched hut that he called home. He used the jar to store drinking water drawn from a well half a mile outside the village.

Every morning before going to work in the fields, Xie Duan would say good-bye to the big snail in the jar, and every evening when he came back from work, he would visit the snail again and let it know of his return. Thus, the field snail became an important part of Xie Duan's life.

Before the arrival of the field snail, Xie Duan's bachelor life had been a dull routine. Each morning he would get up early and go to work in his fields, bringing with him a simple lunch, which was usually corn bread with some pickled vegetables. Every evening he would return home, cook a simple meal, and eat it. Then he would visit a neighbor or two to chat before returning to his hut to sleep. Now that he had the field snail, he thought that his otherwise tedious life had become a little more exciting, but he could never have anticipated how exciting his life was about to become.

One evening Xie Duan came home as usual. As was his custom, he went up to the water jar to greet the field sail, which acted a little weird. Xie Duan did not give its strange behavior much thought, and walked into his hut. A delicious aroma was coming from the hut and greeted his nostrils, making him hungrier. Surprised and curious, he gingerly pushed the door open. Good heavens! On his table were several hot, delicious dishes, ready for him to enjoy.

"Who did this?" he asked himself, scratching the back of his head in bewilderment. "It must be my fellow villagers. They had been helping me until I could take care of myself, but why have they suddenly begun to look after me again, and with such good food? How can they afford it?"

After the meal, the best that he had ever eaten in his life, he went to visit his neighbors to express his gratitude, wondering why they had resumed helping him in such a secretive and liberal manner. The villagers, however, were as puzzled as he was, for none of them knew anything about what had happened.

"Well, it must be a freak accident. Someone may have sent the food to me by mistake," Xie Duan pondered in bed. For the first time, he lost sleep. He began to feel guilty about eating the food, which could have been meant for someone else. He reproached himself for being imprudent and greedy.

The next evening the same thing happened again, much to Xie Duan's astonishment. "No one could be so silly as to make the same mistake twice. There must be something strange going on." This time, he did not eat the food. He wanted to find out who was behind the mischief or act of kindness.

The next morning he got up and went to work as usual. Before noon, however, he stole back to his hut and hid behind the hedged fence that formed the courtyard. He was going to find out what was going on. He was holding his breath and waiting motionlessly when suddenly the lid of the water jar popped open. From the jar emerged a young woman as pretty as a fairy. Xie Duan blinked his eyes a few times as if he were struggling to wake up from a dream. The next moment, he saw the young woman go toward his thatched hut. Stunned by the miraculous spectacle, Xie Duan almost cried out, but he managed not to make a sound. When the young woman entered the hut, he quietly tiptoed toward the window, peeped in, and caught sight of the young woman fixing his meal.

In order to figure out what the young woman had to do with the water jar, Xie Duan tiptoed back to it. There he found the field snail lying still. When he carefully fished it out, he found it to be only an empty shell.

"Could that young woman be a spirit living in the shell?" he asked himself, the snail shell almost slipping from his quivering hand. "No matter who she is, she must like me. Why can't I have a talk with her to find out who she is, and why she is hiding in the shell?"

So thinking, Xie Duan hid the empty shell beneath the hedges. By now he could smell the meal. The young woman must have finished her cooking and be ready to return to the shell. Without hesitation, Xie Duan dashed to his hut and blocked the doorway.

"Who are you? Where are you from?" he asked. Startled, the young woman pushed Xie Duan aside and rushed to the water jar. When she could not find the snail shell, she panicked and began to cry. She asked Xie Duan to give the shell back to her.

"I didn't mean to hurt you," said Xie Duan, following her to the water jar and trying to comfort her. "Please tell me who you are and why you have to hide yourself in the snail shell. Tell me, and I will give the shell back to you."

"I am a fairy, but I want to live an earthly life," the young woman began when she had calmed down, "I have been looking for an honest and diligent young man to become his wife."

"Oh, I am sorry!" the honest, naïve Xie Duan apologized.

"Sorry for what?" the fairy asked, knowing what he was going to say but amused at his expression of embarrassment.

"Well," scratching the back of his head, Xie Duan blushed, "I am sorry for taking the snail home and preventing you from finding a husband."

"I've found one already," the young woman said in a hushed voice.

"Who?" asked Xie Duan, but immediately he found the answer when his eyes met the snail fairy's, which were shy and full of love.

"But . . . but I have nothing," Xie Duan stammered.

"You have all I am looking for," the fairy declared, "honesty, diligence, and kind-heartedness."

When they heard about the love affair, the villagers were as happy as Xie Duan and the fairy. They gave them the best wedding they could. Xie Duan and the field-snail fairy lived happily ever after.

DRAGON PRINCESS

Two dragons playing with a *longzhu* (dragon pearl).
Courtesy of Baihua Literature and Art Publishing House.

To the Chinese, everything has two sides: the yin (negative) and the yang (positive). A dragon, for instance, can either guarantee favorable weather for crops or bring about drought and flood. Therefore, revering dragons has long been a Chinese tradition. Speaking of dragons, one cannot ignore their treasured longzhu *(dragon pearl). The Chinese believe that* longzhu *makes a dragon what it is. Without* longzhu, *a dragon will become powerless, but with it, even a mortal can perform miracles. Armed with this background knowledge, the reader will have a better understanding of the following story.*

A scholar named Liu Yi was on his way to take a national imperial examination. If he passed it, he would be able to get a job as a high-ranking official, which many of the intellectuals of the day aspired to be.

After a long and arduous journey, Liu Yi arrived at Mt. Shishan on the coast of the East Sea, tired and thirsty. Soon he caught sight of a spring at the foot of the mountain. Its still, dark water seemed bottomless. An inscription on a monument dedicated to the spring said that it led to the *longgong* (the Palace of the Dragon King) of the East Sea. Liu Yi quenched his thirst with the spring water and went on his journey, doubtful of the inscription's credibility.

Liu Yi plodded a few miles on a mountain path without coming across a single soul. Just as he was beginning to feel very lonely, he heard the faint melody of a flute in the distance. As he walked on, it became increasingly distinct. Soon he saw the player of the music, a teenage girl herding a flock of sheep along the roadside. She was holding a bamboo flute to her mouth, her hands sticking out from the holes of a *jia* (cangue), a heavy wooden yoke borne on her shoulders and enclosing her neck and arms. Curious, Liu Yi approached her and asked sympathetically, "Who are you? How come you're locked in a cangue?"

"Well," the girl sighed, but did not continue.

"Don't be afraid. I am a scholar on my way to the imperial examination," Liu Yi said, trying to gain her trust. "Tell me what happened to you. See if I can help."

At this, the girl raised her head, the torn and shabby cloth gown she was wearing and the muddy smear on her face not concealing her youth and beauty. Blushed, she ventured, "Are you sure you can help me?"

"Yes!" Liu Yi replied with determination.

"You have to believe me, and don't be scared if I tell you who I am, and why I am in such a miserable condition."

"I trust you," Liu Yi replied, though uncertain what she would say. "Please tell me what happened to you. I will help you no matter what."

"Thank you so much," the girl began tearfully. "I am the third daughter of the Dragon King of the East Sea. He banished me here because I helped the people in the region." The dragon princess then recounted her ordeal. It turned out that the Dragon King of the East Sea had held a grudge against the residents of the region for not showing him enough respect.

"What respect did your father command of them?" Liu Yi could not help cutting in.

"I really don't know why my father suddenly developed an avaricious appetite for cattle and sheep. He demanded that the people send him a buffalo and a sheep every other day as sacrifices." The dragon princess paused a little and went on, "People reluctantly gave up their beasts of burden, because once they lose them, they have to do all the hard work in the fields themselves. For that reason, they missed a few of their offerings. Worst of all, in a matter of a year, their livestock simply ran out."

"What happened next?" Liu Yi asked anxiously.

The dragon princess told him that her dragon father had then punished the people with years of drought, which resulted in a great famine. A large number of people died of starvation, and those who didn't want to sit still waiting for death left their homes to go begging elsewhere. The compassionate princess could not bear seeing the people suffer. She decided to help them. To do so, she had to take possession of the carefully guarded *longzhu* that gave her father all his powers. The princess managed to win the sympathy of her mother, who revealed to her the secret hideout of the Dragon King's precious pearl.

One night the dragon princess waited until the Dragon King was fast asleep, then tiptoed to the hideaway, took the *longzhu*, and stole out of the palace. She dashed to the surface of the sea, splashed out, and soared into the sky in her dragon form. Then she began to fly here and there, holding the magic *longzhu* in her mouth, which gave her the power to bring about rainfall. Overnight she relieved people of their disastrous drought. People rushed out into the rain, beside themselves with joy. The dragon princess was so happy to hear them laughing again.

"You are so kind," exclaimed Liu Yi, who had already fallen in love with the dragon princess.

"Thank you, but my father did not think so," said the princess melancholy. "He would not forgive anyone who dared to touch his *longzhu*, not to mention stealing it. He once had a guardsman put to death just because he was so curious that he took a peep at the pearl in the treasure box without his permission. My father would have killed me if it were not for my mother's plea for leniency."

"Tell me how I can help," Liu Yi said, seething with indignation at the injustice that the princess's cruel father had inflicted upon her.

"But you are going to take the imperial exam! I don't want you to give up this opportunity to better your life."

"If I miss this exam, I can always take another." Liu Yi said earnestly, "But I can't stand your suffering like this one more day. I want you to get your life back."

Liu Yi's sincerity and determination deeply touched the dragon princess. She also fell in love with him. She handed him a letter she had written and asked him to deliver it to her uncle, the Dragon King of the Dongting Lake, which was a thousand miles from where they stood.

"I really don't want you to go. Who knows what will happen on the long journey ahead," said the dragon princess, her moist eyes full of love and apprehension.

"Don't worry about me. Take good care of yourself while I am away. I will get the letter to your uncle as soon as I can." Liu Yi turned and embarked on the long journey. He had to leave immediately, before his will could be so softened that he would not be able to tear himself away from the dragon princess.

"Wait!" The dragon princess called out behind him. "Take this bracelet with you." Seeing Liu Yi puzzled, she explained, "This will help you get in touch with my uncle. When you arrive at the lakeshore, cast the bracelet into the water. Then my uncle will emerge from his palace to pick you up."

Liu Yi thanked the thoughtful and resourceful dragon princess and set out. Day after day, month after month, he crossed numerous rivers and climbed several mountains. He forged on courageously despite many difficulties. As he traveled, Liu Yi lived on the expense money that his parents had given him for taking the imperial examination. However, miles before he reached his destination, the money ran out, even though he did all he could not to waste a single penny. For the last leg of the journey, he had to trade everything he had with him for food, but he held on to the bracelet. He needed it to see the princess's uncle so that he could help deliver her from her misery.

When Liu Yi left the dragon princess, it was early summer. As he approached the Dongting Lake, it was already midwinter. He would have frozen to death if it were not for the moderate Southern climate in the lake region.

At the lakeshore, Liu Yi cast the bracelet into the water. Soon a dragon burst from the surface. When it landed, the dragon assumed the form of a middle-aged scholar, lest he might frighten the young man. It was the princess's uncle, the Dragon King of the Dongting Lake. Liu Yi handed him the princess's letter, in which the princess told her uncle about her mishap and asked him to talk her father into relenting.

Without hesitation, the Dragon King of the Dongting Lake rushed off to meet his brother, the Dragon King of the East Sea, bringing Liu Yi along with him. It took them less than a day to arrive at the East Sea. There, the uncle dragon persuaded his brother to forgive his daughter as well as the people in the region of Mt. Shishan.

Liu Yi's selflessness, courage, and faithfulness won not only the heart of the dragon princess, but also the favor of the dragon parents and relatives. They held a grand wedding for Liu Yi and the dragon princess.

The next morning the dragon princess took Liu Yi to see her royal parents. After brief, formal greetings, she made a request that they allow her and her husband to relocate to the spring at the foot of Mt. Shishan. Knowing how much she loved the people she had helped, Liu Yi expressed his support for her choice. The dragon parents readily consented, and before their departure, the Dragon King gave the *longzhu* to his daughter. The newlyweds lived a happy life, and so did the people of the region, protected by their guarding dragon princess.

THE MAGIC LOTUS LANTERN

Chinese performing arts have played a large role in preserving and disseminating folktales. One example is "The Magic Lotus Lantern." Theatrical performances of this tale appeared as early as the Song (960–1126) and Yuan (1280–1368) dynasties, and it gained renewed popularity in the form of a Chinese dance drama in 1957, a regional opera of Hebei province in 1959, and a movie cartoon in 2002.

In Midwestern China there is a beautiful mountain named Hua. On top of it there is a temple dedicated to the Goddess San Shengmu. People worship this Goddess because they believe that she is always ready to help them. When this story took place, she was busy helping the people of the region fighting a strange epidemic with the magic power of her *baoliandeng* (Magic Lotus Lantern). Even though the disease was under control, she did not stop working because she wanted to make sure that the epidemic would not recur. For this reason, she had to be away from her temple's altar from time to time.

During her absence, a young scholar named Liu Yanchang toured the temple. He was on his way to the capital to take an imperial examination. He burned incense and drew a *qian* (bamboo slips used for divination) after praying to the Goddess San Shengmu, wishing that the goddess would make him lucky enough to succeed in the examination. At the time, the goddess happened to be absent and therefore was unable to give him an answer to the lot he had drawn. Disappointed at the blank *qian*, Liu Yanchang inscribed his complaint on the wall of the temple before continuing with his journey:

Brush in hand, I write with anger,

You the goddess do I blame:

Taking tributes at the altar,

Care you not to give an answer.

When Goddess San Shengmu returned and saw the scathing poem, she decided to teach the insolent scholar a lesson. She asked the gods and goddesses of wind, thunder, lightning, and rain to let loose a downpour while Liu Yanchang was trudging on a winding mountain path. Having nowhere to hide, Liu Yanchang was soaked through. Hit hard by the sudden drop of temperature, he fell ill and collapsed.

Liu Yanchang's misery finally proved too much for the compassionate goddess to bear. She called off the thunder and rain and decided to save Yanchang without startling him. She asked her maidservant Lingzhi to transform into an elderly country woman, while she herself turned into the old woman's daughter. Together they helped the bedraggled and sickened Yanchang into a hut they had just conjured up. There the goddess nurtured him back to health. Then she revealed her true identity, told him the reason for her absence from the altar, and explained the rainstorm inflicted upon him after reading his poem.

Both apologized profusely. Days went by, and Yanchang fully recovered. By then the goddess and the scholar had fallen deeply in love. Marriage naturally ensued. Encouraged by Goddess San Shengmu, Liu Yanchang continued with his journey to the capital to take the examination. Months later, the goddess gave birth to their son, whom she named Chenxiang.

At the same time, Goddess San Shengmu's celestial family had learned about her marriage to an earthly man. Her brother, known as Divine Erlang, found his unruly sister and demanded that she give up the marriage and return with him to their heavenly home.

"I won't abandon my husband and son. If you push, I'd rather give up my sainthood," said Goddess San Shengmu with determination. The angry brother ordered his celestial soldiers to arrest his defiant sister. A fierce battle followed. With the power of her Magic Lotus Lantern, Goddess San Shengmu repelled Divine Erlang and his troops.

A few days later, the frustrated brother sent his magic dog to Goddess San Shengmu's temple, where she kept the Magic Lotus Lantern. While she was attending to her newborn baby, the dog managed to steal the lantern and brought it back to his owner. The Divine Erlang immediately launched a second attack, subdued his sister, and locked her up beneath a huge rock on the western ridge of Mt. Hua. However, before Divine Erlang had a chance to get hold of her month-old son Chenxiang, her maidservant Lingzhi took him and fled to a Taoist priest called the Firebolt Immortal. While Lingzhi helped bring up Chenxiang, the immortal taught him martial arts and magic power.

On the night of his fifteenth birthday, Chenxiang dreamed of a shackled woman claiming to be his mother. He was about to throw himself into her arms when a giant general planted himself between them. The general made Chenxiang call him uncle. Before Chenxiang knew what to say, the general took the woman and vanished.

When Chenxiang told the Firebolt Immortal about the dream, the immortal said, "Everything you dreamed is true." He then told the astounded Chenxiang the entire story of his parents' love affair

---

and his mother's abduction. He then added, "Now that you've grown up, you are able to free your mother from her imprisonment in the rocks."

"I can't wait to rescue my mother, but how can I open up a mountain with my bare hands?"

"You already have all you need: wisdom, strength and courage. Of course, a handy tool or weapon will help . . . ." The immortal paused a second and continued, "Well, you will get it on your way. Go now."

Chenxiang thanked the Firebolt Immortal and Lingzhi, his master and adoptive mother, and set out for Mt. Hua. After days of hardship, he arrived in the valley at the foot of the mountain. Night fell, and a thunderstorm broke abruptly. Forked lightning tore open the darkness and revealed a humongous flood dragon, which blocked his way. Chenxiang wrestled with the dragon until it lost all its strength. Then the beast suddenly exploded. After the cloud of smoke had dispersed, Chenxiang spotted a huge, shiny axe lying on the ground. In fact, the dragon had been the illusion of his master's walking stick. The Firebolt Immortal had been testing Chenxiang's courage and felt secretly satisfied that his student had acquired the tool necessary for the task of rescuing his mother.

With the axe, Chenxiang clambered up the western ridge of Mt. Hua. He approached the huge rock that had kept his mother a captive for the past fifteen years. Divine Erlang's magic dog was watching over the site and guarding the stolen Magic Lotus Lantern, placed on top of the rock. After a brief struggle, Chenxiang subdued the dog and retrieved the lantern.

When Divine Erlang and his army came to his dog's rescue, it was too late, so he challenged Chenxiang to a fight. With his axe and the Magic Lotus Lantern, Chenxiang defeated Divine Erlang and his army with ease. He then admonished his godly uncle for his insensitivity to his sister and nephew's well-being. He also threatened to annihilate his celestial troops and render him entirely powerless if he refused to mend his ways. Divine Erlang promised not to interfere in Goddess San Shengmu's life anymore.

Once Chenxiang was free from any obstruction, he hurled the magic axe with all his might and let it fall on the rock encasing his mother. He did it with force as well as with caution. The rock split open with a loud rumble. From the compartment in its center appeared Goddess San Shengmu, as beautiful and young as Chenxiang had seen her in his dream. Chenxiang threw himself into his mother's open arms. As they descended the mountain, they found Liu Yanchang waiting for them. The parents were thrilled to see each other again after so many years of involuntary separation. The father was particularly happy to meet his heroic son for the first time.

The Firebolt Immortal and Lingzhi had found Liu Yanchang and transported him to the mountain for this family reunion. They had spotted him praying in the temple of Goddess San Shengmu on top of Mt. Hua. It turned out that after he passed the imperial examination, Liu Yanchang had landed a job as a magistrate in a remote county. After a few years he managed to get himself transferred to the Mt. Hua region in the hope of rejoining his wife. When he tried to locate her, he could find neither her or her maidservant Lingzhi. By no means was he aware that he had become a father. He had been a regular visitor to the Temple of Goddess San Shengmu, praying at her altar, wishing that the statue could manifest the goddess herself to him. The sudden appearance of Lingzhi and the Firebolt Immortal made his dream come true.

Goddess San Shengmu and her family thanked Lingzhi and the Firebolt Immortal for all they had done to help them reunite. To prevent Divine Erlang from breaking his promise not to bother them again, San Shengmu gave up her goddess nature, though that meant that she would become as mortal as her husband was. San Shengmu did this with great delight. She knew that a happy mortal life with her husband and son would be more meaningful than an empty life as a goddess.

MONKEY KING AND THE IRON FAN PRINCESS

Tang Seng (The Monk of Tang dynasty) and his three disciples were on their way to the Buddhist holy land in the West to seek the true Buddhist scriptures. They had just said goodbye to a hot summer and were about to enjoy a cool fall when suddenly they felt wave after wave of hot air blowing in their faces as they approached a village. When asked about the strange heat wave, a villager told them that the hot air came from what they called the Mountain of Flames, to their west. It covered an area of 800 square miles.

"No one, not even a bird, can cross it alive," added the villager.

"What can we do?" Tang Seng asked hopelessly.

"There's a way, but . . . ," the villager stopped short.

"What is it? Tell us, please," the impatient Monkey King, Tang Seng's primary disciple, asked politely.

"A magic palm fan can put out the fire on the mountain, but it is in the hands of a female spirit. Nobody has ever been able to get it from her."

"Who is she?" Tang Seng asked.

"No one knows her real name. We all call her Princess Iron Fan."

Monkey King wanted to get to the bottom of this. He poked the ground several times with his thousand-pound iron rod, his versatile weapon, and called up the local god of land. Aware of the power of Monkey King, the god of land told him all he knew about Princess Iron Fan: "She is the wife of Prince Buffalo and lives in the Palm Cave on the Emerald Green Mountain. However, two years ago, the prince took a second wife called Princess Jade Face, a fox spirit. He is now living with the foxy concubine miles away in the Magic Cave on the Thunder-accumulating Mountain and seldom comes to visit Princess Iron Fan. For that reason, she is in a very bad mood."

"I would be the last that she wants to help," thought Monkey King, regretting the sheer coincidence and his poor luck. It turned out that in a previous adventure, Monkey King had conquered a young demon named Red Kid with the help of Guanyin, Goddess of Mercy. To prevent Red Kid from doing harm to humans, Guanyin took him away to serve as her disciple. Red Kid was none other than the son of Prince Buffalo and Princess Iron Fan, and they hated Monkey King for the loss of their son.

"To borrow the magic palm fan from the princess would be a mission impossible," Monkey King thought. Looking at the eyes of his master and fellow disciples, which seemed to beg him for an answer, Monkey King gave his head a few scratches and said, "I'll give it a try no matter what." With that, he leapt on to a cloud and, with a somersault, arrived at the Emerald Green Mountain, miles away.

With great civility and humbleness, Monkey King asked Princess Iron Fan to lend him the magic object. The princess, however, greeted him with her double swords. She wanted to avenge her son on the monkey. Monkey King had to fend off her swords with his iron rod. After a few bouts, the princess could not fight on. As she retreated, the princess took a little object from her sleeve pocket and said a few words of incantation to it, and it suddenly turned into a huge fan. A single swipe of the fan stirred up a wind that carried Monkey King to a great distance, so far that he did not land until the next morning. When he did, he set foot on the Little Xumi Mountain, where Lingji Pusa lived. Monkey King asked him for help, and Lingji Pusa gave him a pill that could help him stand firm even in a hurricane.

With the pill in his mouth, Monkey King returned to the Emerald Green Mountain to challenge Princess Iron Fan again. No matter how hard the princess tried her magic fan, the monkey would not budge an inch. Frightened at his newly gained power, the princess turned and sped toward her cave. However, before the gate completely shut, Monkey King had transformed into a mosquito and sneaked in. When the princess asked one of her attendants to serve her a cup of tea to quench her thirst, the mosquito plunged into the cup without anybody noticing. As the princess drank from the cup, the monkey rolled into her throat and then her stomach. There he stretched his arms and kicked his legs. Princess Iron Fan threw herself on the ground, writhing in anguish. Everyone around was wondering what was happening, when they heard someone calling from within the princess, "Hey, Princess Iron Fan!"

"Who's there? Where are you?" asked the princess.

"Hah, hah, I am Monkey King. I am in your belly. If you don't lend me your magic fan, I will show you all my acrobatic talents here and make a mess of your insides!" Alarmed, Princess Iron Palm begged for mercy. She said she would give him anything in the world if he came out of her.

As soon as Monkey King leapt out of her widely opened mouth, she handed him a huge fan. Monkey King took it and rushed to the Mountain of Flames. He jumped into the air and began to swing the fan. To everyone's surprise, the flames did not go out but, instead, became more violent. Monkey King did not know what had gone wrong. He asked Tang Seng and his fellow disciples to run as fast as they could while he was bringing up the rear. As he was running, the fan on his shoulder heaved up and down, further fueling the intensifying flames, which burnt the Monkey King's buttocks. Ever since, all the monkeys, believed to be the descendants of Monkey King, have had red, hairless buttocks.

After fleeing twenty miles from the fiery zone, Monkey King stopped. He called up the local god of land again and asked why the magic fan had failed to work. The god of land told Monkey King that Princess Iron Fan must have lent him a fake one. "To get the real thing," the god of land took a deep breath and continued, "you may have to deal with her husband, Prince Buffalo."

"Well, another mission impossible that I have to accomplish," thought the monkey. With a somersault, he arrived at the Magic Cave on the Thunder-accumulating Mountain. There he encountered Prince Buffalo's second wife, Princess Jade Face. She tried to stop him from entering the cave. Seeing that she was no match for the monkey, she rushed to her husband, crying for help. When Prince Buffalo saw Monkey King, his resentment overwhelmed his senses. Without listening to the monkey's explanation and apology, the buffalo engaged him in a fight.

They fought a hundred bouts, but neither got the upper hand. Suddenly the buffalo called off the battle, saying that he had an invitation to a party. He left on the back of his Water-evading Golden-eyed Beast. Monkey King followed him closely and stealthily. Seeing that Prince Buffalo and his beast submerged in a deep pool, the monkey transformed himself into a crab and tagged along. While the buffalo was feasting with his friends, the monkey stole his beast, changed to Prince Buffalo's appearance, and galloped to the Palm Cave at the Emerald Green Mountain to see Princess

Iron Fan. Princess Iron Fan was surprised and yet very happy to see her husband. At dinner, the buffalo asked Princess Iron Fan where she had hidden the magic palm fan. She told him that she had it in her mouth.

"I heard that you have lent it to the monkey," Monkey King used his trick of reverse psychology.

"I thought the monkey was smart, but he proved a complete fool." Spitting the real fan into her palm, she showed it to the buffalo and continued, "The one I lent him was a fake. Here is the real one."

Holding the tiny fan, Monkey King pressed her for the incantation. He asked, "But how can I make the little thing bigger?"

"Why, have you forgotten the magic word?" asked the princess.

"Well, I haven't been with you for the last two years, and I don't remember it any more."

The overjoyed and credulous princess revealed the incantation to Monkey King, who tried it and expanded the fan to its original size. He then disclosed his monkey identity to the stunned and mortified princess and dashed out of the cave without delay. In a hurry, he did not think to ask for the incantation to shrink the fan, so he had to carry the jumbo fan on his shoulder as he ran.

In the meantime, Prince Buffalo had discovered that his Water-evading Golden-eyed Beast was missing. He knew that the monkey must have taken it. He also knew where he had gone. Without hesitation, Prince Buffalo set off toward his first wife's cave. Before long he saw the monkey approaching in the distance, carrying the big magic fan. Prince Buffalo immediately transformed into Piggy, one of Monkey King's fellow disciples, and went up to meet him.

"Why are you here?" asked the surprised monkey. In his haste, he failed to recognize the buffalo.

"Our master asked me to meet you and offer you some help," answered the Piggy-looking buffalo. "Here, let me help you carry the fan."

Without a trace of suspicion, Monkey King gave the fan to Prince Buffalo, who shrank the fan, stowed it in his mouth, and revealed his identity. Like Monkey King, the buffalo knew how to transform into many forms. After a hundred bouts of fighting, the buffalo's strength began to dwindle. He attempted to flee in the form of a swan. Monkey King saw through his trick and changed into a hawk, trying to gouge out the swan's eyes. Terrified, the buffalo quickly changed into a white crane. The monkey then turned into a red phoenix, hot on the crane's heels. The buffalo had to land in the form of a musk deer and tried to hide in the woods. Monkey King transformed into a big tiger and started pouncing on it. The deer rolled on the ground and changed into a gigantic white buffalo, as tall as a mountain. The monkey matched the size of the buffalo and fought him with his iron rod, which had grown in proportion. Monkey King had anticipated the buffalo's efforts to flee and had summoned up all the heavenly and earthly gods and goddesses to help entrap him. The buffalo had to surrender, and he agreed to persuade Princess Iron Fan to lend the magic palm fan to Monkey King.

With the genuine fan, Monkey King and the rest of his group came close to the Mountain of Flames. The first swing of the fan put out the flames on the mountain and the ground surrounding it, the second swing stirred up gusts of wind to cool the air, and the third brought torrential rain, which the region had missed for decades. Monkey King then returned the fan to Prince Buffalo and Princess Iron Fan, said thanks and good-bye to the gods and goddesses, and led his master and his fellow disciples across the mountain.

A CRICKET BOY

This is another strange tale from Qing dynastic writer Pu Songling, who also wrote the "Painted Skin," retold in this book. You may have heard of bullfights, cockfights, and dogfights, but you probably have never heard of a cricket fight. You cannot find these crickets in pet stores because the combatants must be mature males. Cricket fighting was a long-standing tradition in China until two or three decades ago, when modern means of popular entertainment began to take the place of many traditional Chinese games, as described in Part 2. Cricket fighting used to be a pastime of both old and young. Like any hobby, when indulged by average people, the sport has a limited impact on society. However, when an emperor became a fan of cricket fighting, it was an entirely different story, as you will see in the tale that follows.

A long time ago, cricket fighting caught on in the imperial court, with the emperor leading the fad. A local magistrate in Huayin, who wanted to win the favor of the monarch, tried in every way to get him the best fighting crickets. He had a strategy for doing so: He managed to get a cricket that was very good at fighting. He then made his subordinates go to the heads of each village and force them to send in a constant supply of fighting crickets. He would send to the imperial court the crickets that could beat the one he was keeping.

Theoretically, everything should have worked smoothly. However, as the magistrate was extremely zealous to please the emperor, he meted out harsh punishment on any village heads who failed to accomplish their tasks. The village heads in turn shifted the burden to the poor villagers, who had to search for the crickets. If they failed to catch them, they had to purchase them from someone else, or they had to pay a levy in cash.

The small insects suddenly became a rare commodity. Speculators hoarded good crickets, buying them at a bargain and selling them for an exorbitant price. Many village heads worked hand in hand with the speculators to make profits. In so doing, they bankrupted many a family.

Cheng Ming was one such villager. The head of his village delegated part of his duties to him because he found Cheng Ming easy to push around. Cheng Ming did not want to bully his fellow villagers as the village head did him, so he often had to pay cash out of his own pocket when he failed to collect any competent crickets. Soon the little properties he had were draining away, and he went into a severe depression. One day, he said to his wife that he wanted to die.

"Death is easy, but what will our son do without you?" asked his wife, glancing at their only son, sleeping on the *kang*. "Why can't we look for the crickets ourselves instead of buying them? Perhaps we'll strike some good luck."

Cheng Ming gave up the idea of suicide and went to search for crickets. Armed with a tiny basket of copper wires for catching crickets and a number of small bamboo tubes for holding them, he went about the tedious task. Each day he got up at dawn and did not return until late in the evening. He searched beneath brick debris, dike crevices, and in the weeds and bushes. Days went by, and he caught only a few mediocre crickets that did not measure up to the magistrate's standards. His worries increased as the deadline drew closer and closer.

The day for cricket delivery finally came, but Cheng Ming could not produce any good ones. He was clubbed a hundred times on the buttocks, a form of corporal punishment in the ancient Chinese judicial system. When he was released the next day, he could barely walk. The wound on his buttocks confined him to bed for days and further delayed his search for crickets. He thought of committing suicide again. His wife did not know what to do.

Then they heard about a hunchbacked fortune-teller who was visiting the village. Cheng Ming's wife went to see him. The fortune-teller gave her a piece of paper with a picture on it. It was a pavilion with a *jiashan* (rock garden) behind it. On the bushes by the *jiashan* sat a fat male cricket. Beside it, however, lurked a large toad, ready to catch the insect with its long, elastic tongue. When the wife got home, she showed the paper to her husband. Cheng Ming sprang up and jumped to the floor, forgetting the pain in his buttocks.

"This is the fortune-teller's hint at the location where I can find a perfect cricket to accomplish my task!" he exclaimed.

"But we don't have a pavilion in our village," his wife reminded him.

"Well, take a closer look and think. Doesn't the temple on the east side of our village have a rock garden? That must be it." So saying, Cheng Ming limped to the temple with the support of a makeshift crutch. Sure enough, he saw the cricket, and the toad squatting nearby in the rock garden at the back of the temple. He caught the big, black male cricket just before the toad got hold of it. Back home, he carefully placed the cricket in a jar he had prepared for it and stowed the jar away in a safe place. "Everything will be over tomorrow," he gave a sigh of relief and went to tell his best friends in the village the good news.

Cheng Ming's nine-year-old son was very curious. Seeing his father was gone, he took the jar and wanted to have a peek at the cricket. He was removing the lid carefully, when the big cricket jumped out and hopped away. Panicked, the boy tried to catch the fleeing cricket with his hands, but in a flurry, he accidentally squashed the insect when he finally got hold of it.

"Good heavens! What're you going to say to your father when he comes back?" the mother said in distress and dread. Without a word, the boy went out of the room, tears in his eyes.

Cheng Ming became distraught when he saw the dead cricket. He couldn't believe that all his hopes had been dashed in a second. He looked around for his son, vowing to teach the little scoundrel a good lesson. He searched inside and outside the house, only to locate him in a well at the corner of the courtyard. When he fished him out, the boy was already dead. The father's fury instantly gave way to sorrow. The grieved parents laid their son on the *kang* and lamented over his body the entire night.

As Cheng Ming was dressing his son for burial the next morning, he felt the body still warm. Immediately he put the boy back on the *kang,* hoping that he would revive. Gradually the boy came back to life, but to his parents' dismay, he was unconscious, as if he were in a trance.

The parents grieved again for the loss of their son. Suddenly they heard a cricket chirping. The couple traced the sound to a small cricket on the doorstep. The appearance of the cricket, however, dashed their hopes, for it was very small. "Well, it's better than nothing," Cheng Ming thought. He was about to catch it, when it jumped nimbly on to a wall, cheeping at him. He tiptoed toward it, but it showed no sign of fleeing. Instead, when Cheng Ming came a few steps closer, the little cricket jumped onto his chest.

Though small, the cricket looked smart and energetic. Cheng Ming planned to take it to the village head. Uncertain of its capabilities, Cheng Ming could not go to sleep. He wanted to put the little cricket to the test before sending it to the village head.

The next morning, Cheng Ming went to a young man from a rich family in his neighborhood, having heard him boasting about an "invincible" cricket that he wanted to sell for a high price. When the young man showed his cricket, Cheng Ming hesitated, because his little cricket seemed no match for this gigantic insect. To fight this monster would be to condemn his dwarf to death.

"There's no way my little cricket could survive a confrontation with your big guy," Cheng Ming said to the young man, holding his jar tight. The young man goaded and taunted him. At last, Cheng Ming decided to take a risk. "Well, it won't hurt to give a try. If the little cricket is a good-for-nothing, what's the use of keeping it anyway?" he thought.

When they put the two crickets together in a jar, Cheng Ming's small insect seemed transfixed. No matter how the young man prodded it to fight, it simply would not budge. The young man burst into a guffaw, to the great embarrassment of Cheng Ming. As the young man spurred the little cricket on, it suddenly seemed to have run out of patience. With great wrath, it charged the giant opponent head on. The sudden burst of action stunned both the young man and Cheng Ming. Before the little creature planted its small but sharp teeth into the neck of the big cricket, the terrified young man fished the big insect out of the jar just in time and called off the contest. The little cricket chirped victoriously, and Cheng Ming felt exceedingly happy and proud.

Cheng Ming and the young man were commenting on the little cricket's extraordinary prowess, when a big rooster rushed over to peck at the little cricket in the jar. The little cricket hopped out of the jar in time to dodge the attack. The rooster then went for it a second time, but suddenly began to shake its head violently, screaming in agony. This sudden turn of events baffled Cheng Ming and the onlookers. When they took a closer look, they could not believe their eyes: The little cricket was gnawing on the rooster's bloody comb. The story of a cricket fighting a rooster soon spread throughout the village and beyond.

The next day, Cheng Ming, along with the village head, sent the cricket to the magistrate and asked for a test fight with his master cricket, but the magistrate refused on the ground that Cheng Ming's cricket was too small.

"I don't think you have heard its rooster-fighting story," Cheng Ming proclaimed with great pride. "You can't judge it only by its appearance."

"Nonsense, how can a cricket fight a rooster?" asked the magistrate. He ordered a big rooster brought to his office, thinking that Cheng Ming would quit telling his tall tales when his cricket became the bird's snack. The battle between the little cricket and the rooster ended with the same result: The rooster sped away in great pain, the little cricket chirping triumphantly on its heels.

The magistrate was first astonished and then pleased, thinking that he finally had the very insect that could win him the emperor's favor. He had a golden cage manufactured for the little cricket. Placing it cautiously in the cage, he took it to the emperor.

The emperor pitted the little cricket against all his veteran combatant crickets, and it defeated them one by one. What amused the emperor most was that the little creature could even dance to the tune of his court music! Extremely pleased with the magic little creature, the emperor rewarded the magistrate liberally and promoted him to a higher position. The magistrate, now a governor, in turn exempted Cheng Ming from his levies in cash as well as crickets.

A year later, Cheng Ming's son came out of his stupor. He sat up and rubbed his eyes, to the great surprise and joy of his parents. The first words he uttered to his jubilant parents were, "I'm so tired and hungry." After a hot meal, he told them, "I dreamed that I had become a cricket, and I fought a lot of other crickets. It was such fun! You know what? The greatest fun I had was my fight with a couple of roosters!"

Pu Songling was a prolific writer, and his works have been translated and published in many sources. A current collection you may wish to check out is Pu Songling, More Strange Tales from Ancient China, *translated by Herbert A. Giles (Torrance, Calif.: Heian International Publishing, 1996).*

Tales of Love and Romance

The freedom to love is something taken for granted today, but in ancient China it was an ideal for which young people had to struggle or even die. Parents, or elder brothers in the absence of the patriarchs, arranged marriages for their children or sisters, and they were usually concerned only with obtaining the financial gains or political advantage from the marriage. Parental or fraternal intervention sometimes resulted in tragedies, as related in "Butterfly Lovers" and "A Peacock Flying Southeast." Lovers in "Cowherd and Weaving Girl," "Xu Xuan and His White-snake Wife," and "A Romance of Zhang Gong and Cui Yingying" were luckier, owing to the help of loyal and sympathetic servants, animals, and fowls. Love might be lost for the "Forsaken Wife" and "Meng Jiang" because of their loved ones' betrayal or death, but the tenacity and courage these women displayed in their adventurous search for their loved ones have made an indelible impression.

The bride (with her face covered with a scarf) and the bridegroom greet each other
to consummate this traditional marriage ceremony in front of the bridegroom's parents,
who arranged their union. In the old days, the couple might have never
seen or even known each other before the bridegroom removed the scarf.

THE BUTTERFLY LOVERS

"The Butterfly Lovers," or "Liang Shanbo and Zhu Yingtai," is one of the four classic love stories of the Han Chinese. Some argue that the tale is based on two real people who lived a thousand years apart but were accidentally buried in the same grave. But most Chinese would rather see them as contemporaries. Whatever historical backgrounds there could be are irrelevant to such a timeless folktale. Its celebration of love as an individual's choice is as universal as that of Shakespeare's Romeo and Juliet.

Once upon a time a pretty and intelligent young woman named Zhu Yingtai lived in a wealthy family. With each passing day, her desire to go to school intensified. However, in her day schools were open only to male students. Parents would not allow their daughters to mingle with the opposite sex under any circumstances. Like the daughters of other families of means, Zhu Yingtai could only receive homeschooling. "It is not only the knowledge found in the books that interests me," she would tell her parents and friends when they asked why she was bent on going to a school since she already had a good education at home, "but the outside world also fascinates me. I want to see it and feel it."

Refusing to give up her dream, she never stopped trying to persuade her father to send her to school. Finally her father had had enough of her pestering pleas. One day, when Yingtai made the same request again, he said, "You can't expect me to consent unless you can turn yourself into a man."

"Fine!" Yingtai replied, biting her lips and holding back her tears as she left the room. Her father was secretly pleased with the effects of his tactic, thinking that this would be their last conversation about her going to a school.

The next day, Yingtai's maidservant reported that her mistress was ill and was confined to bed in her *guifang* (woman's private chamber). Her father had to send for a physician. In about an hour, a physician came. Yingtai's father found something familiar about the young man, whom he had never seen before.

"Have we met?"

"No. I am new to this town," answered the physician. "Tell me what's wrong with your daughter."

"She said she is listless and does not feel like eating or even getting up," the father said, and repeated what the maidservant had told him. He seemed to have cast off his doubts of the young physician's competency. He even began to like him, thinking of making him his son-in-law.

"From the symptoms you described," said the physician, "I can tell that your daughter has contracted some strange disease that calls for a special prescription."

"Are you sure?" asked the father in surprise, "You haven't even seen your patient yet."

"I don't have to because I know it," the physician replied with confidence. "Let me prescribe her some special medicine and she'll be all right."

"Please do," urged the worried and curious father. Nevertheless, his eyes almost popped when he saw what was written on the prescription: dragon's antlers, celestial empress's musk, and the water of life from the vase of Guanyin, Goddess of Mercy!

"Where in the world can we get these things?" Yingtai's father asked, regretting having thought of making his daughter marry this absurd young man. "You must be kidding!" Seeing his reddened face, the young physician could not repress his laughter. Taking off his hat, he asked, "Didn't I look manly enough to you, Dad?"

Now that Yingtai had proved she could pass very well for a young man, her father had nothing to say; and he consented to her going to the nearest boarding school, which was eighteen miles from home. In order not to reveal her identity, her father gave her enough money so that she could rent a house separate from the dormitory for the male students. He also ordered her maidservant to go with Yingtai to help with the daily chores. Both would dress and act like males.

Zhu Yingtai, along with her maidservant, bade farewell to her parents and set off to the boarding school. Stopping at a restaurant halfway through the journey, Yingtai met a young man. Yingtai learned that he was going to the same school. He introduced himself as Liang Shanbo, from a farmer's family, not far from Yingtai's home. After lunch they set out for the school together. As they walked and talked, Yingtai and Shanbo's friendship bloomed. Before reaching the school, Shanbo, not knowing Yingtai's female identity, asked that they become sworn brothers. Yingtai readily consented. They told each other their birthdays. As Shanbo was a year older, he became the elder brother and Yingtai, the younger. Dropping to their knees, they kowtowed three times, and finally, they vowed to Heaven that even though they were not born in the same year, they would die on the same day. Yingtai felt lucky that liquor, an important part of the ceremony, was not available at the moment. She really would not know how to handle that, as she had never had a taste of liquor in her life.

Inseparable at school, the two friends also shared the same views in class discussions. One day the teacher was lecturing on the Confucian perception that women were inferior to men. To the surprise of the entire class, Yingtai objected that women could be as intelligent as men, given equal opportunities. Their "inferiority" was due not to their nature, but to the oppression of the male-dominated society. All the students jeered, wondering why a fellow male student should speak up for the "weaker sex." Liang Shanbo stood up in defense of Yingtai's argument. He said firmly, "I agree with Yingtai, not because he is my brother, but because there is a whole lot of truth in what he said. Take my mother, for example. She is every bit as smart as my father, but she did not have a chance to receive any formal education. She was illiterate not because she did not want to study or was unable to learn. She was so because her father would not let her be otherwise. Then it was my father who prevented her from going to school after their marriage."

"That argument is not adequate. We are talking about people we know, that is, people of consequence," one student said, and was echoed by the others.

"How about Mulan?" retorted Shanbo.

Zhu Yingtai suddenly felt that Shanbo stood very tall, and the sunlight from the window behind him shrouded his masculine figure with something like a halo. She had never felt so close to a man. She realized that she was falling in love with him. However, she had to suppress her feelings because in the eyes of Shanbo and all the other fellow students, she was a "he."

Since Yingtai and her maidservant lived separately from the male students, they had no difficulty concealing their female identity. One incident, however, was a close call. One day, Yingtai fell

Chef skillfully slicing crispy skin off Beijing roast duck before serving in famous Beijing Quanjude Roast Duck Restaurant.

East meets West: Tang dynasty-style building used for the site of a KFC fast-food restaurant.

Sample of Chinese dishes, which number in the hundreds, if not thousands.

Chinese painter applying brush-pen, colors,
and water to rice paper.

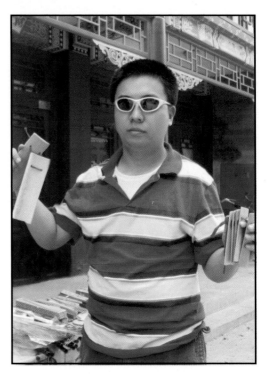

Hao, the author's son, demonstrating how
kuaiban (bamboo clappers) are used while
clapper-storytellers tell stories.

Dresser costuming Beijing opera actor before a show. Only a male actor playing a military or
characteristic role wears a mask of paint. He usually paints his face himself. Courtesy of the
Guandong Huiguan Theater, Gulou Cultural Street, Nankai District, Tianjin, China.

Girls of the Dai ethnic group, dancing. China has fifty-six ethnic groups.

Girls of the Hani ethnic group, singing. Both the Dai and Hani are in South China. Courtesy of Gao Shiyu.

Children playing a traditional game at Tianjin's Quanyechang Elementary School. Facing the challenge of multimedia games, schools are making efforts to revive traditional children's games by making them part of their physical education and extracurricular activities.

Craftswoman embroidering portrait of Deng Xiaoping, the former Chinese leader who started China's economic reform in the late 1970s.

Collection of Chinese crafts: embroidery, cloisonné, triple-colored glaze, dolls, kites, clay figurines, and marbles and snuff bottles painted in the inside.

A bird's-eye view of Tianjin, the author's hometown. Courtesy of the Foreign Investment Office of People's Government of Hedong District, Tianjin, China.

View of countryside in South China through train window.

Lovely country girl. The overwhelming majority of Chinese families love their daughters, though many still prefer to have sons.

Boy climbing a "cliff" on the premises of Warner Brothers cinema in China. Indoor and outdoor sports are becoming increasingly popular among the Chinese.

Schoolchildren at aquarium at Tianjin Natural Museum.

Girl posing at Badaling, a section of the Great Wall in Beijing open to visitors worldwide.

Three Towers in Yunnan Province in South China. Courtesy of Gao Shiyu.

Army of Terra Cotta Soldiers and Horses in Xi'an, excavated during the 1970s. It has become a new world wonder.

Server at a teahouse demonstrating the art of tea drinking, with Chinese calligraphy as the backdrop.

Tianjin *guqu* (drum and singing) storyteller telling a story with the accompaniment of a Chinese dulcimer and a *banhu* fiddle. The tradition still hangs on although seriously challenged by popular culture.

ill and did not show up in class. Being a sworn brother, Shanbo insisted on moving into her residence so that he could take care of her day and night. Yingtai vehemently declined, saying that she already had a servant, and her illness might be contagious.

Three years' school life had solidified Shanbo's brotherly affection for Yingtai and Yingtai's love for Shanbo. Soon they graduated. By now, Liang Shanbo and Zhu Yingtai found it difficult to part from each other. Shanbo wanted to walk Yingtai home. She readily accepted his offer. Considering this to be her last chance to express her feelings to her beloved Shanbo, Yingtai suggested that they have a verse contest to make the eighteen-mile journey interesting. She then explained the rule of the game: One of them would come up with the first line and the other would match it with the second. They had to create the verses about whatever they saw on their way. Shanbo said he liked the idea, and seeing a woodchopper passing by, he began:

"There comes a woodchopper in haste,

Though tired, he intends no time to waste."

Yingtai replied with two questions:

"For whom is he toiling?

With whom are you traveling?"

Oblivious to Yingtai's affectionate hint, the innocent Shanbo replied in a matter-of-fact tone:

"He is working for his wife,

I am traveling with my friend."

"It could be the other way around," Yingtai said, in a seemingly casual manner.

"You must be crazy!" The naïve Shanbo reminded Yingtai, "You are a man. How can you be my wife?" Then he added, "Well, if you were a woman, I would certainly marry you." At this Yingtai blushed. The unsuspicious Shanbo started another verse as they came up to a bridge:

"Brother with brother stands above the water;

Fish after fish swim beneath the bridge."

Feeling melancholy, Yingtai rejoined:

"Fish that swim together may quickly be apart;

"We that stay together may shortly be asunder."

"Come on, Yingtai! What has happened to you? How come you are so pessimistic? Fish would never separate if they weren't caught. As for us, we can always visit each other. Haven't you heard the proverb: 'Only mountains never meet'?" The dense Shanbo could not fathom the heart of a young woman like Yingtai.

Yingtai suddenly cheered up as she caught sight of a pair of mandarin ducks, symbol of long-lasting love, playing on the water. "See, over there, a couple of *yuanyuang*!" She decided to attempt a bolder hint, and started:

"For life they're a loving couple, never parting from each other.

In case I'm the female bird, do you want to be my partner?"

"Don't be silly, Brother Yingtai," said Shanbo, "Even if you were a mandarin duck, you would be a drake."

Mandarin ducks, Chinese cultural symbols of eternal love.

As they approached Zhu Yingtai's home, Yingtai had to make her proposal more obvious within the limit of social norms that forbade young people to express their love explicitly.

"I have a twin sister, who looks, thinks, and acts exactly like me." Yingtai told Shanbo, "Come to my home to propose to her after you get home and have had some time with your parents." Prompted by the sense of imminent, and perhaps permanent, separation, Yingtai had to resort to this white lie, which, she thought, would hurt nobody. Embarrassed as she was, she could not afford to let go the opportunity of making the man that she had loved for three years her lifelong companion.

She added, "I will introduce you to my parents when I'm home." Shanbo thanked his good friend, without the slightest idea that the sister she referred to was none other than Yingtai herself. Before the two realized it, they were near Yingtai's village. They had to say good-bye. Shanbo promised to come back to propose to Yingtai's sister.

When Shanbo returned to Yingtai's home a few months later, he was shocked to find that his sworn brother Zhu Yingtai, who had studied with him in school for the past three years, was the beautiful young twin sister he had mentioned. He apologized for his denseness in failing to understand Yingtai's hinted proposal.

Shanbo asked Yingtai's parents to give their daughter to him in marriage. Instead of giving their sanction, they asked him a lot of questions. They were particularly interested in his family's social and financial background, for in their days, the concept of *mendang hudui* (marriage between families of the same status) was deeply entrenched in the Chinese mind. When Yingtai's parents learned that Shanbo was from a family of moderate means, they rejected his proposal outright. Shanbo left Yingtai's home in despair. The despondent Yingtai did not know what to do. Tears were her companion day and night.

When a spoiled young man named Ma Wencai sent a matchmaker to propose marriage to Yingtai, Yingtai's snobbish parents readily accepted, because he was from a wealthy family. Ma

Wencai was a classmate of Yingtai and Shanbo. Yingtai knew how selfish and insolent he was. In fact, no one in the class liked him. In a society where filial piety was as important as national allegiance, Yingtai's objections, no matter how vigorous, proved useless. Her parents had made up their minds not to let their daughter marry a poor scholar like Shanbo.

Back home, Shanbo pined away, thinking of Yingtai day and night. Without her, his life seemed empty. Soon he fell fatally ill. On his deathbed, he asked his grieving parents to bury him at the side of the road where he had seen his beloved Yingtai home.

When news of Shanbo's death came, Yingtai was surprisingly composed. Her tears seemed to have dried up. She unexpectedly gave up the fight against the marriage arranged by her parents. When the wedding day arrived, she dressed herself carefully. She first slipped into a white gown, worn for the occasion of mourning, and then put on a bride's red robe. Before the wedding procession set out, Yingtai asked to visit Shanbo's grave on the way to her bridegroom's home. "Or I would rather die than get married," she threatened. Her bridegroom's relatives were very reluctant to satisfy her demand, for they deemed it ominous for a wedding to be mixed up with a visit to a graveyard. However, knowing that Yingtai meant what she said, they had no choice but to comply.

When the wedding procession arrived at Liang Shanbo's burial ground, Zhu Yingtai asked to halt her sedan chair. When she flipped the curtain open and stepped out, her appearance stunned everyone: she was in a white mourning gown. She had removed the red robe in the sedan.

Zhu Yingtai rushed to Shanbo's grave, threw herself upon it, and began to lament. She sobbed, "Shanbo, I'm here with you. I'm sorry I'm late, but wait and take me with you." As if her words were a spell, suddenly a storm sprang up. A loud crack of thunder was followed by a streak of lightning, which split the grave open. Wasting no time, Yingtai jumped into the crevasse, which then closed itself.

The sky cleared as fast as the storm had struck. When the startled relatives and participants in the wedding procession pulled themselves together, they saw a pair of beautiful butterflies flying out of the grave. They were dancing joyously in the free air under the sunny sky. Even today, the Chinese believe that the butterflies are the undaunted spirits of the faithful young lovers.

A FORSAKEN WIFE AND HER UNFAITHFUL HUSBAND

The theme of youzi sifu (traveling husbands and waiting wives) permeates Chinese literature and folklore, as is evident in many of the tales retold in this book. It has to do with the 1,300-year old keju (imperial examination) system. Before its abolition in 1901, this was the only way for Chinese to get into government positions. In a society where men had the final say, this system was open only to male scholars, and the highest imperial examinations were always conducted in the capital. To take the examinations, married men had to leave their spouses behind. Ideally, they would come back for them after they passed the exams, so they could both enjoy their improved life. However, that was not always what happened. When the fictional character Qin Xianglian decided to fight her abandonment and won, she vented the anger of all women victims and became a legend, respected by the Chi-

nese from generation to generation. Today, Chen Shimei, the name of Qin's husband, has become synonymous with "a man unfaithful to his wife."

Long ago, there lived in Central China a scholar named Chen Shimei. Living with him were his invalid, elderly parents; his loving, caring wife Qin Xianglian; and their two young children, a boy and a girl. While Chen Shimei devoted himself to studying for the coming imperial examination, Xianglian took care of the family. Life was hard, but she looked forward to the day when her husband would have passed the examination and returned home with fame and fortune.

When the examination season came, Chen Shimei bade farewell to his parents, wife, and children. He promised to come back to them as soon as he obtained a lucrative government position upon his success in the exam. In tears, Xianglian told him, "Don't worry about us. I will take care of your parents and our children. Come back to us no matter whether you succeed or not. We all wish you good luck!"

Three years passed, but not a single word came from Chen Shimei. Qin Xianglian and his parents were worried, wondering if he had encountered some misfortune. Xianglian wished to go to the capital, where she knew the examination took place every year, to find out what had happened to him. But in addition to the long distance and cost of such a trip, she had to look after her young children and her aged parents-in-law, whose health was deteriorating with each passing day.

As if Qin Xianglian's misery were not enough, a serious drought hit her region and soon resulted in a famine. Xianglian had to sell her belongings to purchase medicine for her parents-in-law. She could not prevent worry, hunger, and sickness from ruining their lives. When her parents-in-law died, like a dutiful daughter, Xianglian managed to give the elderly couple a decent burial before she became penniless. Having no idea what would become of her and her children, she placed all her hope on finding her missing husband. On many occasions, she indulged in the wishful thinking that her husband had succeeded in the imperial examination and become a high-ranking official. He must have been too busy to come home for a visit. If he had known that disaster had devastated his hometown and took the lives of his parents; if he had known his wife and their children were at the brink of starvation, surely he would have returned?

One day, while she was out begging, a neighbor came up to her and told her something that gave her a glimmer of hope. He said that he had been to the capital lately and seen her husband there.

"My husband is still alive?" asked Qin Xianglian, both happy and incredulous. The neighbor suspected that the new *fuma* (emperor's son-in-law) must be her husband, Chen Shimei.

"Are you sure? Misidentifying an emperor's relative is no joke!" Xianglian warned.

"I don't think I can mistake him, because I grew up with him and know him too well, don't I? I know how he looks, talks, and moves. I can recognize him even though he is in an official's robe."

"Did you talk to him?" Xianglian asked impatiently.

"Who am I to speak to an emperor's son-in-law?" retorted the neighbor. "I could not even come close to him while he was surrounded by his guardsmen."

Qin Xianglian decided to pay the *fuma* a visit at any cost, particularly when she had nothing to lose. The next day she set out for the capital, taking along her two children. Assuming that what the neighbor had said was true, Xianglian was going to have a talk with her husband and try to convince him to help his family.

The emperor's son-in-law was indeed Chen Shimei. He had not only passed, but excelled at the examination. His performance caught the attention of the emperor, who wanted to marry his daughter to this new *zhuangyuan* (The Scholar). Finding him to be in his late twenties, the emperor hesitated, for at his age, he must have been a married man, or he could be so abnormal that he was simply unmarriageable. When asked about his marital status, Chen Shimei said that he was a widower without children. He told the emperor that he had remained single since the death of his wife so that he could concentrate on his studies. Desperate for wealth and rank, Chen Shimei took the risk of lying to the monarch, a capital offense at the time. His marriage to the princess made him one of the most powerful and wealthy men in the country.

Qin Xianglian and her children begged their way to the capital. When they finally approached the mansion of the *fuma*, two guardsmen blocked their entrance. When they heard Xianglian's story, however, they relented and let them "break in" and "chased" them to the *fuma*'s living room. The sudden appearance of his wife and children startled Chen Shimei.

"How dare you break into a *fuma*'s mansion?" yelled Chen Shimei, treating them as if they were total strangers. He almost relented when his two children clung to his sleeves and called him "Dad," but he immediately recollected himself, thinking, "I must be iron-hearted, or my head could roll." He could not afford to let the emperor and the princess know that he had lied to them. He did not want to give up what he had: the princess, the money, the power, and the prestige. He had his wife and children ejected from his mansion before the princess could find out what was going on.

The sympathetic guards told Xianglian secretly that the only person who might be able to help her was the old Prime Minister. They said he was one of the few high-ranking officials in the capital who had a sense of justice.

"A Prime Minister is next only to the emperor in power and prestige. No one else would be in a position to confront the *fuma*," they added.

"But I know nobody in the capital. How can I get in touch with the Prime Minister?" Xianglian asked.

The guards paused a few seconds, and one of them came up with an idea. He said, "The Prime Minister goes to the court every day along the same route. You can stop him on his way and tell him your story then and there."

The next day, Qin Xianglian did as the guards had suggested. The interruption irritated the Prime Minister at first, but when he heard her story, he was shocked by the *fuma*'s betrayal and deceit. He knew Chen Shimei had committed a capital crime, but he would not want to ruin him, thus making his wife widowed and his children fatherless. He wanted to help the *fuma* avoid capital punishment, if he would tell the truth. He hoped to see the family reunited. He told Qin Xianglian what to do.

The next evening, the Prime Minister invited Chen Shimei for dinner at his mansion. In the middle of the feast, the Prime Minister suggested that they have some fun while eating. When a ballad singer was ushered in, a *pipa* (lute) in her arms, Chen Shimei recognized Xianglian. He realized that the Prime Minister had tricked him. Enraged, he wanted to leave on the pretext that he was not feeling well. The Prime Minister, however, pretended not to know anything about the relationship between his two guests and insisted that Chen Shimei stay and listen.

At the request of the Prime Minister, Qin Xianglian gave a few plucks on the *pipa* and began to sob out her sufferings and the fate of her parents-in-law while her husband was away taking the imperial examination. The Prime Minister meant this to be a subtle way of educating Chen Shimei so that he could change his heart and avert fatal consequences. Chen Shimei, however, would not heed the Prime Minister's kind admonishment. Instead, he stormed out of the mansion, accusing the Prime Minister of poking his nose into a *fuma*'s affairs. Xianglian thanked the embarrassed and indignant

Prime Minister for doing what he could. Despondent over her husband's cold-heartedness, she left the capital with her children, not knowing where to go.

Chen Shimei saw his wife and children as liabilities. He feared that as long as they existed, they could come to ruin his life at any time. So he hired an assassin named Han Qi, lying to him by saying that Qin Xianglian was his former lover who had come to blackmail him. He wanted Han Qi to kill the family on their way back home. Before Han's departure, Chen Shimei demanded, "Come back to me when you finish. I need you to show me their blood on your sword. If you fail, I'll have you destroyed with your own blade."

Chen Shimei had not anticipated that Han Qi was an honest and righteous man. When Han Qi learned the truth from Xianglian, he spared the family's lives by taking his own, knowing that he would lose it anyway at the hands of Chen Shimei for betraying him. At his request, before his death Xianglian took his bloodstained sword as evidence and returned to the capital. She was going to bring the murderous Chen Shimei to the High Court.

In those days, officials were largely corrupt, and they often shielded one another. Judge Bao Zheng of the High Court was allegedly the most upright in his time. Qin Xianglian's case, however, was not an ordinary one because it involved the royal family. Fully aware that the arrogant *fuma* would deny everything in the courtroom, Judge Bao Zheng came up with an idea. He invited Chen Shimei to chat in his office, in the hope of reasoning him into admitting his wrongdoing. When Chen Shimei came, he found it to be another trap. Bao Zheng calmed him down and assured him that he would get him a lenient sentence if he reconciled with his wife, Qin Xianglian. "I hope that you won't reject my offer." Bao Zheng said. "You have to understand that each of your offenses—lying to the emperor, neglecting your parents, and committing a murder—each deserves capital punishment."

"I don't think you can do anything about it even if this woman's allegations are true," retorted Chen Shimei in an overbearing manner. "Tell you what: I've already told my story to the princess and her mother before I came here. They've already pardoned me and don't want the wicked woman and her children to tarnish our royal reputation."

"I'll believe it when I see it!" the indignant Bao Zheng exclaimed. He ordered Chen Shimei to be arrested and brought to his courtroom. Sure enough, both the princess and her mother were waiting there to ask for Chen Shimei's release.

"How dare you stand in front of the royal family? Drop to your knees to show respect to Your Highness!" demanded the princess, flaring up at the sight of Qin Xianglian, who entered the courtroom with her children behind Judge Bao Zheng.

"By tradition," Xianglian began, composed, "you are but a concubine in our family. You ought to kowtow to me because I am the legal wife!" Her smart retort enraged the princess, who would have torn this insolent countrywoman into pieces but for Judge Bao Zheng's intervention.

Before long, the Chief Eunuch (the emperor's closest attendant) brought the emperor's decree of pardon to the court. As the pressure was mounting, Judge Bao Zheng thought it wise to seek a compromise. He offered Qin Xianglian a decent sum of money and asked her to drop the case. Qin Xianglian was terribly disappointed. She chided the judge, "I heard that you were the most just and brave judge in the country, but now I've finally learned that crows are black everywhere." Before Judge Bao Zheng could say anything in his defense, she continued, "How can you, a man known for his integrity, bribe me into forgiving such a heinous murderer as this man?"

Qin Xianglian's taunt struck Judge Bao Zheng as a wakeup call. Taking off his hat and putting aside his seal—both were symbols of his office—he said with determination, "I would rather give up my position or even my life to uphold justice than protect a criminal, no matter who he is." He then sentenced Chen Shimei to death and had him executed.

A PEACOCK FLYING SOUTHEAST

Originally a full-length narrative poem, this 2,000-year-old folktale is extremely popular among the Chinese. The metaphoric title "A Peacock Flying to the Southeast" comes from the first sentence of the poem: "A peacock flying to the southeast/Looks back every five li." It is an allusion to the theme of the tale, that is, the reluctant divorce of a young couple that eventually led to their destruction. The cause of the tragedy was the social norms of the time, when males determined the fate of females; and parents, the fate of their children.

Like mandarin ducks and butterflies, peacocks are also Chinese cultural symbols of love.
Courtesy of Baihua Literature and Art Publishing House.

On a gloomy morning, a carriage rolled along a country road. Sitting in it was a young woman, sad but stoic. Following the carriage was a young man on horseback, sobbing with grief. They had been a happily married couple until the young man's mother forced them to separate. They were now heading for the home of the young woman's parents.

The young man's name was Jiao Zhongqing and the young woman Liu Lanzhi. They were both from well-to-do families. Jiao Zhongqing worked as a clerk in the county magistrate's office in a big town a few dozen miles from home, so he had to rent a house close to his office. His widowed mother disliked urban life and therefore refused to live there with him, so Zhongqing had to leave his mother with his newly married wife Liu Lanzhi to take care of her. Lanzhi did not complain. Instead, she promised to be a dutiful daughter-in-law, as her parents had taught her to do since her girlhood.

"Don't worry about me," she would say, whenever Zhongqing came back home and apologized for the situation.

However, if he had known, Jiao Zhongqing would have had a lot to worry about, for no matter how hard Lanzhi tried, his fault-finding mother seemed to be implacable. In fact, she always hated anyone that she deemed competition for her son's attention. In order to drive her daughter-in-law away, she did all she could to annoy and torment her. She forced Lanzhi to start working before dawn and gave her so much to do that she couldn't go to bed until midnight.

Lanzhi's life was a nightmare, but for months she submitted to her mother-in-law's abuse without telling her husband. She loved him too much to bother him. Lanzhi knew that Zhongqing was already suffering enough from his boss, who was as hard to please as his mother. Besides, she was too kind to see the mother-and-son relationship estranged because of her. Lanzhi endured the hardship and suffering quietly, hoping that her forbearance would eventually change her mother-in-law's attitude toward her. Months passed, but her efforts proved fruitless. Instead of changing her mind, her mother-in-law even stepped up the oppression. Finally, Lanzhi had had enough. She decided to let Zhongqing know the truth.

On a traditional holiday, Zhongqing returned home, only to find his wife Lanzhi depressed. When asked, the hesitant Lanzhi told him everything. Zhongqing could hardly believe his ears. His father had died when he was a little boy. His mother had taken very good care of him since.

"How could such a caring mother be so cruel to my wife? Isn't Lanzhi taking good care of her?" Zhongqing asked himself. His mother's good health and the tidiness of the house were a positive answer to his question. Taking a closer look at the once pretty face of his wife, he suddenly realized why it had been so haggard lately. He also realized why his wife, thin as she was, kept losing weight.

Zhongqing might be a dutiful and submissive son, but he found his wife's misery too much to ignore. He plucked up enough courage to confront his mother. Lanzhi stopped him, saying, "I really don't mean to hurt the relationship between you and your mother. I just want you to listen so that I can feel better."

"But my mother has to listen to me once." With that, Zhongqing left for his mother's chamber.

"Why have you been so mean to Lanzhi?" asked Zhongqing, after he greeted his mother unemotionally. "Don't you think I'm already lucky enough to have a wife like her? The way I see it, she's been treating you very well. Can't you repay her kindness with at least a bit of the care you lavished on me?" Zhongqing's abrupt, nonstop questioning took his mother by surprise. She had never expected her obedient son to be so daring as to take his wife's side and stand up against his own mother.

Now her anger knew no bounds. "She must be the cause of his revolt," she said to herself. The more she thought so, the more enraged she became. "How dare she send you here to challenge me?" fumed the mother. Pounding her gnarled fist on the *kang* and stomping her little feet on the dirt floor, she blurted out what had been on her mind all the time: "Let her go. Divorce her now!"

The unexpected backlash overwhelmed Zhongqing, for disobedience to parents in his time was as serious an offense as treason today. He could have divorced Lanzhi simply by writing her a letter to proclaim his desire, for that was all a husband needed to send a wife away in those days, so long as he could justify his action by demonstrating that he had one of the *qichu* (seven reasons for being divorced).

Zhongqing could not disobey his mother, but he did not want to separate from his beloved wife, either. He loved her, and besides, he knew who was in the wrong. Caught in the middle, Zhongqing did not know what to do. He tried to calm his mother, which he found impossible. At her insistence, he verbally agreed to let Lanzhi go. In fact, he wanted to buy Lanzhi some time with a strategy of disengagement: He asked his wife to go back to her parents' home temporarily while promising to bring her back after his mother vented her anger.

Lanzhi did not blame Zhongqing for letting her go. She knew that he was in an awkward position. She even felt thankful because it had already taken him a lot to confront his domineering mother. She knew that his feelings and promises were sincere, but deep in her heart she felt that things might not happen the way he intended.

Calmly, she thanked him, "You don't have to get me back. Do you remember the wintry day when I married into your family? Ever since, I have been trying everything I can to make your mother happy. Can you recall a single incident where I insisted on having my own way? Day and night I kept working all by myself. I tried cautiously not to make any mistake. But in the end, she still made you divorce me. Are you sure that I still have any chance of being part of the family?" Zhongqing remained speechless, tears welling up in his eyes.

Alarmingly composed, Lanzhi started to tell her husband what to do with her belongings. Showing him her dowry wardrobe of magnificent dresses and shoes packed in about seventy trunks, she said, "Since I am good-for-nothing any more, these are not worth very much either. So they may not be good enough to give to your future wife as gifts. Now that we are not going to see each other again, I'll leave them to you as a souvenir so that you'll remember me."

Day broke with the rooster's crow. Lanzhi began to dress herself. Carefully she put on her embroidered skirt. She tried several different styles before finding one that satisfied her. She did the same with her shoes and jewelry. Her dexterous fingers looked like ivory and her red lips like ruby. Gently she stepped out of her chamber, like a bride as beautiful as a fairy.

Unperturbed, she went to say good-bye to her mother-in-law, who was still seething with anger. Ignoring her tantrum, Lanzhi began, "As I was a country girl, I did not receive much education in civility. I am sorry that I am not good enough to be your son's wife. I am also sorry that I will not be able to take care of you even though you have bestowed so much upon me. As I am leaving for my parents' home, I really worry that you have to do the family chores all by yourself."

Then Lanzhi said good-bye to her young sister-in-law, tears trickling down her face. "When I first came, you were just learning to walk. Now that you are a big girl, please take good care of your mom. When the festivals for girls come on the seventh day of the seventh month each year, think of me as your playmate and companion." So saying, she got into the carriage waiting outside the courtyard, her eyes blurred with tears.

Watching the house that she used to call home fade into the distance, Lanzhi knew very well that she would never have a chance to return to it. She knew that Zhongqing's mother would never accept her. Looking ahead to where her parents' home lay, she saw a very gloomy future. She was fully aware of what would be in store for her. Her elder brother, who lived with and provided for her widowed mother, was selfish, snobbish, and authoritarian. In a male-dominated society, he was the master of the house in place of his deceased father. Lanzhi feared that he would marry her off in no time and would not give her the time to wait for her mother-in-law to come around.

Lanzhi's home drew near. Before they parted, Zhongqing and Lanzhi pledged their faithfulness to each other. They vowed, "If we can't live as husband and wife in this world, we will in the next!"

As Lanzhi had anticipated, her mother and elder brother were very displeased to see her back. To the mother, a divorced daughter was a disgrace to the family. It meant that the family had not given her enough education to make her a qualified wife and daughter-in-law. To her brother, her coming home presented a financial burden. He planned to turn the liability into a moneymaking opportunity.

Before long, a rich family learned of Lanzhi's return and sent a matchmaker to propose. When her mother asked Lanzhi to accept the proposal, she sobbed: "I can't betray Zhongqing because he's never abandoned me. You may tell the matchmaker that I'm not in the mood to think of remarrying at the moment." Looking into the entreating eyes of her poor daughter, her mother relented and sent the matchmaker away, much to the dismay of Lanzhi's brother.

A few days later, a high-ranking official dispatched his deputy to Lanzhi's home to propose on behalf of his son. Lanzhi was about to decline the proposal when her brother stopped her. He was not going to allow a golden opportunity to associate with a rich and powerful family to slip away.

He scolded Lanzhi, "Are you crazy? What is in your mind when you give up a marriage like this? How can a clerk compare with a man of such noble birth? Don't expect me to support you the rest of your life!" As if that were not enough, he added, "If you don't say yes to this marriage, you have to get out of my house!"

The nightmare that Lanzhi had anticipated came true. Seeing no other alternative, she resigned herself to the arrangement, with boundless grief. The day before the wedding, everyone was busy preparing for it but Lanzhi. She remained dazed the entire day. When evening set in and darkness prevailed, her heart was as heavy as the curtain of the night. She could not help running out of her room to find some privacy so that she could cry her heart out.

In the darkness outside her house, she heard a horse galloping toward her in the distance. When the traveler halted and jumped off its back, he turned out to be Jiao Zhongqing. He had learned of Lanzhi's "change of heart" and hurried all the way to find out why.

"Ever since I returned home, my mother and brother have been pressing me to remarry," Lanzhi explained. "What would you expect me to do?"

"My congratulations on your newly acquired ladyship!" gibed the helpless Zhongqing. "While riches and honor lie ahead of you, my future will be nothing but a grave."

"How can you say that?" Lanzhi sobbed, "Don't you see that we are both the victims of our oppressive families? If you don't want to live, let us meet in the other world as we promised." They held each other tightly, with fathomless sorrow, as they realized that this would be their last time together alive.

Back home, Zhongqing said to his mother, "It's so windy today, and I feel so cold. Your son is like a flickering flame that's about to go out at any time. Never complain about what you deserve. I wish you happiness and longevity!"

Zhongqing's forboding words struck fear in his mother. "You are from a well-known family and have a decent job in the government," she said, tyring to talk him out of his suicidal impulses. "How can you die for the sake of a woman who is beneath your dignity? You don't have to feel guilty about divorcing her. If you like, I'll talk with our neighbor and ask them to marry their daughter to you right away. She is a hundred times better than Liu Lanzhi!"

"We'll talk about that tomorrow," said Zhongqing listlessly, forcing a bitter smile. "It is late, and both of us are tired. I just want to go to sleep. I'm tired. I want to go to sleep . . . ." He turned and shuffled off to his bedroom.

After seeing Zhongqing off, Lanzhi did not return to her chamber. Instead, she ran to a pond nearby, tears running down her cheeks unchecked. When Lanzhi's family members and relatives came out to look for her, it was too late—she had drowned. Zhongqing hung himself on a crabapple tree in his backyard the same night.

The two remorseful families buried Lanzhi and Zhongqing together in the same grave. On one side of it, they planted a pine tree, and on the other, a phoenix tree. As the trees grew, their branches entwined and their leaves became entangled. Among the foliage, there appeared a pair of *yuanyang* (mandarin ducks), singing to each other from dawn to dusk. Until this day, people still believe that the *yuanyang* perching on the trees above the grave were the spirits of the faithful husband and wife, Jiao Zhongqing and Liu Lanzhi.

COWHERD AND WEAVING GIRL

As discussed in the chapter on Chinese religion in Part 1, followers of Chinese popular religion believe that Heaven and Hell are each governed by a monarchical hierarchy, modeling the mundane world. Of the three monarchs, the celestial Yuhuang Dadi (Jade Emperor of Heaven) was deemed the supreme ruler. Legends claim that Yuhuang Dadi had seven fairy daughters, of whom the youngest was the prettiest. There are quite a few tales about her. The one retold here is the most popular.

Once upon a time there was a young man, handsome, diligent, and honest. Orphaned in his early teens, his wicked big brother and his sister-in-law drove him out of the house, giving him no other possession than a weak, old buffalo. The buffalo, however, proved to be very loyal to its young owner, trying its best to relieve him of the toil in the paddy fields. The two became inseparable friends. Gradually people began to forget his real name, Dong Yong, instead calling him Cowherd.

Meanwhile, the youngest of the seven celestial princesses known as *Qixiannü* (the Seventh Fairy) had grown tired of the privileged but secluded life in the Heavenly Palace. She longed for an earthly life below, which she had been watching from her chamber with great interest. That was a very perverse idea, in the opinion of her parents and her sisters. Nevertheless, the *Qixiannü* had made up her mind to pursue what she deemed to be her own happiness.

One day, the princess sneaked out of the Heavenly Palace and descended onto the earth, where she transformed herself into a young countrywoman who had lost her way. She staggered along the country path beside the paddy fields where Cowherd was working. He stopped to ask where she was heading and if she needed any help.

"To tell the truth," the fairy began, "I am *Qixiannü*. I've been watching you working with your buffalo friend for a long time."

"How come I didn't see you watching me? There is nothing to block my view here." the innocent Cowherd asked.

"Of course you didn't. I was up there," the fairy giggled, pointing to the sky with her slender finger.

Realizing his folly, Cowherd blushed. "Oh, I've heard of you."

"Do you like me?" asked the fairy boldly.

"I—I like you very much," Cowherd stuttered, his heart thumping hard.

"I like you, too. In fact, I want to be your wife," the fairy proposed. To Cowherd, it was a very unconventional move. He could not believe his ears. "Me, a poor cowherd, marry you, a fairy and daughter of the Jade Emperor of Heaven?"

"So what?" questioned the fairy.

"Don't you see how poor I am? Except my old buffalo, I have nothing. How can I bear seeing you suffer with me?" explained Cowherd.

"Don't worry. I know how to weave the best cloth in the universe, and I know you are a hard worker in the fields. With our honest labor, we will have a happy life," the fairy assured him. They married happily, and in two years they had a son and a daughter. While Cowherd worked in the fields with the buffalo, his fairy wife wove at home to help support the family. The villagers all admired her excellent weaving skill and eventually gave her the nickname Weaving Girl.

The family was enjoying a moderate, peaceful life until Weaving Girl's celestial parents found her missing and traced her to the village. It was believed that a day in heaven amounted to a year on earth, so the years she had spent with her mortal husband and children were but a few days in heaven. The Jade Emperor and the queen were enraged that they gave their daughter an ultimatum: either come back home immediately or see her husband and children destroyed. A loving wife and mother, Weaving Girl would never let her cruel parents hurt her husband and children. She had to surrender to her cruel parents and return to the Heavenly Palace. With great sorrow, she parted from her distressed husband and children.

The bereaved Cowherd had a hard time calming the motherless children and tucking them in. He did not know what to do without his beloved wife. He went to the stable to see his old pal, the buffalo, whose tacit friendship had all along been his solace. This time, he got more than he had expected.

"Dong Yong," the buffalo began to speak, to the great astonishment of Cowherd. "I'm dying. When I'm gone, skin my body." Hearing the buffalo's last words, Cowherd's feelings went quickly from shock to despair and sorrow.

"No, I can't," Cowherd replied categorically.

"Do as I bid you. You have no time to waste. After you get my hide, sew it into a coat. Put it on, and it will take you to the Heavenly Palace. Then you and your children will be able to join your wife." With that word, the old buffalo dropped to the ground and breathed its last.

Cowherd was seized with grief and gratitude. For the sake of the children who missed their mother so much, he trusted what the buffalo had said and did as it requested. After burying the carcass, Cowherd sailed into the air, carrying his young son and daughter, each in a basket on either end of a shoulder pole.

Seeing Cowherd coming closer and closer to the Heavenly Palace, the Queen of Heaven drew a deep line across the sky with her hairpin. Instantly there appeared a torrential river, blocking the advance of Cowherd. The river is known to the Chinese as *Yinhe* (Silvery River), which Westerners call the Milky Way. The Queen of Heaven meant to separate the couple forever with this insurmountable obstacle.

However, magpies from all corners of the world, deeply touched by the devotion of the young couple and angered by the cruelty of the celestial parents, flocked to help Cowherd. It took them a year to gather together. Numbering in the thousands of millions, they formed a bridge so that Cowherd and Weaving Girl could at least meet briefly.

The reunion of Cowherd and Weaving Girl happened to be the seventh day of the seventh Chinese lunar month, which falls sometime in August. By the way, the occasion known as qixi (Eve of the Seventh Day) has since become the Chinese Valentine's Day, and the term queqiao (magpie's bridge) has found its way into the names of many Chinese matchmaking agencies.

The original author or authors of the tale must have drawn inspiration from observation of the astronomical phenomenon, because the most prominent feature in the sky on a midsummer night in the northern hemisphere is the Milky Way, flanked by the Lyra and Aquila constellations. Altair, the brightest star in Aquila, with two smaller, bright stars on either side of Altair, is believed to be Cowherd carrying his two children. Vega, the most brilliant of the Lyra constellation, is believed to be Weaving Girl. The four smaller stars in a diamond shape beside Vega are supposedly her weaving shuttle.

The tale has inspired numerous Chinese literary creations, generation after generation. The following poem, written by an anonymous poet in A.D. 210, is but one example:

> Star of Weaving Girl, clear and bright,
>
> Her dexterous hands busy on the loom,
>
> But days have gone by with nothing done;
>
> Only tears are raining down in volume.
>
> The Silvery River, clear and shallow,
>
> How far could the couple be apart?
>
> Yet, divided by the flowing waters,
>
> They could only face each other in silent gloom.

Magpies, symbols of good news. Courtesy of Baihua Literature and Art Publishing House.

MENG JIANG WAILS AT THE GREAT WALL

The Great Wall is not exactly a single linear structure. The word "wall" should really be plural, for the Great Wall consists of many walls, built and rebuilt over a period of 2,200 years. Put together, the walls have an unbelievable length of more than 50,000 kilometers (31,069 miles). The section built during the Ming dynasty (1368–1644) alone extends 6,000 kilometers (3,728 miles). That is about the distance between Miami, Florida, and Anchorage, Alaska. A pride of the Chinese today, the Great Wall was, however, a source of misery for those who built it. The story of Meng Jiang is a metaphorical testimony to the sufferings of the millions who contributed to, and perished for, the construction of this wonder of the world.

There once lived, in the same neighborhood in a village south of the Yangtze River, a Meng family and a Jiang family. Both were elderly couples without children. Being good neighbors, they helped each other when in need. As their ages advanced, their desire for children grew stronger and stronger. They knew that eventually they would be too old to take care of themselves, let alone one another.

One spring a miraculous plant took root in a plot between their houses. The elderly couples took good care of the tender sprout, as if it had been a child. In a few days the magic plant grew into a vine. The two families tended it with more care. In late summer the plant blossomed, and when the flower withered, it gave birth to a bottle gourd. The gourd grew larger and larger, until it was as big as a gigantic pumpkin. Because the huge bottle gourd weighed too much on the vine, the elderly couples constructed a trellis to support the vine and hung a plaited mat to hold up the gourd so that it would not fall prematurely.

When the bottle gourd was ripe, the Meng and the Jiang families decided to share the fruit of their labor. They carefully halved the gourd, and opening it, they could hardly believe their eyes: in the center of the gourd there slept a baby girl! Her smiling face with two dimples seemed to say that she was having a sweet dream. When she opened her sparkling eyes, the little girl looked as if she already knew who the elderly couples were. Turning to the Meng couple, she called, "Mommy," and turning to the Jiang couple, she uttered, "Daddy." The two elderly couples were thrilled, though astonished by the extraordinary birth of the little girl and her startling precocity. The elderly couples decided to raise the girl together. They gave her the name Meng Jiang, a combination of the two families' last names. The four elderly parents did all they could to make sure that Meng Jiang had an appropriate upbringing. Under their loving care, Meng Jiang grew up to be a civil and diligent young woman. Everyone in the village liked her.

One late afternoon, Meng Jiang was weeding her Jiang parents' garden when a young man leapt over the fence. The sudden appearance of a wretched young man took Meng Jiang aback. The young man panted vehemently. After a long while, he managed to wheeze out an apology for his trespassing. The commotion alerted Meng Jiang's parents. When they came out to see what was happening, the young man apologized profusely again and, having regained his breath, began to tell his story.

He was Wan Xiliang, a young scholar of a well-to-do family from a prefecture a few hundred miles away. He had lived a peaceful life until The First Emperor of Qin launched his ambitious project to connect all the walls constructed by the states he had conquered and build them into a single defense system (known today as the Great Wall). He was drafting millions of male laborers, one from each family of three adult males and two from each family of five. As the only adult son of his family, Wan Xiliang was a candidate for the draft. People knew what the laborers' fate would be: Nine out of ten would never come back alive.

"I am dodging the draft, not because I don't want to serve our country," Wan Xiliang said at the end of his story, trying to justify his action, "but I just don't see the point of building those walls at the cost of so much money and so many lives."

"We understand what you are saying, son," the Jiang father put in, "We are just lucky that we have only a daughter. Thank heaven the emperor is not drafting women yet."

The Meng and Jiang parents' sympathy seemed to have calmed Wan Xiliang. Suddenly he had a fit of dizziness and collapsed. When he came to, he found himself lying on the *kang*, attended by Meng Jiang and her parents.

"I am so sorry," Wan Xiliang said to them. "I was just tired and hungry. I haven't had anything for two days. Now I feel much better. I'll leave right away. I just don't know how I can thank you enough for saving my life." So saying, he sat up and was ready to get off the *kang* when Meng Jiang and her parents stopped him.

"At least you need to rest for a few more days," they said, "You are still too weak to move around. Besides, the recruiters must be looking for you."

"But, it is . . . it is inconvenient . . . ," stammered Wan Xiliang, and blushed as his eyes met Meng Jiang's.

"Don't worry. You may stay here with us," said the Jiang father, "and Meng Jiang will live with her Meng parents. So there won't be any inconvenience at all." Apparently he had read Wan Xiliang's mind.

Wan Xiliang stayed. Hiding from public view, he pursued his studies while waiting for things to blow over. The Jiang parents treated him as if he were their son. Months passed, and nothing happened. In the meantime, Meng Jiang went back and forth between her Meng and Jiang parents. In due course the two youngsters felt in love. The subtle changes in their feelings toward each other did not escape the observant parents. They had them married, inviting only a small circle of close friends to the wedding because they did not want too many people to know about Xiliang.

As an old Chinese saying goes, "There is no wall that is entirely proof against a draft of wind." A villain, who had been coveting the beauty of Meng Jiang for some time, eventually found out about the marriage of Meng Jiang with Wan Xiliang. Out of jealousy, he managed to discover Xiliang's identity and reported him to the authorities. Soon the emperor's men knocked at the newlyweds' door. They seized Wan Xiliang and sent him to the Great Wall's construction site a thousand miles away, in the far north.

Meng Jiang wished that her husband could survive the ordeal, and she told herself every day that she would be able to see him soon. However, months passed without hearing anything from him. Summer gave way to fall, and now winter was setting in. Still not a word came from her husband. Meng Jiang's worries grew as the days went by, and so did her parents'. The falling temperatures reminded her that when Xiliang left, he did not have winter clothes with him. She often dreamed of Xiliang shivering in bitter cold. She set her mind on visiting him at the construction site. She wanted to bring him the warm clothes that she had made for him.

As she reluctantly parted with her loving elderly parents, Meng Jiang assured them that she would be back as soon as she found Xiliang. Despite all the imaginable and unimaginable difficulties lying ahead, she embarked on the quest for her husband. She had no other means of transportation than her own feet. She walked and walked toward the north, climbing over many hills and crossing numerous rivers. As she trudged along, the temperature became increasingly colder.

One snowy day she fell sick. Before she could reach a small village lying ahead of her, she sank into the snow and fainted. When she came to, she found herself lying on a cattail bed. An old woman was at her side. Evidently the woman was the owner of the cozy little cottage. She had found Meng Jiang in the snow and nursed her back to life. As soon as she felt better, Meng Jiang thanked the kind old woman and prepared to resume her journey. She insisted despite the old woman's warning that she was still feeble and that the weather could become worse at the construction site.

After untold sufferings, Meng Jiang reached the Great Wall's construction site at long last. There she saw thousands upon thousands of laborers toiling against the bitter wind and in the icy snow, carrying bricks and hauling stones while being brutalized constantly by the guards and foremen. None of the laborers seemed sufficiently fed and clad. She saw many of the laborers fall, never able to rise again. The horrible scene made Meng Jiang worry about her husband Wan Xiliang all the more. She wished that she could see him immediately.

Forgetting her fatigue and hunger, she promptly started the impossible task of finding Xiliang among the countless laborers. She started her search from the west end of the Great Wall and moved toward the east. Finally, as she approached the end of the Wall on the east coast, she came across a group of laborers from her hometown. One of them was from her village. When Meng Jiang asked him about Xiliang, he did not know what to say. Their silence told Meng Jiang what she feared to know.

"Tell me the truth, please. Live or dead, I need to see him." Meng Jiang requested.

The laborers finally told her what had happened. "Wan Xiliang died of the unbearable working conditions only a month after his arrival," they said. Because too many people died each day, the guards forced the laborers to bury the dead inside the walls as they built them. Therefore, the only place where Meng Jiang could find her dead husband would be the Great Wall itself.

Although it wasn't unexpected, this tragic news was still a shock to Meng Jiang, and she fainted. When she regained consciousness, she had to face the harsh reality that not only had she lost her beloved husband, but she also was unable to see his body. Her grief was inconsolable. Dropping to her knees in front of the Great Wall, she burst into tears. For three days and nights, Meng Jiang wept and wailed. Toward the end of the third day, she was still crying when, all of a sudden, there came a loud crashing sound, followed by a series of deafening rumbles. As thick clouds of dust dissipated, it became clear that an 800-mile segment of the Great Wall had collapsed, exposing countless white bones in the debris. Stunned, Meng Jiang was at a loss what to do; how could she possibly tell which skeleton belonged to her poor husband Wan Xiliang?

A man suggested that she drip some blood from her finger onto a bone to see if the blood soaked into it. "If it does," he said, "the bone must be Xiliang's." Whether this was science or superstition, Meng Jiang did not care. She wanted to find Xiliang. She bit her finger and began the painful task of identifying the bones. No one was sure whether it was a stroke of luck or an instance of divine intervention, but before long Meng Jiang found Xiliang's skeleton, a hairpin still clutched in his skeletal fingers. The hairpin further confirmed the identity of the bones, for Meng Jiang had given it to Wan Xiliang as a remembrance when he was taken away.

The news that a little woman had caused a large section of the Great Wall to collapse enraged the First Emperor of Qin, who happened to be on a tour on the east coast of China to look for elixir of eternity. He ordered that Meng Jiang be arrested and brought to him. He would watch her be executed. But when he saw the beauty of the young woman, he immediately changed his mind. He spared her life and wanted her to be his concubine. Knowing that she would have no chance to escape, Meng Jiang complied.

"Becoming a concubine of the First Emperor has been the dream of many young women. I feel extremely honored to have this opportunity," Meng Jiang said sarcastically, but the dense emperor took her words as a compliment.

When the emperor's maids of honor tried to take her away from the execution ground, Meng Jiang stopped them. "Wait a minute," she said, then turning to the emperor, "I have three requests. If you don't satisfy them, I'd rather die."

"Tell me," responded the emperor, curious about what she wanted to ask of him.

"First, give my husband a decent burial," started Meng Jiang.

"That is easy," the emperor responded.

"Then you must lead the funeral procession," Meng Jiang continued.

"Well . . . ." The emperor hesitated, knowing that only the first son of a deceased parent should lead his or her funeral procession. It was an insult to an emperor. However, the temptation of having Meng Jiang as his concubine far outweighed his ego.

"Fine, I'll do it. What is your last request? I hope it will be an easy one."

"Sure, it should be a piece of cake for you. Because I'm an inlander, I have never been to the sea. I want to have a boat tour on the high sea, and I want you to be my company."

If he resented the first two humiliating requests, the emperor actually liked the idea of taking Meng Jiang to the sea. He thought he was seeing the romantic side of Meng Jiang. Without hesitation, he readily consented to her demand.

After Wan Xiliang's funeral, the First Emperor of Qin took Meng Jiang to the sea. The ship set sail in the midst of fanfare and cheers. Several leagues off shore, the emperor ordered that the wedding ceremony begin. Before the maids of honor could get hold of Meng Jiang, she had maneuvered herself to the edge of the starboard.

Glaring at the emperor, she pronounced, "I would rather die than live by the side of a butcher like you!" Then, she threw herself overboard and vanished in the roaring waters. Mysteriously, her plunge stirred up surprisingly large tidal waves, which nearly wrecked the ship.

After Meng Jiang's death, people said that the Dragon King of the East Sea was behind the tidal waves. Sympathetic to Meng Jiang, the Dragon King took her as his honorable guest and created the waves in an attempt to destroy the tyrant.

A ROMANCE OF ZHANG GONG AND CUI YINGYING

Chinese love stories often ended in tragedy, as shown in "A Peacock Flying Southeast," "Butterfly Lovers," and "Cowherd and Weaving Girl." This tale, however, is one of the few exceptions. Originally a sad story, over time it evolved into one with a happy ending. A character in the story named Hongniang has a lot to do with this reversal of fortune, earning her a reputation comparable to that of the Western Cupid and a place in the Chinese lexicons. The term Hongniang is synonymous with "matchmaker," but with a commendatory connotation.

A long time ago, a prime minister named Cui Peng died. His wife, Madam Cui, and daughter, Cui Yingying. escorted his coffin back to his hometown, hundreds of miles from the capital. Among the entourage was Yingying's maidservant, Hongniang. As they approached the town of Puzhou, they heard that an army of bandits had been harassing the town and its surrounding areas. Madam Cui had every reason to worry, for the large number of valuables she brought with her and the beauty of her daughter were huge risk factors. Besides, the small number of guards that Madam Cui commanded was no match for the bandits.

From a local farmer, Madam Cui learned of a nearby sanctuary, the famed Pujiu Temple. Its numerous yards and houses were ideal accommodations for the living, and its sacred environment was a perfect temporary resting place for the dear departed. Madam Cui decided to take refuge in the temple. There she hoped to buy some time and figure out how to cope with the situation.

Meanwhile, a young scholar named Zhang Gong stopped at the same temple. He was on his way to the capital to take an imperial examination. He had just called on a friend, known as the White Horse General, stationed a hundred miles from Puzhou. Having heard of the beauty and fame of Pujiu Temple, Zhang Gong had always wanted to visit it. When he arrived at the quiet, wooded temple in the suburbs of Puzhou, he found it to be a perfect place to study for the examination, which was to take place in a few months. He determined to stay until the examination day approached. He settled down in a small courtyard, which happened to be next to a bigger one where Madam Cui and her daughter Cui Yingying took shelter. Separating the two yards was a brick wall as high as a person, with its top part hollowed out so that people in the two yards could see each other.

Night fell. Zhang Gong studied for awhile. Tired and bored, he took a break to write a poem. When he finished, he could not help reading it aloud, loud enough for the residents in the next yard to hear:

"Quiet in the blooming spring,

Alone in the serene night,

Why in the moonlight clear,

Not a pretty girl I sight?"

No sooner had he stopped reading than a tender female voice drifted over the wall that separated the two courtyards:

"Confined to my lonely chamber,

For nothing my youth I squander;

I wish the one that listens yonder

Could be the understanding chanter."

Apparently Zhang Gong and Cui Yingying, who had chanced to see each other during the day, were now in love. However, in a society where communication between a young man and a young woman without their parents' permission was taboo, the two youths could only use veiled love poems to express their affections. Even so, they ran the risk of being discovered and chastised by Madam Cui. Cui Yingying's clever and understanding maidservant Hongniang agreed to serve as their secret liaison.

The next morning, Hongniang accosted Zhang Gong, who in turn asked her to pass a handkerchief to her mistress. On it was a new veiled love poem. Hongniang knew that even though Cui Yingying loved the young scholar, she might feel too embarrassed for her maidservant to act openly as a go-between. Hongniang had to help in a roundabout way. Instead of handing the handkerchief to Cui Yingying in person, she placed it on her mistress's dresser without her knowing it, so that she would pick it up herself. Cui Yingying read the poem and got the message, but she was too shy to respond in writing.

Days passed without a word from Cui Yingying. Zhang Gong's anxiety intensified. Then, out of the blue, there came an opportunity. The bandits' chieftain, Sun Feihu, had learned that Madam Cui and her beautiful daughter Cui Yingying were staying in the Pujiu Temple. Laying siege to it, he demanded that Madam Cui marry her daughter to him. Otherwise, he would storm the sanctuary and take Cui Yingying by force. Facing the threat of grave danger, Madam Cui had to deploy a stalling tactic. She told the chieftain that it would be improprate for her daughter to get married before her father's burial. She asked him to put off the wedding until they lay the deceased prime minister to rest. Sun Feihu gave Madam Cui a grace period of half a month.

Madam Cui had won some time, but she did not know what to do with it. As days went by, her worries weighed heavier. Both the mother and the daughter were at their wit's end. Finally, Madam Cui made a difficult decision. She gathered all the people in the temple and announced, "I will marry my daughter to anyone who can pull us through."

To Cui Yingying's relief and pleasure, Zhang Gong offered to help. He managed to sneak out of the temple and escaped through the bandits' encirclement. Then he purchased a horse from a local and galloped to where his friend, the White Horse General, was stationed. Surprised, White Horse General asked Zhang Gong why he came in such a hurry. Zhang Gong told him what had happened and asked him to rescue Madam Cui and her daughter.

The general came to the temple and wiped out the bandits. Together they captured the chieftain Sun Feihu and turned him over to the authorities. Madam Cui and Yingying were both very grateful for his help. Particularly thankful to White Horse General was his friend Zhang Gong, because having saved the Cui family from a catastrophe, he would certainly be able to marry his beloved Cui Yingying.

After seeing off White Horse General, Zhang Gong went to see Madam Cui.

"What are you here for?" asked Madam Cui, as if nothing had happened. In fact, she knew clearly what the young scholar's motive was, but how could she honor a promise made for the sake of expedience? She pondered, "Being the daughter of a prime minister, Cui Yingying is from a noble family. Zhang Gong, however, is but a poor scholar. Unless he can pass the imperial examination, he will be nobody. How can I marry my daughter to such a poor and pedantic bookworm?" Madam Cui would have thought aloud but for Zhang Gong's presence.

In answer to Madam Cui's question, the unsophisticated Zhang Gong answered, "I am here to propose to your daughter."

"Don't you know that she is still in mourning and not in a position to talk about marriage?" questioned Madam Cui, who launched an offensive as her defense.

"Do you still remember what you promised?" the perplexed Zhang Gong asked, alarmed at Her Highness's forgetfulness.

"I didn't promise anything," asserted the woman. "I said what I said because of the urgent situation. Protecting the family of a prime minister voluntarily is any subject's responsibility. Don't you think so?"

Zhang Gong was so stunned at Madam Cui's blatant breach of her promise and so angry at her abuse of the dead minister's authority that he could hardly speak. "Well, since you like Yingying so much," Madam Cui said in a conciliatory tone, with an attempt to mitigate the tense situation, "I'll let her treat you as a brother."

Frustrated at Madam Cui's ingratitude and betrayal, Zhang Gong fell ill and pined away. Seeing this, the sympathetic Hongniang suggested that he play a love tune on his lute so that Yingying could hear him. Touched by Zhang Gong's musical message, Cui Yingying responded with a letter inviting Zhang Gong to see her the next evening. She asked Hongniang to deliver the message to him and arrange for them to meet in secret. She did not care about her maidservant's direct involvement in her love affair any more. In fact, she felt she needed all the help Hongniang could provide.

With the assistance of Hongniang, Zhang Gong and Cui Yingying met and spent the night together for the first time. As their trysts became more frequent, Madam Cui found out what was going on. She summoned Hongniang to her chamber and gave her a good beating, blaming her for what she thought to be her daughter's corruption. To Madam Cui's surprise, Hongniang did not try to deny her role in the secret love affair. Instead of apologizing for what she had been doing, she pointed a finger squarely at Madam Cui, saying, "It is you who made the secret love affair possible."

"How dare you!" Madam Cui was furious. "What have I done wrong?"

"You said you would marry Yingying to anyone who could get us out of the danger that would corrupt Yingying anyway, but when Zhang Gong took all the risks to get us help from White Horse General, you ate your words," accused Hongniang.

Pausing a little, she went on, "You could have given Zhang Gong some monetary award and simply sent him away, but you didn't. You chose to let him stay with us and make Yingying his sister. Then how can you prevent the two lovers from getting together? Don't you think you are responsible for what they're doing?"

For all her anger at the maidservant's insolence, Madam Cui found it hard to refute her. Seeing Madam Cui speechless, Hongniang continued, "If you let the situation get out of hand, it will reflect badly on the reputation of the Cui family. Besides, you don't want to be charged with negligent parenting, do you?"

In the end, Madam Cui had to accept the young couple's relationship, but she adamantly refused to let them live as legal husband and wife. She ordered Zhang Gong to concentrate on his studies for the imperial examination and leave for the capital to take it when the time came. She told Zhang Gong not to return for her daughter unless he passed the examination and became a high-ranking official. The young couple parted reluctantly, uncertain of what was going to happen to their relationship in the future.

The next spring, Zhang Gong took the exam, passed it, and got a high-ranking position in the imperial government. He rejoined Cui Yingying, who had by this time returned to the capital. The snobbish Madam Cui had no more reasons to stand in their way. The couple lived a happy life thereafter.

As to the whereabouts of Hongniang, no one knows for sure. Some say she is still living with her mistress, while others claim that she quit her job and returned to her hometown, where she happily married her childhood boyfriend

The maidservant Hongniang helps the young scholar and the young woman.

XU XUAN AND HIS WHITE-SNAKE WIFE

A number of Chinese tales have connections with one or more physical locations of the country. The beauty of the West Lake in Hangzhou, a city known as "heaven on earth," inspired the tale retold here.

One early spring morning, Xu Xuan, a young salesclerk in a drugstore in the suburbs of Hangzhou, went to visit a Buddhist abbot named Fahai in the Temple of Golden Hill at the West Lake. A benefactor of the temple, Xu Xuan was a frequent guest of the abbot. Anticipating wet weather, which was a common occurrence in that region during the spring season, Xu Xuan brought with him an umbrella.

Sure enough, it began to drizzle as Xu Xuan reached the West Lake and was ready to cross the Broken Bridge, so called because of its conjunction with a dike that ended abruptly. He was secretly rejoicing at his foresight when he encountered two beautiful young women, staggering head-on into the rain. Too late to dodge them, he had to shake his own hands to greet them awkwardly as he was holding the umbrella. You see, in ancient China, men and women were not supposed to touch each other unless they were husband and wife. The two seemingly embarrassed young women responded with a bow. Offering his umbrella to them, Xu Xuan ventured to ask who they were and where they were going.

The women were, in fact, the incarnations of snakes. Now that they could assume the form of humans after years of strenuous self-cultivation, they had given up their secluded serpentine lives and come out of hiding to see the world. Grateful as they were to Xu Xuan, they would not give away their identity to a stranger.

"My name is Suzhen White," the woman in white answered, blushing. Pointing to her younger companion in blue, she continued, "This is Xiao Qing, my maid and friend."

"We've been to the grave of Lady White's husband, who passed away a few days ago." Xiao Qing responded, secretly feeling pleased with her quick wit.

As their eyes met, Xu Xuan and Lady White immediately felt drawn to each other. Before Xu Xuan could ask where she lived, Lady White offered to meet him the next day at the same location so that she could return the umbrella. Xu Xuan was only too glad to accept the offer of a date from such a beautiful young woman.

Their meeting the next day and subsequent meetings eventually led to marriage. Xu Xuan quit his job and opened a drugstore of his own with the help of Lady White and Xiao Qing. The medicinal herbs, blessed by Lady White's magic power, were miraculously effective. As a result, their business boomed. Their drugstore attracted a lot of people who would otherwise have gone to the Temple of Golden Hill to pray for a cure. However, their success seriously affected the temple's donations—an impact that Xu Xuan and Lady White did not mean to create, nor were they aware of it. Soon they began to suffer consequences.

Pretending to be a customer, Fahai, the abbot of the Temple of Golden Hill, paid a visit to Xu Xuan's drugstore. With his magic insight, Fahai knew Lady White and her maid to be the incarnations of supernatural snakes, and he immediately realized who had caused his loss of revenue. He made plans to get rid of Lady White and her maid.

The next time Xu Xuan visited his temple, Fahai revealed Lady White's serpentine origin. Dumbfounded and shaking his head in disbelief, Xu Xuan said, more to himself than to the abbot, "It can't be true. She is as good a human being as anybody!"

"Well, believe me or not, you're going to suffer in the end." Using a scare tactic, the vicious abbot continued, "She may love you enough not to hurt you intentionally, but you will surely get poisoned through close contact with her in the long run."

"No, you are lying!" Xu Xuan tried not to believe the abbot.

Fahai's patience was wearing thin. "Well, seeing is believing," he said. "Follow my instructions and you'll find out for yourself." Casting a spell upon Xu Xuan to make him credulous, the devilish Fahai told Xu Xuan what to do.

Back home, Xu Xuan sent Xiao Qing away, secretly doctored a glass of wine with a dab of *xionghuang* (a kind of arsenic), and offered it to his wife at dinner. The unsuspecting Lady White took the potion gladly, thinking of it as a gesture of love. No sooner had she drunk the toxic wine than she revealed her former identity as a white python. The horrific sight threw Xu Xuan into a life-threatening coma.

Knowing who was behind her husband's folly, Lady White decided to bring him back to life. She knew that only *lingzhi* (a magic herb) could revive him, but it grew on a treacherous cliff on the Golden Hill, closely guarded by Fahai's lookouts. Overcoming untold difficulties, Lady White managed to obtain the herb without Fahai and his guardsmen finding out.

The herb could save Xu Xuan's life but not his soul, which had been snared by Fahai's evil spell. Lady White tried to assure her husband that she had become a normal human being and would never return to her reptile past so long as he would not use the malicious concoction. Xu Xuan, however, refused to believe what she said. He would not forgive her even after she told him that she was expecting their baby. On the contrary, he looked upon Fahai as his savior and, forsaking her, sought refuge in the Temple of Golden Hill.

Lady White did not want to give her husband up, knowing that what he had said and done was involuntary. Together with Xiao Qing, she challenged Fahai to a fight. She tried to flood his temple with the water she called up from the West Lake with her magic charm, but each time she raised the water level, Fahai would move the dike higher with his supernatural energy. Eventually, Lady White had to give up the fight for fear of harming her unborn baby. As she retreated to the Broken Bridge with the help of Xiao Qing, Lady White was too exhausted to walk further.

The bridge brought back the memory of her first encounter with Xu Xuan. Love and anger overwhelmed her at the same time. Meanwhile, the only thing on Xiao Qing's mind was how to avenge her mistress on her ungrateful husband.

They crossed the bridge and were about to settle down under a tree at the West Lake when they spotted a bedraggled man staggering down the bridge behind them. It was none other than Xu Xuan. During the turmoil of the battle between his wife and Fahai, he had somehow shaken off the spell and fled from the temple. He was trying to catch up with his wife, apologize to her, and reconcile with her. Seeing the wretched and remorseful Xu Xuan, Lady White immediately forgave him. The hot-tempered Xiao Qing, however, would not be so lenient. She wanted to teach him a good lesson. Only after Lady White's repeated pleas did she relent.

The couple soon greeted their newborn with great joy. However, their peaceful life did not last long. A month later, the heinous Fahai shattered it again. He invited a celestial army to fight Lady White and Xiao Qing. In the end, they subdued Lady White, who was still weak from childbirth, and imprisoned her under the Tower of Thunder Ridge near the West Lake. Xiao Qing narrowly escaped capture.

For a decade, Xiao Qing improved her martial skills and cultivated her magic powers. Then she returned to stage a surprise counterattack, defeated Fahai and his xiabing xiejiang (Shrimp soldiers and crab generals), and rescued Lady White from the dungeon beneath the Tower of Thunder Ridge, before burning the tower to ashes. She encased Fahai in the body of a crab. The Chinese today still claim that they can find Fahai's figure inside the bodies of crabs.

Lady White fighting *xiabing xiejiang*.

Myths, Legends, and Immortals

Gods and goddesses, immortals and super beings, and legendary heroes and heroines may have never physically existed in history, but they have always been part and parcel of the psyche, or collective mind, of a culture. Han Chinese, unlike some peoples of other cultures, often considered these mythical and legendary beings to be as human as you and I. "Guanyin, Goddess of Mercy" was portrayed as mortal before she became a follower of Buddha, and "Mazu, Mother Goddess of the Sea" was seen as earthly prior to her ascendance to heaven. So was Lü Dongbin, who helped the needy with "A Dancing Crane" and his fellow "Eight Immortals Crossing the Sea," who acted like children. "Gun and Yu," who conquered the deluge, would have been taken for ordinary tribal leaders but for their supernatural powers.

The hero Bao Zheng and heroines Mulan and Mu Guiying, commander-in-chief of the "Yang Family Generals," might have no supernatural background at all, but they were invested with superhuman prowess either by mystic beings like the "Fox Fairy" or simply by the people who have orally passed on the stories of their laudable deeds. The interesting aspect of Mulan and Mu Guiying lies in the paradox that they were so highly regarded in a male-dominated society. They proved to be as good as, if not better than, the other sex.

Xiwangmu (**Queen Mother of the West**), **a powerful goddess of death and longevity in Chinese popular religion, sitting on the terrace. Courtesy of Baihua Literature and Art Publishing House.**

GUANYIN, GODDESS OF MERCY

Guanyin is the Chinese version of Avalokitesvara, who is one of the Buddhist enlightened beings known as bodhisattva, or pusa *in Chinese. Guanyin is so popular in China that the name is almost synonymous with* pusa. *Prior to the Song dynasty (960–1126), Guanyin was still masculine in appearance. Over time the Chinese followers feminized the deity, for a woman figure would better embody Guanyin's compassion for hearing and answering their prayers.*

The belief in Guanyin has a far-reaching impact on the Chinese mind, as is evident in many of the tales retold in this book. For example, the almighty, fearless Monkey King was but a child in front of Guanyin. He sought her help whenever he was in trouble, her mediation whenever he was in a dispute, and her judgment whenever he was treated unfairly.

The Chinese have also made great efforts to humanize and Sinicize Guanyin. A famous Chinese classic of the Ming dynasty (1368–1644), Soushenji (Record of Searching for Deities) *is one of these endeavors and serves as the basis for the tale that follows.*

According to *Soushenji*, Guanyin was originally the incarnation of Shi Shan, the third son of Elder Shi Qin, a Buddhist abbot from the state of *Jiuling Guzhu* (Eagle Ridge in a Lonely Bamboo Forest). The family of Shi had been doing good deeds for three generations. One day, however, when a bandit leader came to beg, Shi Shan's three sons refused to show him mercy. In retaliation, the bandit leader then rallied his men and massacred 300 people in the village of the Shi family. The atrocity of the bandits enraged Yuhuang Dadi (the Jade Emperor of Heaven), who blamed the three brothers for driving the bandits to revolt. Despite their history of charity, he locked up the brothers in a celestial prison for life.

In the state of Beique there lived King Miao Zhuang and Queen Boya. To punish the king for his bloody conquests in the process of establishing his kingdom, Yuhuang Dadi deprived him and his wife of their fertility. They frequented a Buddhist temple to repent and pray for mercy. Finally Yuhuang Dadi relented. He thought of the three Shi brothers and set them free. He let them be reborn into the House of Miao Zhuang to become their daughters. Shi Shan became the youngest daughter and got the name Miao Shan. The birth of the three sisters was phenomenal: They came into the world accompanied by a wisp of fragrance and a flash of dazzling light.

Guanyin bestowing children on the infertile parents. Courtesy of Baihua Literature and Art Publishing House.

Miao Shan was intelligent and eager to learn even when she was a small child. As she grew into a young lady, her parents tried to marry her off because, according to the social norms of the time, keeping an unmarried grown-up daughter would be a disgrace to the family. Miao Shan, however, refused repeatedly. At their wits' end, her parents locked her up in a chamber in the backyard garden. There, taking advantage of her quiet, sequestered environment, Miao Shan meditated and became a devout Buddhist believer, as she had been in her previous existence as Shi Shan. No matter how King Miao Zhuang and Queen Boya reasoned with her, Miao Shan would not change her mind. She told her parents that she had devoted herself to Buddha and would never think of worldly affairs such as marriage. Her sisters, both married by now, came to see her and, using themselves as examples, tried to persuade her, but in vain.

One day, Miao Shan decided to leave for a nearby nunnery called the Temple of White Peacock. She wanted to be part of the 500-nun community there. Her parents let her go with great reluctance. Before her departure, Miao Shan apologized to them, "Father and Mother, I'm sorry that I have to leave and can't take care of you any more. But when I become a *pusa*, I will come for your salvation."

In the temple, Miao Shan worked and studied hard. When Yuhuang Dadi learned that she had become a nun, he ordered all the celestial deities to assist her and made her transition to a nun's life easier. The hustle and bustle of the celestial deities working at night scared the other nuns so much that they complained of Miao Shan to her parents. Her father came with his soldiers and tried to get Miao Shan back. When she rejected his demand, the father became so furious that he decided to burn the temple down. Three times did Miao Shan save it from the flames by biting her finger and sprinkling the blood from the wound over the structure.

King Miao Zhuang became even more wrathful. He arrested Miao Shan and condemned her to death. Her queen mother wanted to give her a chance and ordered that Miao Shan be imprisoned in the *lenggong*, where the king banished his disfavored concubines. The queen hoped that with time and persuasion, her daughter would eventually come around. Nevertheless, the queen was wrong, because Miao Shan would not give in at all.

When the execution day came, the local *tudiye* reported her imminent death to Yuhuang Dadi. The heavenly emperor had her enshrouded with a magic red light to fend off the executioner's hatchet. Frustrated, the brutal father ordered Miao Shan to be smothered with a red satin scarf. Before she gave her last breath, a large, white tiger dashed into the execution ground, snatched the dying Miao Shan, and ran toward a black forest. There, the King of the Underworld gave her a tour of his kingdom. Unable to bear seeing the dead suffering, the merciful Miao Shan closed her palms in front of her bosom and started to pray and chant. Suddenly all the shackles on the tormented dead came loose and broke into pieces. The King of the Netherworld had to cancel her ledger of death and return her to this world.

Soon, Buddha took Miao Shan as his disciple. Nine years later, she became a bodhisattva or *pusa*. The Chinese now prefer to call her Guanyin, Guanshiyin, or Guanyin Pusa. She is believed to have a thousand eyes able to perceive people's miseries and a thousand hands able to deliver them from their sufferings. She had two close disciples: a boy named Shan Cai (Good Fortune) and a girl called Long Nü (Dragon Princess). The following tale explains how Dragon Princess became Guanyin's disciple.

The Dragon King's beautiful daughter, Dragon Princess, was the apple of his eye. Fearful of possible dangers the outside world might pose to her, he never allowed her to venture out of the *longgong* (Dragon Palace), which was in the sea.

On land, humans were celebrating the Lantern Festival, bringing the half-month Chinese New Year season to a new height. Dragon Princess could not resist her curiosity. She pestered her father to let her go and take a look, as she often did. The Dragon King, however, categorically rejected her request, as usual.

When night fell, the princess slipped out of the palace and went on shore. She disguised herself as a country girl and went into town, where the Lantern Festival party was in full swing. Hundreds upon hundreds of lanterns with diverse designs lit up the streets as if it were day time. The exquisite colors and decorations of the lanterns simply captivated Dragon Princess. She had never imagined that the human world could be so beautiful! She was enjoying herself when a splash of water fell on her head and her body. Someone living on the second floor of a house along the street had tossed his cold tea out of his window. The sudden occurrence terrified the princess, because she realized that when her body touched water, her dragoness nature would reveal itself. Her transformation would scare the people and thus create a stampede, which would definitely ruin the Lantern Festival celebration. Trying to get back to the sea before her metamorphosis took place, she dashed toward the seaside, elbowing and nudging through the crowd. She ran and ran, and only a few feet before she could reach the water, she fell and turned into a big fish, flopping and flapping on the sand. She had tried all she could not to turn into her dragoness body in order to minimize the impact of her transformation on the humans who would see her. As it happened, two young fishermen had just returned from the sea and disembarked from their fishing boat. They were amazed at such a big, strange fish. One of them wanted to set it free; the other, however, suggested that they sell it together with the fish they had caught, for some extra money. Without knowing that it was Dragon Princess, they carried the big fish downtown.

Dragon Princess's plight did not escape the discerning eyes of Guanyin while she was meditating in the Purple Bamboo Forest. The Goddess of Mercy could not let anything bad happen to the princess. She asked her disciple, Shan Cai, to go and buy the fish.

"But how?" asked Shan Cai, perplexed. "We have no money."

"You silly boy!" Guanyin admonished him good-humoredly and smiled. "Go and take with you some of the incense ashes."

"After all, you are my master!" commented Shan Cai as he received the ashes from Guanyin and left for the fishing town on his lotus glider. When he arrived, he found the two fishermen peddling their fish downtown, with a crowd around marveling at the big, strange fish. People made various comments about the fish, but none would make an offer to buy it because it was too big and too expensive. A grey-bearded man suggested that the fish be cut into pieces. Shan Cai hated the idea but pardoned the old man for not knowing the identity of the fish. The senseless suggestion, however, scared the wits out of Dragon Princess. Just as one of the fishermen raised his hatchet to cut the fish, a boy monk stopped him, saying, "I'll buy the whole fish."

"Aren't you monks vegetarians?" the fisherman asked tauntingly.

"Yes, we are, because we don't kill," responded the young monk. "I am buying it because I want to release it into the sea." He handed the two fishermen his money and asked them to help carry the fish to the seashore. As soon as they let go the fish in the water, it splashed its tail a few times, as if to express its gratitude. Then it submerged into the depth of the sea. The two fishermen rejoiced at their good fortune, but when they took a close look at what they had in their hands, it was nothing but incense ashes.

The disappearance of the princess had thrown the *longgong* into chaos, and the dragon father into distress. He had ordered his marine servants and guardsmen to search for his daughter in and above the sea. Before he realized where his daughter could have gone, his daughter had returned from her adventure. The fuming father demanded that she tell everything about her absence. When the princess mentioned the young monk who had saved her life, the father became worried. He knew that the monk must have been Shan Cai, Guanyin's disciple. He feared that Guanyin might report the negligence of his guardianship to Yuhuang Dadi. The more he worried, the angrier he became at his daughter, blaming her for the mess. His wrath drove him so crazy that he turned his daughter out of his palace.

Now that she had nowhere to turn, Dragon Princess began to weep helplessly. Guanyin heard her cry and sent Shan Cai to help her again.

"Do you recognize me?" Shan Cai asked.

"You are the monk who saved my life!" said the princess, smiling, tears still lingering on her cheeks. "I haven't had time to say thanks yet."

"Don't thank me. I'll take you to someone for whom you really should feel thankful," said Shan Cai.

When they arrived in the Purple Bamboo Forest, Shan Cai introduced Dragon Princess to Guanyin. Guanyin liked the grateful princess very much and asked her if she wanted to be with her, like Shan Cai. Dragon Princess readily accepted the offer. Guanyin made Dragon Princess her second disciple and called her Long Nü, or Dragon's Daughter.

When the Dragon King learned that his daughter had become Guanyin's disciple, he regretted driving her away. He wanted her to come back, but each time he asked, Long Nü rejected him. She told him that she still loved him, but her love for Guanyin was greater. Besides, she enjoyed being away from the seclusion of his *longgong*.

MAZU, MOTHER GODDESS OF THE SEA

Mazu, meaning "mother" in a Fujian dialect, is a Chinese marine goddess. Like many of the Chinese gods and goddesses, she was a deified human being. The worship of Mazu is very popular in the coastal areas of Mainland China, Hong Kong, Macao, and Taiwan. Chinese emigrants also took the belief to other places of the world. "Macao" means "a temple of Mazu." The city got the name when one of the first Portuguese colonizers asked a local what the name of the place was. The local mistook the subject of the question as the temple of Mazu, which the colonizer happened to be pointing at while questioning him.

Once upon a time, on an island in the East China Sea, there lived a fishing family named Lin. They were popular among their fellow villagers because they were always willing to help anyone in need. Although the Lin couple had six children, only one was a son. They were worried that if something should happen to the only male heir, the family line would break. Keeping a family line unbroken was a serious matter to the Chinese. They prayed to Guanyin, Goddess of Mercy, for another boy.

One night the wife dreamed that Guanyin gave her a pill and said to her, "I know you are a good couple, and you deserve someone to carry on your good deeds when you are not able to do so. Here is a pill of fertility. Take it, and you will be pregnant." Before she had time to thank Guanyin, the wife awoke from her dream. In her hand she was holding the pill. She took it and waited to see what was going to happen. Sure enough, in a month, she began to expect a child. However, she waited month after month, but the child did not come into being. When finally the long-overdue time of birth arrived, a strange phenomenon took place: a flash of red light shot across the room, followed by a fragrant draft of air. In its wake, the child was born. It was a girl. Though disappointed that it was not a boy, as they had prayed and wished for, the parents loved her all the same. As she never cried, they called her *Mo Niang* (Quiet Girl) and named her Lin Mo. Unlike her cheerful and outgoing peers, Lin Mo was quiet and pensive even when she was only four years old.

One day, Lin Mo's parents took her to the Buddhist temple where they prayed. The image of Guanyin, Goddess of Mercy, mesmerized the thoughtful young girl. Gazing at the saintly statue of Guanyin, Lin Mo gained spiritual revelation. Soon she became a devoted Buddhist.

On an early morning, an elderly monk came to visit the Lin family. He asked to see Lin Mo and taught her a secret charm, which gave her the magic power to tell the future and visit a place without physically being there.

One afternoon Lin Mo was praying in her chamber when an elderly nun came asking for alms. The nun said she was from the Temple of West Mountains. She got some food from Lin Mo's parents and was about to leave when Lin Mo came out of her chamber and stopped her, saying, "Sister, the sago trees in your Temple of West Mountains have bloomed. Could you bring me a flower next time you come?" The nun thought that the girl was being naughty and pulling her leg, for she knew that the temple was a dozen miles away, and when she had left it that morning, the sago trees had shown no sign of blooming at all.

"How do you know?" the puzzled nun asked.

"I've just been there, and I saw the flowers on the sago trees," said Lin Mo, "I didn't want to pick them without your permission."

The nun left, shaking her head in disbelief. Back in the temple, however, she was stunned to see the sago trees full of colorful blooms. She realized that the little girl possessed exceptional power of extrasensory perception. Her amazement became even greater when she turned around and saw Lin Mo standing behind her, asking for the flower.

During Lin Mo's teenage years, a strange encounter on a spring morning further enhanced her magic powers. That day she went on an outing with some friends. While her friends were indulging themselves by frolicking and chasing each other around, the contemplative Lin Mo felt drawn to a fountain. When she reached it, she looked into the water, which was as clear as a mirror, so she could see her reflection distinctly. She sat down at the edge of the fountain and began to tidy up her hair. Suddenly, a divine being emerged from the water. He gave the unperturbed Lin Mo two bronze tablets with encrypted incantations inscribed on them. When her friends asked what the inscriptions meant, Lin Mo said, "I don't know yet, but I will study them hard and make sense of them."

Back home, the young Lin Mo set about deciphering the sealed book on the bronze tablets in earnest. By cracking the codes, she gained the power of exorcising ghosts, averting disasters, and curing diseases. With her newly acquired ability, Lin Mo gave a great deal of help to her fellow villagers who were in need.

One of her deeds was to confront two demons, called *Shunfenger* (Sharp Ears) and *Qianliyan* (Sharp Eyes). The huge statues of *Shunfenger* and *Qianliyan* are integral parts of a Mazu temple. They always stand on either side of its entrance.

One dark evening a tempest started, and in its wake came the two demons. They began to victimize the people on land and at sea around the island Lin Mo's family and their fellow fishermen called home. Lin Mo fought the demons with her silk scarf. Each time she shook the scarf, it called up a huge sandstorm, and sand blew into the demons' ears and eyes, rendering them powerless. Eventually they surrendered to Lin Mo. With her healing power, she cleaned the sand out of their ears and eyes. The demons pledged allegiance to Lin Mo and vowed to assist her in fighting other evil spirits.

On the eighth day of the ninth Chinese lunar month in the year 987, a day before the *Chongyangjie* (Double Ninth Festival), Lin Mo said to her parents and siblings calmly, "I'm going to celebrate *Chongyangjie* this year on the hill tomorrow. Thank you for your kindness, understanding, and support all these years!" None would have imagined that she was going to become a deity, and her physical being would never come back to them.

The next morning, Lin Mo, then twenty-eight, bid farewell to her family and went toward the hill, the highest point of the island. As soon as she reached its zenith, heavy clouds began to shroud her. All of a sudden, a bedazzling light shot out of the clouds, which then gradually dispersed, leaving nothing behind. People believed that the light had carried Lin Mo to heaven, where she was sainted as Goddess Mazu.

Since then, there have been over a dozen purported sightings of Mazu. Many Taiwanese believe that Mazu helped their forebear Koxinga, known to mainland Chinese as Zheng Chenggong, and his army free the island from Dutch occupation in 1662. Koxinga was a Chinese general of the Ming dynasty (1368–1644) who resented the invasion of the Qing (1645–1911) and meant to use Taiwan as his base to stage a comeback and restore the Ming dynasty.

Another alleged incident took place in 1683, when General Shi Lang of the Qing dynasty launched an offensive to take the Penghu Islands in the Taiwan Strait before seizing the island of Taiwan from Koxinga's descendants, asserting independence. Later, when asked why they were so brave in the battles, some of General Shi Lang's soldiers claimed that Mazu had shown up and assisted them in their fighting.

A picture of *Mazu*. Courtesy of Baihua Literature and Art Publishing House.

A DANCING CRANE

This is a folktale associated with Lü Dongbin, one of the baxian (Eight Immortals), whose tale is retold later in this chapter. According to legend, Lü Dongbin has a strong sense of justice and often defends the weak and helps the needy.

The immortal Lü Dongbin was roaming the country. One day he came to the town of Hanyang. As he wandered its streets and enjoyed its beauty, he did not forget the true purpose of his travels: to find a needy and honest person to help. Because Lü Dongbin looked like a beggar, no one would think of him as an immortal. A day had passed, and he had not yet found what he regarded as an honest person in need of his help.

Evening came, and Lü Dongbin felt both tired and hungry. He went into a restaurant, but the server drove him out, fearing that he might not be able to pay for the food. He went into another and had the same experience. When night fell, he had almost exhausted all the restaurants in town, and he found himself at the outskirts, where there were fewer people and less traffic.

A banner on a shop, fluttering in the breeze, caught his attention. It said "The Xin Family Restaurant." He entered it. An amiable middle-aged man came up and greeted him. During their conversation, Lü Dongbin learned that his name was Xin Shi, and he was the owner of the restaurant. Xin Shi seated Lü Dongbin and asked a server to bring him a pot of hot tea and a menu. Looking at the entrees listed on the menu, Lü Dongbin appeared to be embarrassed. Finally, he told the owner and the server that he was penniless. Then, taking off his ragged, dirty gown, he asked if he could trade it for a bowl of noodle soup. Unlike the owners of the other restaurants Lü Dongbin had encountered downtown, Xin Shi did not show any sign of annoyance. Instead, he asked the server to bring food. When Lü Dongbin asked him why he treated a beggar like him so well, Xin Shi answered, "Anything may happen in our lives. I'm a restaurant owner today all right, but how can I be so sure that I won't be in your position in the future? I wish I could be respected and taken care of if that happens."

Lü Dongbin nodded without saying a word. Over the next months, he roamed and begged during the day, and returned to the Xin Family Restaurant in the evening. He ate and stayed in the restaurant. He did so for half a year, without paying a single cent. He observed Xin Shi, his family members, and the employees, but could not see a single sign of displeasure and contempt. When he apologized and promised to pay them if his fate should take a turn for the better, Xin Shi would say, "Don't worry. Pay me back whenever you can."

At first, Lü Dongbin wondered if the restaurant owner saw through his disguise and knew he was an immortal. His doubt evaporated when he found that Xin Shi treated every poor customer with the same courtesy. "No wonder he is not making money," pondered Lü Dongbin. He also discovered another reason for the unprofitableness of the restaurant: its location. Because it was on the outskirts of the town, it had a limited clientele. Most of the customers were poor transients. Looking at the slightly stooped figure of Xin Shi, Lü Dongbin realized that this was exactly the person he had been looking for—honest and in need of help.

One evening, when Lü Dongbin came back from a day's wandering he asked Xin Shi to dine with him. Over a cup of wine, Lü Dongbin asked why Xin Shi did not have a good business even though his food, the service, and the environment of the restaurant were excellent. He wanted to see if Xin Shi was business-minded enough to help himself later. Xin Shi told him that the restaurant, though close to the beautiful Yangtze River, was a little far from downtown.

"Besides," Xin Shi added, "it has been only a year since I became its owner."

"Looks like it is high time I paid for what I owe you all these months!"

"No, no. I know you can't afford anything. I am willing to help."

"I, too, am willing to pay for your kindness" Lü Dongbin insisted. Pausing a little, he asked a server behind Xin Shi, "Could you get me a pen and some ink?" Despite his bewilderment, the server did as requested. Lü Dongbin surveyed the restaurant, dipped the brush pen in the ink, and drew a crane on the wall facing the entrance. The bird arched its long neck, extended its wings, and bent one of its slender legs, as if to dance.

Courtesy of Baihua Literature and Art Publishing House.

When he finished, Lü Dongbin gave Xin Shi a flute and said, "Whenever you play the flute, the painted crane will jump off the wall and dance." Xin Shi tried the flute, and sure enough, the crane raised its head, retracted its wings, and squatting a little, jumped off the wall. When it landed on the floor, the bird began to dance with extreme elegance. When Xin Shi played the flute again at Lü Dongbin's suggestion, the crane flew back to the wall and became a painting again.

Before Xin Shi could thank him, Lü Dongbin began, "I hope that the dancing crane will attract more customers, and each of them will become your voluntary advertiser." Pausing a second, the immortal added, "Soon you will become wealthy. I hope this will be enough to pay you for your kindness to a beggar." So saying, Lü Dongbin left the restaurant and vanished in an instant.

In no time, the Xin Family Restaurant became known far and wide for its dancing crane in addition to its quality food and service. Xin Shi quickly became wealthy, but he was still as charitable as he had always been.

One day, Lü Dongbin returned to the Xin Family Restaurant, to the happy surprise of Xin Shi and his family. They were only too glad to see him again and wanted to treat him to a big dinner. Lü Dongbin declined and said, "Now that the restaurant is well established, and this area has become as prosperous as downtown, I don't think you'll ever need the crane any more," Lü Dongbin said, smiling.

"I agree," said Xin Shi. "Besides, the crane has been working so hard that it deserves a long-overdue break."

Lü Dongbin produced a flute from a pocket in his wide sleeve and played an enchanting tune. The painted crane hopped onto the floor and came up to Lü Dongbin, who mounted on its back. The next moment, the Xin Family and their customers saw the bird fly out of the window carrying Lü Dongbin, and disappear in the distant sky.

Today, tourists to Hanyang, which has become part of the city of Wuhan, will see a pavilion on top of a hill at the Yangtze River. Local legend tells that Xin Shi, the restaurant owner, built the pavilion in memory of Lü Dongbin and his dancing crane after their departure.

EIGHT IMMORTALS CROSSING THE SEA

There are numerous xians (immortals) in popular Chinese beliefs. They are men and women who have acquired the status of gods and goddesses. The best known are the baxian (Eight Immortals): Tieguai Li, Zhongli Quan, Zhang Guolao, Lü Dongbin, He Xiangu, Lan Caihe, Han Xiangzi, and Cao Guojiu.

Tieguai Li limped, with his hallmark iron crutch. His handicap was the result of a mistake made by his disciples, who burnt his physical body while his spirit traveled elsewhere. When the spirit returned, it had nowhere to reside but the dead body of a lame beggar. Zhongli Quan was a general. After a lost battle, he was introduced to an immortal, who taught him to become one himself. Zhang Guolao used to be a magician. After he became an immortal, he formed the habit of riding a white donkey while facing backward. When the donkey was not in use, he could fold it up like a piece of paper and place it in a leather pouch. Lü Dongbin became an immortal when he met the God of Fiery Dragon. Later, he learned swordsmanship from another immortal. After that he became the champion of the weak. He Xiangu is the only female immortal of the eight. She was good at telling fortunes. Lan Caihe is known for his childlike face, which never aged. Han Xiangzi was a dandy and alcoholic. Cao Guojiu, being the father of an emperor's wife, used to be very powerful and wicked. He narrowly escaped execution for his misdeeds. After his pardon, he repented and became an immortal.

Most of *the time, the baxian went their own ways to do their miraculous deeds. The tale of the dancing crane (above) is an example of Lü Dongbin's adventures. The most significant gathering of the Eight Immortals was when they tried to cross the East Sea together—a well-known legend, retold as follows.*

The Eight Immortals met again at a party given by *Xiwangmu* (the Queen Mother of the West), Goddess of Death and Immortality. Her authority is only less than that of Yuhuang Dadi, Jade Emperor of Heaven. Living on top of Mt. Kunlun, she had an orchard of magic peaches. A bite of the fruit would make a mortal live forever. However, the peaches ripened only every thousand years, and when they did, *Xiwangmu* would invite all the deities, including the Eight Immortals, to a party at Mt. Kunlun, where she would share the peaches with them.

Since *Xiwangmu*'s liquor was very tasty, the Eight Immortals drank to their hearts' content. When they left the party, they were all intoxicated. Looking down from the clouds on which they traveled, they saw the East Sea seething with waves in the distance.

"I've heard a lot about the East Sea and its fantastic mirages, but I've never been there. How about taking a tour of the East Sea while we are in high spirits?" suggested Lü Dongbin.

"We're all drunk; we'd better pick another day," Zhang Guolao advised.

"There aren't many chances for a reunion like this. Let's go for a visit and have some fun together," Zhongli Quan recommended.

"Let's go," responded the other immortals unanimously. So saying, they sailed to the east on the clouds. When they arrived above the East Sea, they were amazed by its magnificent billows and its endless expanse.

Lü Dongbin again made a proposition, saying, "We can cross the sea on the clouds with ease, but it is boring. How about crossing it with the tools we have so that we can show our different magic talents?"

Everyone liked the idea. Tieguai Li cast his crutch into the water and sailed on it as if it had been a boat; Zhongli Quan floated on his horsetail whisk; Zhang Guolao traveled on his donkey; Lü Dongbin, on his vertical bamboo flute; Han Xiangzi, on his flower basket; He Xiangu, on her bamboo cover; Lan Caihe, on his jade clappers; and Cao Guojiu, on his jade tablet.

At the time, the Dragon King of the East Sea was holding a court meeting, when suddenly there came from the surface above a flash of white light, illuminating every nook and cranny of his palace. He ordered his elder son Mojie to find out what was going on. The elder dragon prince emerged with his *xiabing xiejiang* (shrimp soldiers and crab generals) and saw the Eight Immortals crossing the sea, each with a treasure as his or her vehicle.

Lan Caihe's jade clappers seemed particularly appealing to the dragon prince. Although there were millions of rarities in his father's palace, he had never seen anything so intriguing. He dragged Lan Caihe down to the bottom of the sea, locked him up in a dungeon, and confiscated his jade clappers, which lit the palace as brightly as the sun. The Dragon King was so proud of his son that he rewarded him with a celebration party.

When the rest of the immortals reached the other coast, they found Lan Caihe missing. Initially, they thought that he must have lagged behind. After they waited for a long time and he did not show up, they determined that something must have gone wrong.

"You should have listened to me," complained Zhang Guolao. "See what's happened to us drunkards?"

"Well, since you suggested that we travel on the sea instead of on the clouds, you've got to go and get to the bottom of it," Zhongli Quan said to Lü Dongbin,

"Fine! I'll be back soon with what I discover," responded Lü Dongbin. He left and scoured the surface of the sea, but could not find a trace of Lan Caihe. "It had to be the Dragon King," he suspected. He shouted at the waters below, "Listen, you dragons! If you don't let Lan Caihe go, I will dry up the sea with my magic fire!"

The elder dragon prince emerged and responded angrily, "How dare you talk so loud and so big! I won't release Lan Caihe, but instead, I will make you his mate in my prison." Enraged, Lü Dongbin drew out his magic sword and charged at the dragon prince, who fled back to the bottom of the sea. Lü Dongbin then cast his magic gourd into the sea. Instantly, one gourd turned into millions, and all together, they produced a sea of flames with tremendous heat that brought the sea to a boil.

"Let that Lan Caihe go and keep his clappers only," Dragon King ordered his son. "Hurry and release him before that lunatic dries up the sea!" Reluctantly, the dragon prince released Lan Caihe. Lü Dongbin called off the fiery attack and returned to the immortals with Lan Caihe. As the immortals celebrated their victory, Lan Caihe, however, remained unhappy. When asked, he said the dragons were still in possession of his treasured clappers.

"Let's go get the clappers back and dry up the sea in revenge!" Tieguai Li shouted.

"Hold it, hold it!" Zhang Guolao calmed Tieguai Li down and suggested, "Let Dongbin go back again and ask the dragons for the clappers first. If they refuse to return the clappers, then we'll be justified in setting the fire." Everyone agreed. He Xiangu volunteered to assist Lü Dongbin.

In the air above where the Dragon Palace was supposed to be, Lü Dongbin and He Xiangu demanded that the dragons return the jade clappers. "If you don't," they threatened, "we'll start to burn the sea again!" Dragon King, who now regretted setting Lan Caihe free, dispatched Moji to get Lü Dongbin. After a few bouts of fighting, the dragon prince realized that he was no match for the immortals. He was about to run away when He Xiangu caught him with her bamboo cover. While he was struggling, trying to flee, Lü Dongbin killed him with his sword.

The astounded Dragon King then sent his second son to fight the two immortals. In the heat of fighting, Lü Dongbin cut off the younger dragon prince's right arm. The prince managed to return to the palace but died soon after. Vowing to avenge the premature death of his two sons, Dragon King came out to fight the immortals with the help of his 100,000-strong *xiabing xiejiang*.

Tieguai Li and Lü Dongbin released the magic flames from their bottle gourds and soon dried the sea up and took over the Dragon Palace. The defeated Dragon King of the East Sea fled to the South Sea, where he told his story to its sovereign.

"What? They killed your two sons, dried up the sea, and took your palace just for a set of clappers?" the Dragon King of the South Sea roared with rage. "They've gone too far. We have to teach them a lesson."

"But how?" asked the Dragon King of the East Sea.

"In your palace," the Dragon King of the South Sea said with a cunning smile. "They are doomed in your palace." Seeing the baffled face of the Dragon King of the East Sea, he went on, "When they fought on land and on the surface of the water, they had an advantage over you and your sons. Now that they are on the dried seabed, the advantage will be ours, for we can easily flood them with the water from other seas."

"Marvelous! Let's contact the Dragon Kings of the North and West Seas so that we can get enough water."

After their day's fighting, the Eight Immortals felt tired and went to sleep in the deserted and dry palace of the Dragon King. In the wee hours, Zhang Guolao was wakened by a strange humming noise coming all around from the distance. He listened closely, and the humming turned into low rumbling. "Get up! The tsunami! It's coming all around us! Hurry, we've got to run!" However, his alarm came too late, for roaring waves closed in as hundred-foot-high walls. Tieguai Li and Lü

Dongbin tried to fend off the water with their fiery gourds, but it was no use. However, they found that wherever Zhang Guolao turned, the water would make way for him. The immortals were overjoyed at this unfound magic power of his. Following him, they escaped to the shore.

The Dragon Kings of the North, South, and West Seas helped the Dragon King of the East Sea regain his palace. Finding no trace of the immortals, they thought they must have perished in the tsunami they had created. They held a feast to celebrate their victory.

The humiliating defeat vexed the Eight Immortals. They racked their brains to figure out how to retaliate. Finally, Lü Dongbin broke the silence, saying, "If they could attack us with water, and our fire was not powerful enough, then why can't we fight them with earth?"

"Tell us how," urged the others.

"Let's push Mt. Tai into the sea and fill it with its dirt," said Lü Dongbin.

Together the Eight Immortals toppled Mt. Tai and pushed it into the East Sea. The Dragon Kings narrowly escaped the calamity and retreated to the South Sea again.

"What more can we do?" asked the Dragon King of the East Sea, weeping with despair.

"Cheer up, my brother," said the Dragon King of the South Sea, " In my opinion, the Eight Immortals have committed four counts of capital crimes punishable by the laws of Heaven: killing the Dragon King's sons, burning his palace, moving Mt. Tai, and jamming the East Sea."

"You're clever. We should've realized this earlier. Let's file charges in the High Court of Heaven and let the Jade Emperor deal with them," the Dragon King of the West Sea said excitedly, as if he already saw the immortals locked up in the celestial penitentiary.

The Jade Emperor heard the case and dispatched his heavenly army to conquer the immortals. The battle had been raging for days when Guanyin, Goddess of Mercy, appeared to intervene. She said to the Eight Immortals and the Dragon Kings of the four seas, "A fight will eventually be over, but in the end, both opponents will get hurt. That has been true from time immemorial. I've consulted Buddha and Laozi, and I've just talked with the Jade Emperor. They all wanted me to help you get reconciled. What do you say?"

"We'll take your advice," said the Eight Immortals and the Dragon Kings unanimously.

"I hear that it all started because of a set of clappers. Where are they now?" asked Guanyin. Lan Caihe showed her the clappers, as bright as the sunlight. Guanyin took the brightest two pieces out of the set and handed them to the Dragon King of the East Sea, saying, "These are for you as a remembrance of your sons, whom you can't bring back to life."

The Dragon King thanked Guanyin and asked, "For your sake, I accept the death of my sons, but where do we live since the palace is already ruined and the East Sea is filled with the debris of Mt. Tai?"

"Ah," said Guanyin with a smile of confidence. "Follow me." When they came to the seashore, she placed a forefinger beneath the tip of Mt. Tai jutting out of the sea, and with a slight upward jerk, lifted the mountain from the waters. She then replaced the mountain where it had been. Soon the East Sea resumed its previous depth and expanse. After thanking Guanyin, the Eight Immortals and the Dragon Kings apologized to each other and went their own ways.

Eight Immortals crossing the sea. Courtesy of Baihua Literature and Art Publishing House.

BAO ZHENG AND THE FOX FAIRY

In the Song dynasty (A.D. 960–1279) there was a family named Bao. The Baos had three sons, of whom Bao Zheng was the youngest. On the evening of his birth, it rained heavily and thunder rumbled so loud that his expectant mother could not go to sleep. She was tossing in bed when, all of a sudden, a thunderbolt crashed right above the roof of her chamber. She was frightened, wondering why it was aimed at her. Eventually she went to sleep. In her sleep, she dreamed of giving birth to a child with an extremely dark complexion. The moment it came into being, the baby began to speak, saying "Mom" and "Dad." The child's precocity scared the mother, and she woke up instantly. When she told her dream to her husband, Lord Bao, he was surprised, too, because he had just dreamed the same dream!

Before dawn, Bao Zheng was born. However, enwrapped in thick afterbirth, he looked like a flesh ball. Lord Bao said to his eldest son and his daughter-in-law, "This child is abnormal. It must be a bad omen for our family." His second son's wife said to Lord Bao, "We'd better throw the flesh ball away. You've already had two sons; what is the use of having a monster such as this?" At her suggestion, Lord Bao asked his second son to put the flesh ball in a basket and throw it away.

Back home, the eldest son's wife said to her husband, "I had a different dream from that of your parents. In mine, your little brother was a child of nobility. He will be the smartest of you three when he grows up. Go and ask your brother where he has discarded the child." When asked, the younger brother said that he had left the basket on the slope of the other side of the mountain. The eldest brother went to look for Bao Zheng in the direction that his younger brother had given him.

In the meantime, a prowling tigress had found the deserted flesh ball. When she licked the after-birth open, the tigress found a chubby boy of dark complexion. Just as she was starting to eat him, the tigress saw a golden halo hovering around his body. The tigress balked at eating this extraordinary child. Instead, she nestled down beside him and warmed him with her body heat. The tigress decided not to leave the baby until someone came to claim him. The newborn Bao Zheng was not afraid of the wild beast at all. He nudged the tigress until she realized that he wanted her milk. The tigress happened to be a new mother; she nursed Bao Zheng, and her milk was said to have sown the seed of Bao Zheng's courage, which he would display when he grew up and became a public official. He would be so courageous and upright that he even dared to challenge the emperor. People would say that he had *hudan* (the courage of a tiger).

When the eldest brother approached, the tigress left quietly, knowing that the boy was safe now. The tigress was right. The eldest brother carried Bao Zheng to his home without telling anyone in the extended family. His wife, the mother of their three-month-old son, named Bao Mian, became Bao Zheng's wet nurse. Later, when he grew up, Bao Zheng called his sister-in-law *saoniang* (sister-in-law mother).

For seven years, Bao Zheng's eldest brother and *saoniang* kept his adoption a secret. At a party to celebrate Lord Bao's birthday, the sight of his grandson Bao Mian reminded him of his castaway son Bao Zheng. Lord Bao said sadly, "If my youngest son were not dead, he would be as big as Mian now." At this, Bao Zheng's *saoniang* said to Lord Bao, "Are you sure you are still missing your youngest son?"

"Sure I am," replied Lord Bao, a bit puzzled at the question.

"Do you want to see him?"

"What? He's still alive?" Lord Bao's bewilderment turned into amazement.

"Yes, he is!" Immediately, Bao Zheng was brought into the presence of Lord Bao, his real father.

Bao Zheng's appearance was Lord Bao's best "birthday present." Everyone in the family was happy to see the boy except Lord Bao's second son and his wife. The husband said to his wife, "This is very bad news. Bao Zheng looks so smart that when he grows up, he will certainly become someone. Then he will take revenge on us for throwing him away. What shall we do?" "We've got to get rid of him," his wife said cold-bloodedly.

Lord Bao hired a private teacher to tutor Bao Zheng and Bao Mian. Bao Zheng was not only intelligent but also diligent. He studied hard and learned very fast. Seeing this, the second brother and his wife became even more worried. They went to Lord Bao to try to frame Bao Zheng. They lied, telling him that Bao Zheng was wasting his time, and suggested that the idler be penalized. Lord Bao had always trusted the couple, so he made Bao Zheng quit school and herd the family's cow.

While attending to the cow, Bao Zheng had a strange encounter. On a fine day, there suddenly came a thunderbolt, followed by a series of rumblings and lightning. It turned out that the God of Thunder was trying to destroy a fox fairy to prevent her from becoming a goddess. While dodging the thunderbolt, the fox ran into Bao Zheng. With no time to ask for permission, she crawled beneath his gown. Seeing that Bao Zheng had a sign of sainthood on him, God of Thunder had to refrain from launching his strikes, fearing that he might hurt the boy. Grateful to Bao Zheng for saving her life, the fox fairy vowed to repay him. After that incident, she followed Bao Zheng's every move without his knowledge, acting as his guardian angel.

Bao Zheng's second brother and his wife were bent on killing him. While he was away attending to the cow, his second sister-in-law had big stones piled around the edge of a well where Bao

Zheng would come to draw water for his cow. That evening, when Bao Zheng arrived at the well, she pretended to weep. He went up to her and asked, "Sister-in-Law, what are you crying for?"

"I dropped my gold hairpin into the well. If I can't fish it out, your brother will beat the hell out of me," she lied.

"Don't worry! I'll get it for you." As he spoke, Bao Zheng clambered down the shaft of the well with the help of a rope. When he was halfway down, his second sister-in-law began to push the stones into the well, intending to kill him.

Meanwhile the fox fairy had a premonition of her savior's danger. Riding on the clouds, she rushed to his rescue. The fox did not know how to swim, so she summoned the God of the Well and asked him for help. She said, "Bao Zheng has saved my life. Please save his for my sake!" "No problem," said the God of the Well. Seeing the stones falling, he transformed into an old dragon woman and led Bao Zheng to safety in the depth of the well. Bao Zheng was surprised to see how brilliant the bottom of the well was and asked why. "Because of a magic mirror," answered the God of the Well. He then gave the mirror to Bao Zheng. The same mirror would serve as Bao Zheng's "mirror of perception" when he grew up and became a judge. It would help him identify evils that were otherwise indiscernible.

The God of the Well in the form of an old dragon woman.
Courtesy of Baihua Literature and Art Publishing House.

The wife of the second brother was rejoicing at Bao Zheng's quick death when suddenly she saw the boy tossed out of the well by a gush of water, unharmed. "He's really lucky," said the woman in bewilderment and fear. Now even more determined to get rid of Bao Zheng, she came up with another idea. The next day, she went to Lord Bao and told him that Bao Zheng was abusing the family cow. She asked Lord Bao to extend Bao Zheng's working hours and have her take supper to him in the evening. Lord Bao consented. She then mixed arsenic in the pancakes and fried eggs she cooked and took them to Bao Zheng.

Again, the fox fairy sensed the danger and rushed to save Bao Zheng. Because she was not a goddess yet, she could not speak human language. She turned to Bao Zheng's cow for help, saying, "You must save your master because the food he is about to eat is poisoned." Hearing this, the cow went up to Bao Zheng and knocked the pancakes and eggs out of his hands.

"My dear cow, we are friends, aren't we? Why don't you let me eat my supper?" asked Bao Zheng, baffled. The cow knelt down and wept. Bao Zheng wondered what was wrong with the animal.

"No matter what, I have to feed my hungry stomach," he thought aloud, and gathering up the food, prepared to eat it. The cow tried to warn Bao Zheng by nudging him, but Bao Zheng became so angry that he threatened to hit it. Desperate, the cow snatched the food and swallowed it. Instantly it dropped dead. Only then did Bao Zheng realize what had happened.

Back home that evening, Bao Zheng told Lord Bao about his second sister-in-law's attempt to kill him. Although doubtful about what his son had said, Lord Bao would rather err on the cautious side. He allowed Bao Zheng to resume his studies.

Bao Zheng studied hard, and in several years he became quite a scholar. It was time for him to take the imperial examination, which was scheduled to begin in the capital, hundreds of miles away. If he passed the examination, he would have a chance to get a high-ranking position. He left home and started out for the capital. The next day, however, he got lost. When he asked a farmer for directions, the farmer laughed at him, saying, "What? You take the imperial examination? If you can pass, I will plant my garlic upside down!"

Although humiliated, Bao Zheng walked away without saying a word. He then asked another farmer, but again could not get a reasonable answer. Suddenly he realized the reason for these responses: He looked ugly because of his extraordinarily dark complexion. He gave up asking for directions. As the day of the examination was nearing, Bao Zheng became concerned: He might well miss it. Just then, the fox fairy came to help him again. Unable to speak to him, she appeared in his dream as a young woman when he took a nap under a tree.

"Hey, don't you know that even if you know the direction, you will surely be too late for the examination?" asked the fox fairy.

"What can I do?" Bao Zheng asked earnestly.

"Take this broom and ride on it. Don't open your eyes before you are told to do so. Otherwise, you'll fall from it and get killed."

"Thanks! I won't," replied Bao Zheng with excitement and gratitude.

Sure enough, when he woke up, Bao Zheng found a broom beside him. He got on it, and it suddenly began to fly. He closed his eyes, as the girl in the dream had told him to. He felt the wind whistling by, and soon he heard someone saying, "You can open your eyes now." When he did, he found himself safely on the ground in the capital. He was just in time for the examination, where he scored the highest. As a result, Bao Zheng won the title *zhuangyuan* (The Scholar) and became Judge of the High Court. However, he never again heard from the fox fairy. He firmly believed that she had become a goddess.

MULAN FIGHTS IN THE GUISE OF A MALE SOLDIER

Other than a sketchy poem (see www.wku.edu/~yuanh/China/mulan.htm), information about Mulan is very sparse, giving rise to speculation about her family name, birthplace, nationality, and the time frame of her activities. The most acceptable argument is that Mulan is the embodiment of more than one heroine of Northern Wei (A.D. 386–581), an ethnic state of China. Northern Wei fought several wars against the Huns, or Xiongnus. The image of Mulan has been popular among the Chinese for several reasons. In a culture that emphasizes loyalty to one's rulers, love for one's parents, and respect for one's siblings, she had it all. Her disdain of fame and wealth makes her even more admirable.

Sometime in the fourth century, one of the nomadic Hun, or Xiongnu, tribes, led by Tu-Li Khan, launched an attack against its southern neighbor, Northern Wei, one of the several states of a split China. Emperor Xiaowen of Northern Wei had been concentrating on building up his state's economy and raising the living standard of his people. To reduce military expenditure and increase agricultural production, he sent his national reserves home to engage in farming in times of peace and would call them in when the state was threatened with a war. Now that the Xiongnus had begun raiding the border regions of Northern Wei and were ready to launch an all-out invasion, Emperor Xiaowen ordered Commander He to mobilize the nation's reserves.

Among the soldiers in reserve was a cavalier captain named Hua Hu. In his late forties, Hua Hu was no longer as able as he had been in the last war, two decades earlier. When the order came for him to rejoin the army, he had just recovered from a devastating illness, which made him even

---

weaker. Despite his difficulties in fighting, he had no choice but to go, for the recruiters, who often did things by the book, would not care about his physical condition. The government allowed reserves to have their sons answer the call in their place, but Hua Hu's son was only six. His two grownup daughters could not help because women were not recruited as fighters in the Northern Wei army.

The normally talkative Hua Hu was struck dumb by the mobilization order. He sighed all day long and appeared absent-minded. He did not fear fighting at all; what he was worried about was that his poor health would prevent him from rendering effective service to his country. He wished that his son were old enough to serve in his stead, but . . . alas!

Hua Hu's moodiness took a toll on his youngest daughter, Mulan. Her happy giggles gave way to sighs of worry as she watched her sister preparing the armor for her invalid father. Mulan was pretty, intelligent, and energetic. Unlike her tacit, meek big sister, whose aspiration, like any average Chinese young girl, was to find a good husband and become a good wife and mother, the extrovert, tomboy Mulan desired to become a heroic warrior like her father used to be. Since childhood she had learned all the marshal arts that her father could teach.

"What's the matter?" asked her big sister as Mulan sat motionless next door at her loom, with shuttle in hand, sighing again and again.

"Nothing," Mulan replied, trying to look as normal as she could. In fact, the biggest decision in her life was brewing in her mind. She felt that she had mastered enough fighting skills to take her father's place. The only problem, though, was that she was a female. The recruiters would never allow a daughter to fight for her father.

"What am I going to do?" Mulan asked herself. When she could not find an answer, she sighed. That was how her sister figured out something was wrong with her. In the eyes of the big sister, Mulan had always been a little girl. She felt that way because of the untimely death of their mother. She had assumed her mother's role in taking care of her father, her "little sister," and her baby brother.

That night Mulan lost sleep for the first time. She tiptoed to the room next door, where her sister had been working on their father's armor. She found it on the *kang*. Apparently her sister had left it there after she had mended it. Mulan could not resist putting it on. When she tucked her beautiful hair into the helmet and looked into a mirror, she saw a young male soldier staring back at her in amazement.

"I got it!" Mulan almost cried out with joy. The way she appeared in the armor gave her enough confidence to pass for a male soldier. Without hesitation, she picked up a pair of scissors from her sister's sewing kit, looked into the mirror, and cut her hair as short as that of a young man. Thanks to the loose attire worn in her time, particularly the stiff armor, the female features of her body would not present much of a problem. As for her pierced ears, after removing and stowing away her earrings, she would make sure that no one could come close enough to discover the tiny holes.

The next morning Mulan told her father and sister her plan. At first they objected that she was a woman and eventually would betray her own identity. In the end, she talked them into agreeing to let her go. After all, it was the best alternative they had. With the armor on, Mulan went about purchasing the horse, the saddle, and all the necessary accessories. Then she said goodbye to her father, sister, and little brother, who were very reluctant to see her leave.

"Don't worry about me. You know how good I am, Dad. I won't let you down," Mulan said from horseback.

"Take good care of yourself!" her father and sister said almost in unison. The sight of Mulan as a handsome, gallant male soldier, however, gave them some comfort and confidence.

"Come back to us when the war is over" were her little brother's words.

"I will. Be a good boy while I am away," Mulan felt that her little brother had suddenly grown up.

Mulan had no difficulty passing for a man soldier before the recruiters; however, despite her disguise and precautions, living and fighting as a female among male soldiers proved to be a daunting task. Even though frequent fighting and marching made it easier for Mulan to hide her identity, there were still close calls. When she was promoted for her bravery to the position of general, the troops threw a party to welcome their new commander. Having no prior experience with alcohol, Mulan had to tell the soldiers that she was suffering from a stomach disorder and must temporarily refrain from drinking. For ten years she managed to keep her identity hidden. In the eyes of her soldiers and junior officers, she was always the resourceful, courageous, and demanding general.

During a decisive campaign against Tu-Li Khan's intruding army, Mulan brought her intelligence and bravery into full play. At the time, Commander He was defending a vital fortress and asked Mulan to send him supplies. Mulan summoned Zhang Ying, one of her best lieutenants, to her headquarters. She ordered him to rush the supplies to Commander He. Before his departure, Mulan asked him to be very cautious, as enemy scouts were everywhere along the route.

The Xiongnu commander Tu-Li Khan, a very cunning military strategist, outsmarted Zhang Ying and intercepted his convoy. Zhang Ying and some of his men survived the ambush, but when they retreated to the base, they had to leave all the supplies with the enemy. Instead of punishing Zhang Ying, Mulan took the responsibility upon herself, saying, "I shouldn't have underestimated our enemy. This is not the time to point fingers. We have to figure out how to get the supplies back and send them on to Commander He without further delay."

Mulan and her officers worked out a plan. Someone had to get into Tu-Li Khan's camp to fight from within while the main forces attacked the enemy from outside. Mulan insisted on going to Tu-Li Khan's camp. When she met Tu-Li Khan, she pretended to surrender with the troops she had brought along. She claimed that because she had lost the supplies, she would definitely lose her life when her superior learned of her negligence. Tu-Li Khan did not totally trust Mulan. He asked her to get him the entire stock of supplies. Mulan agreed. She asked Tu-Li Khan for a convoy of camels to help her accomplish the task.

When she came back with the first loads of food and fodder, Tu-Li Khan was very pleased. Mulan invited him to watch her soldiers shipping the rest of the supplies across the Heishui River from her camp. Hours had passed and the soldiers had shipped only a third of the total amount. Tu-Li Khan complained to Mulan that her soldiers were loafing on the job and demanded that she spur them on. Mulan suggested that the Khan come over the river himself and urge the soldiers to speed up. She said, "Now that I have surrendered, my soldiers might have a grudge against me. But they may fear your authority."

The arrogant Khan did not give her words a second thought. With a small army of his generals and bodyguards, he crossed over the Heishui River. Mulan's army, led by Zhang Ying, ambushed the enemy as they were about to land. Tu-Li Khan and his men became Mulan's captives without much resistance because the surprise attack caught them unprepared. Placing her sword on the neck of Tu-Li Khan, Mulan demanded that he order his soldiers on the other side of the river to surrender, which he did.

With the captives and the retrieved supplies, Mulan and Zhang Ying arrived at Commander He's fortress just in time. Commander He praised Mulan highly and made sure that Emperor Xiaowen knew of Mulan's role in bringing the war to a victorious conclusion.

In the capital, Emperor Xiaowen summoned Commander He and General Mulan to his imperial court. He wanted to promote them and award them generously. Mulan declined, much to the surprise of the emperor and his courtiers. After thanking the emperor, Mulan asked that the award be distributed among her officers and soldiers. She said that it would be impossible for her to fight victoriously without their bravery and dedication. She also asked for an honorable discharge instead of the high-ranking official title that the emperor wanted to confer on her. She told Emperor Xiaowen that her only desire was to return to her family. She asked for only a small convoy of camels with some presents for her father, sister, and brother. Emperor Xiaowen, impressed, granted her requests.

Mulan's aging father, her married sister, and her teenage brother, as well as her sister's husband and their young children, were all very happy to see her. Her brother and brother-in-law butchered a pig and a sheep so that her big sister could prepare a feast to celebrate her homecoming.

A few months later, a group of her former comrades in the army came to visit their General Mulan. She greeted and welcomed them into the house in her colorful woman's attire. Mistaking her for a sister of Mulan, they asked her where Mulan was.

"Here I am," Mulan said calmly, with a strangely familiar smile.

"You must be joking!" responded the visitors. "Our general is a man."

Mulan, her elegant, long hair flowing down to her shoulders, looked as feminine as any pretty young woman of the day, except that years of military service had etched a lot of maturity on her face. When Mulan put the armor back on and told them the entire story, the men's eyes popped and jaws dropped. They could not imagine that all these years they had been fighting alongside a woman general!

"How did you manage to do that?" her comrades could not help asking.

Pointing to the domestic rabbits running around in the courtyard, Mulan revealed the secret of her success in the deception. "You can tell a male rabbit from a female one when they are not hopping around, because the male rabbit's feet go hop and skip, and the female rabbit's eyes are muddled and fuddled. However, when two rabbits run side-by-side close to the ground, how can you tell which is a male and which is a female?"

How true! Her comrades recollected the days and nights when Mulan lived, marched, and fought with them. They knew that it would take more than a rabbit analogy to understand her heroism.

WOMEN GENERALS OF THE YANG FAMILY AND COMMANDER-IN-CHIEF MU GUIYING

For several thousand years, the Chinese had treated men as more important than women. Official records often depicted women as dynasty-busters who demoralized emperors. Folklore, however, was not so biased. Tales such as "Mulan" and the one retold here even extolled them as heroines.

The Song dynasty had waged a protracted war against Great Liao, a nomadic tribal state in North China. People of Great Liao were of Hun origin, known to the Han Chinese as Xiongnus. Bent on conquering the Song dynasty, the Xiongnu army, mostly cavalry, started one war after another. Facing Great Liao's invasion, the Song Court split into two factions; one wanted to fight and the other was eager to surrender, with the emperor wavering in between.

Leading the Song army were generals from the Yang Family: the old Commander-in-Chief Yang Jiye and his eight sons. They were known as the *Yangjiajiang* (Yang Family Generals). They fought courageously and won many battles. However, the emperor misplaced his trust in a pacifist, who went to war reluctantly. He was Pan Renmei, a commander of another Song corps. In a decisive battle, Pan Renmei refused to send reinforcements, as he was supposed to do according to the war plan. His betrayal cost the lives of the old Commander-in-Chief, Yang Jiye, and five of his sons. Of the three who survived, one gave up his military career to become a monk, another was caught and surrendered, and the eldest brother, Yang Yanzhao, was the only one left to lead the army in his father's place. His wife, son, sisters, and sisters-in-law took the places of his dead and missing brothers. Because they were mostly female, people called them affectionately *Yangmen nüjiang* (Women Generals of the Yang Family).

For a time, the war was at a stalemate. To break the impasse, the Xiongnus enlisted a Han Chinese defector named Lu Zhong to strategize their military actions, because he not only knew the Song army well, but also was an expert in deploying all kinds of battle arrays. He was best known for his new invention: the formidable *Tianmenzhen* (Heavenly Gate Array). He trained the Great Liao troops hard every day to familiarize them with the array. When he was finally convinced that the troops were invulnerable, he challenged the Song army to break his *Tianmenzhen* within a hundred days. "Otherwise," he threatened, "the army of Great Liao will overrun the entire land of Song."

The Song army tried various tactics to break the *Tianmenzhen* but failed. As the deadline drew near, everyone in the Song Camp began to worry. They did not mind fighting to the last drop of their blood, but they were concerned for their homeland: If they failed, the Song dynasty would fall into the barbarians' hands and their people would suffer miserably.

Yang Yanzhao, the Commander-in-Chief, called a meeting to brainstorm a countermeasure against *Tianmenzhen*. The Chief of Staff remembered a woman named Mu Guiying and recommended her to Commander Yang Yanzhao. He told the Commander that Mu Guiying was a young woman, the only daughter of a rebel Song general camped in the nearby mountains. The general had been training Mu Guiying in martial arts and military strategies since her childhood. The father had offended the emperor with his forthright criticisms and had fled to the mountain with his army to avoid persecution.

"What does the story have to do with *Tianmenzhen*?" an impatient general could not help cutting in.

"Good question. I'm just coming to it," replied the Chief of Staff. "The general was a friend of Lu Zhong . . . ."

"You mean they are not friends any more?" asked Yang Yanzhao.

"He died, just a few months ago, of heart failure. Probably the harsh life in the mountains took a toll on his health," responded the Chief of Staff. He continued, "When he was Lu Zhong's friend, they had nothing they wouldn't share with each other. Therefore, he knew Lu Zhong's military stratagems very well. After Lu Zhong's defection to the Xiongnus, he was so angry with his betrayal that he developed a series of countermeasures against all the arrays Lu Zhong could come up with."

"But he's dead," another general interrupted the Chief of Staff.

Women Generals of the Yang Family and Commander-in-Chief Mu Guiying   139

"That's why I mentioned his daughter, Mu Guiying. Knowing his days were numbered, he passed the entire military secret to her."

Hearing this, everyone felt a sense of hope and relief. Commander Yang Yanzhao was particularly happy. For the first time in many days, the generals could see a smile on his face. He immediately ordered his son Zongbao, a promising young general, to find Mu Guiying and ask her for the countermeasure against the *Tianmenzhen* array. He demanded that he be back by sunset the same day or he would suffer serious consequences.

Leading a small task force, the young general set out in early morning. Before long, Yang Zongbao and his men arrived at the mountain where Mu Guiying and her rebel army were stationed. On his way, Yang Zongbao saw a big bird and shot it with his arrow. The bird fell, tumbling down a few hundred yards away in the woods. When his men went to retrieve the game bird, however, a group of women soldiers had already taken it. They got into a squabble, each side claiming that its commander had shot the bird. The women soldiers were maidservants and bodyguards of Mu Guiying. When Zongbao met Guiying, they immediately felt drawn to each other. Trying to resolve the dispute, they asked their soldiers to examine the bird. What they saw amazed them all: two arrows planted almost in the same spot on the bird's neck, one belonging to Yang Zongbao and the other to Mu Guiying. The two young admirers immediately fell in love. Fully aware of his mission and his father's order, Yang Zongbao tried not to reveal his feelings, but Mu Guiying, a born rebel who loathed traditional conventions, had no intention of concealing hers. When Yang Zongbao asked her for the countermeasure against *Tianmenzhen*, she said that since she did not have it with her on the hunting trip, he had to come to her headquarters to get it.

Yang Zongbao followed her to her camp in the depths of the mountain. There, to the surprise and embarrassment of Yang Zongbao, she proposed marriage to him and asked that the wedding be performed immediately. Otherwise she would not give him the countermeasure. Yang Zongbao told her he had to return to his father before sunset or he would face a court-martial. At this, Mu Guiying laughed.

"You think it's a laughing matter?" Zongbao asked, half puzzled, half angry.

"Court-martial? Don't treat me like a fool. I know the military and its disciplinary system. The Commander-in-Chief is the judge and the jury. I don't think your father would kill his own son, especially when you are a rare species in the Yang Family army."

"You really don't know my father," Zongbao explained, "He is well known for his impartiality and seriousness."

"Well, you don't mind taking some clubbing on your buttocks for getting a pretty and capable wife like me, do you?" challenged Guiying.

"No," Zongbao replied.

"Then stay."

Out of love and necessity, Zongbao complied, thinking that a night's delay would not matter too much. "Even if I brought the countermeasure back this evening," he comforted himself, "the Song army would not be able to launch a counterattack in the dark."

"Now that I have done all you asked me to, you've got to let me go as early as possible tomorrow," Zongbao said to Guiying.

"I will let you get back to your camp before sunrise."

Early next morning, Yang Zongbao returned to his father with the countermeasure, anticipating his anger and bracing himself for some corporal punishment. It turned out that he had underestimated his father's wrath. Apart from the delay, a marriage with a rebel without his consent added to his fury. He sentenced Zongbao to death. The commander's mother, wife, aunts, and the other generals all rallied to ask for leniency.

"I've lost my husband and almost all my sons to the enemy," the Commander's mother said, "I won't let you take my grandson from me." Yang Yanzhao explained, "I love him as much as you do, but if I make this case an exception, how do you expect me to enforce discipline among our troops? How then can we defeat our enemies, with disobedient officers and soldiers like Zongbao?"

In the meantime, Mu Guiying had stolen after her husband and had been monitoring the entire event. She had not anticipated that the father could be so cruel to his own son. Seeing her newly married husband on the guillotine, she cared no more about her own safety and decided to meet her father-in-law face to face. She pleaded for leniency on her husband's behalf, saying that she was the one to blame, as she loved Zongbao so much that she had prevented him from returning on time.

The Commander-in-Chief readily set his son free. As it turned out, he had been using his son as bait to recruit Mu Guiying to serve in his army. He knew that a great mind was worth a hundred times more than a single military tactic. He firmly believed that Mu Guiying would be a great asset to the already famous Women Generals of the Yang Family. To enforce military discipline, he granted his son a stay of execution and put him on probation. After announcing the sentence, he added, "I will pardon you if you two can help us break the *Tianmenzhen* array."

Mu Guiying did not disappoint her father-in-law. Her military talent was well known to allies and foes alike. The next day she led the Song army in breaking the first move of the formidable *Tianmenzhen* array. Limited as it was, a success after so many frustrations was a tremendous boost to the Song army's morale. At long last, they tasted victory. Yang Yanzhao decided to pass on his commanding authority to Mu Guiying. It was a shocking move, for there had never been a woman Commander-in-Chief in the entire history of China. The other officers supported the decision, completely convinced of her capability.

Mu Guiying took the command with great confidence. She reviewed the troops and taught them the tactics to break the rest of the moves of the *Tianmenzhen* array. She then organized a counterattack. She ordered a well-trained brigade to break *Tianmenzhen* so that the enemy would not be able to advance. At the same time, she sent a surprise detachment to cut off the enemy's supply line by burning their food and fodder to ashes. "Without their supplies," she said, "the Xiongnus' men and horses will be disabled." Sure enough, when the detachment had accomplished their task, the Xiongnus retreated. They attempted to return to their base, Youzhou, a fortress that they had taken from the Song army in previous battles. As the Xiongnus approached the city, panic swept through their troops, for they saw the banner of the Song army flying high on top of the fortress. It turned out that Mu Guiying had anticipated the enemy by taking back the fortress. Seeing that everything was moving as smoothly as she had planned, Mu Guiying launched a general offense. The Song generals and soldiers fought bravely and soon routed the confused enemy troops.

Through their patriotism and heroism, the Women Generals of the Yang Family, and their Commander-in-Chief Mu Guiying in particular, won the hearts of the Chinese from generation to generation.

GUN AND YU CONQUER THE DELUGE

The big flood that overran the better part of China in its early history was comparable in scale to the biblical deluge. However, the Chinese tale has no connection with religion. Instead, it treats the inundation merely as a natural disaster, and a demigod's conquest of the flood is simply a celebration of men's wisdom and resolve. You will be surprised to learn that people had the idea of surveying land from the air long, long ago.

Once upon a time, the Chinese were suffering a great deluge, caused by the God of Water named Gonggong. He was the same deity who had bumped his head on Mt. Buzhou and broken a part of the sky many, many years before. For no reason at all, he suddenly became unhappy again and let loose all the water he could summon, covering an extensive part of China, which was at the time under the leadership of King Yao. The flood drowned a large number of King Yao's people. To survive, the rest managed to clamber up the mountains, only to find themselves at the mercy of the birds and beasts of prey that had lost their food sources due to the calamity.

Sympathetic with the plight of King Yao's people, Gun, a giant of great strength and the grandson of the Heavenly King, took some of the king's treasured *xirang* (magic earth) and came to the earthlings' rescue. He sprinkled a little of the *xirang* here and there into the water, and it expanded immediately into high hills and dykes, deterring the rise of the roaring water.

Unfortunately, the Heavenly King found out that Gun had stolen his treasure. So he sent Zhurong, the God of Fire, to punish Gun. In a fight, Zhurong killed Gun at the foot of Mt. Yushan, to the great joy and relief of Gonggong, who was fleeing from Gun.

Soon Gonggong staged a comeback with his flooding water, which, however, could move no farther once it reached Mt. Yushan, where Gun was lying, his eyes still wide open. Gun would not close them in death because he was still deeply regretful that he had failed to help King Yao and his people, so much so that his spirit, unwilling to leave his body, was keeping it from decaying. Eventually, a new life began to grow in his body. This was Great Yu. With Great Yu's birth, Gun turned into a yellow dragon and vanished.

When the Heavenly King learned of Gun's dedication to fighting the deluge, he was deeply touched. He began to regret having had him killed. To demonstrate his remorse, he gave all his *xirang* to Great Yu and made him the leader in the fight against the big flood, like his father. By the time Great Yu returned to earth, King Yao had passed away. His successor, King Shun, was only too glad to see him and granted him the authority to rally all the human and material resources available in his domain to fight the big flood. King Shun also assigned Great Yu a dragon called Yinglong to assist him.

The thought that Great Yu, merely a youngster, should have the courage to lead so many people in fighting him made Gonggong, the God of Water, very angry. In retaliation, he raised the water level ten *zhang* (100 feet) higher. The renewed flood swept away the dykes that Great Yu had just built with his *xirang*, resulting in the loss of many more lives.

Determined to defeat Gonggong, Great Yu called a conference on Mt. Huiji to work out a better strategy against the sinister God of Water. A sluggish giant named Fangfeng came late to the meeting. Great Yu had him executed for his tardiness and used his example as a warning. In consequence, all the gods took Great Yu's orders seriously and went about their tasks earnestly. With his disciplined army of gods, demigods, and humans, Great Yu soon put Gonggong and his army to flight.

Now that Gonggong was gone, Great Yu had time to deal with the water. He learned a lesson from the past, that is, that water was not to be blocked, but to be diverted to the sea while checking it from overrunning too much of the land. He ordered a giant turtle to carry the *xirang* that he had and follow him wherever he went. He sprinkled some of the magic earth on the area where water ran deep. When *xirang* dropped into the water, a plateau or a mountain would rise out of it, the size of which depended on the amount administered. Great Yu also asked Yinglong, the dragon assistant, to fly in the air to show him the way to the sea, so that he could divert the water toward it. Yinglong used his tail to mark the land, and Great Yu had a canal cut through it accordingly.

Great Yu worked and lived together with the gods and people. He worked so hard that his face was tanned, his thighs scraped, and his calves rubbed hairless. His example encouraged more people to join in the fight against the deluge, and in a few years, the entire land of China, except the Yellow River drainage area, was free from inundation. Great Yu was inspecting the topography of the Yellow River area when, all of a sudden, a giant merman emerged from the swirling water. He introduced himself as the River God, presented a slate to Great Yu, and resubmerged. Great Yu studied the strange inscriptions on the slate and realized that it was a plan for water control. The plan greatly facilitated his efforts to fight the flood. He soon reached Longmen (Dragon Gate), a tall mountain range that blocked the Yellow River from flowing into the sea.

While he was inspecting the mountain, Great Yu found a cave. Inside, the spirit of a primordial sovereign gave him a bamboo tube, which was a magic land-measuring device. With the bamboo tube, Great Yu pinpointed the location where he could open up a channel to let the Yellow River through. With a magic axe, he cleaved a great opening in the mountain range and released the penned up water in the Yellow River. Torrents roared toward the East Sea. Somewhere downstream, Great Yu cut another mountain range into three sections so that the Yellow Rive could wind through them. That location has since become known as Sanmenxia (The Three-gate Gorges).

Great Yu had devoted all his time and energy to water control, and in consequence, he was still a bachelor at thirty. When people asked him to think of marriage, he told them that he would do so when he got divine indication. As he said this, a snow-white fox with nine tails trotted up to him. It bowed and disappeared. Great Yu remembered a popular local rhyme:

"One who sees a white fox of nine tails will become the king; one who marries a girl of Tushan will become prosperous." For this reason, he married a girl whose family name was Tushan. The girl's first name was Nüjiao.

Four days after the wedding, Great Yu had to leave for the water-control site. He relocated his wife Nüjiao to a town in the north and promised to rejoin her when his water-control troop went her way. When they did, however, Great Yu was too busy to see Nüjiao. He missed the chance to visit her three times, and Nüjiao became very worried about him. She asked that he take her to the water-control site with him so that she could attend to him. Great Yu consented. Nüjiao told her husband to beat a drum when he was hungry, and she would send food to him.

Great Yu thanked his wife and went to work. They were to dig a tunnel through a mountain. As the rock was very hard, they made very little progress. In desperation, Great Yu transformed himself into a huge bear and began to dig the tunnel with his paws. While he was digging, some stones that he kicked up happened to hit the drum, which called in his wife. The sight of her husband being a gigantic bear not only scared her but also humiliated her. She shrieked and turned to run. Eager to offer an explanation, Great Yu followed her. In a hurry, he forgot to change back to his human form. His pursuit horrified Nüjiao, who turned into a big rock before he reached her. Great Yu called her and begged that she come back to him, but in vain. In the end, he asked that she give him the baby she had conceived. At his words, the rock cracked and gave birth to a boy. Great Yu named him Qi, which means "born from a rock."

At Mt. Tongbai, Great Yu and his water-controlling force defeated Gonggong, who fled to the farthest corner of the earth. However, they did not find their work at all easier. Every day great winds and sandstorms would spring up to harass them and hinder their progress. From a captured sprite, Great Yu learned that a lieutenant of Gonggong, a powerful, monkey-like demon called Wuzhiqi, was behind the malevolence. He would not admit defeat and stayed behind to resist Great Yu. After a fierce battle, Great Yu caught Wuzhiqi and imprisoned him beneath Mt. Guishan.

The victory was decisive. At long last, the Chinese could live and work in peace again. Great Yu thought that it was time he returned to his heavenly home, but people loved him so much that they wanted him to stay and succeed King Shun after he passed away. Great Yu agreed, and he ruled as benevolently as his predecessors. He worked conscientiously even in his old age. He died during a hunting trip at Mt. Huiji and was buried on the sunny side of the mountain. Each spring and fall, flocks of birds came to visit his tomb and trim the grass on it with their beaks.

Moral Tales

Each moral tale teaches a lesson. "A Compassionate Scholar and an Ungrateful Wolf" cautions us not to be lenient to our enemies; the "Twin Sisters and the Magic Malan Flowers" encourages us to satisfy our desire in an honest way; the "Painted Skin" and "Monkey King Strikes the White-bone Demon Three Times" warn us against hideous evils in beautiful disguise; "Laozi's Prophecy" tells us not to judge a person by his or her appearance; "A Foolish Old Man Trying to Remove Two Mountains" shows that perseverance pays; and "A Man with a Dog's Leg" demonstrates that what goes around comes around. As you read, you may find more than meets the eye.

LAOZI'S PROPHECY

Laozi was a great ancient Chinese philosopher and the father of Taoism. People believe that he authored the sacred book Tao Te Ching (The Way of the Tao). *His real name was Li Er. Laozi means "Old Saint" in Chinese. There are many legends about him. Following is one of them.*

Laozi was traveling to the west. One day he came to a county named the Gate of Secluded Valley. It was named after a pass in its territory, where the Great Wall ran through it.

Xi was the county's magistrate, and he invited Laozi home to see his twin sons. They were almost three years old. One was called Older Brother and the other, Younger Brother. Older Brother seemed to be dull though good-natured. Younger Brother, on the other hand, looked bright.

Jingling a few pieces of gold in front of his twin sons, Magistrate Xi hoped that they would smile and please Laozi. He then asked Laozi which of his two sons would be able to take care of him in his old age.

Laozi was about to give him an answer when a neighbor of Xi's cut in, "Of course the smart-looking Younger Brother will make you happy."

"I am sure he will become somebody when he grows up," added another.

Without a word, Laozi took a *yuanbao* (a piece of gold) from Xi and held it up to Older Brother.

"Son, tell me what this is," he asked.

"Gold," said Older Brother, looking puzzled.

"You want it, son?" Laozi asked.

"Yes."

"So, slap your dad in the face and it will be yours. Or I'll give it to your brother."

No matter how hard Laozi coaxed, Older Brother would not raise even a finger to his father. Laozi then turned to Younger Brother and made the same offer: "Slap your dad in the face and this gold *yuanbao* will be yours." Without hesitation, Younger Brother gave his father a good slap, snatched the *yuanbao*, and waddled away happily.

Magistrate Xi was not at all angry. Instead, he felt proud. He preferred Younger Brother's quick mind to Older Brother's inaction. He was sure that he could rely on Younger Brother for support in his old age.

Laozi did not agree, saying, "You are wrong, my brother. Trust me. Older Brother is the one that will support you."

"How come?" The magistrate could not believe his ears.

"Because Older Brother values affection while Younger Brother loves money." Seeing both the magistrate and his neighbors still unconvinced, Laozi continued, "If nothing out of the ordinary happens, my prophecy will eventually come true." So saying, he left the magistrate's home and resumed his journey west.

Magistrate Xi did not give much thought to the prophecy until a few decades later. He was now retired and confined to bed because of old age and illness. Older Brother, the one who had refused to slap him in the face for a piece of gold, was attending to him day and night. He did not have the time and money to raise a family. To buy food and medicine for his father, he had sold or pawned almost everything he had. Finally, when there was nothing left, he had to go begging so that he and his father could survive.

In the meantime, Younger Brother had become a wealthy merchant. Unlike Older Brother, he did not care about his father at all. He even refused to visit him when asked. He said that if he went to see the old magistrate, he would lose a lot of business and money. When Older Brother begged him to see his father for the last time, Younger Brother yelled, "Let him die. I don't even have the time for his funeral!"

Back home, Older Brother told Xi what the Younger Brother had said. The dying magistrate now remembered the Old Sage's prophecy.

A COMPASSIONATE SCHOLAR AND AN UNGRATEFUL WOLF

This is a very popular Chinese tale. It teaches people not to show mercy to those who are evil by nature. The term Dongguo xiansheng *(Mr. Dongguo) has become a synonym in Chinese for "a naïve person who gets into trouble through being softhearted to evil people" (Wu 1999). For the same reason, the word* Zhongshanlang *(wolf of Zhongshan) refers to a person who repays kindness with ingratitude.*

Mr. Dongguo was a pedantic scholar, known for his kindheartedness and gullibility. One day he went to the state of Zhongshan to try his luck at an imperial examination. He wanted to pass it so that he could get an official position. With him was a donkey, carrying over its arched, skinny back a big sack of bamboo books, which Mr. Dong needed to study for the examination. [A bamboo book was a series of bamboo strips stringed side by side. When not in use, it was rolled up like a bundle. Books of bamboo were much heavier and bulkier than books of paper. A bamboo book bundle might only have as many words in it as there are on a few pages of this book.]

A bamboo book sample.

Mr. Dongguo was trudging along on a country road when all of a sudden a big, grey wolf plunged in front of him. Mr. Dongguo was transfixed with terror, while his donkey, throwing the sack of books on the ground, ran for its life. By the time Mr. Dongguo had collected himself and thought of fleeing, it was already too late, for the wolf had come up under his nose. Shutting his eyes, the scholar resigned himself to his fate. However, to his great astonishment, Mr. Dongguo heard the wolf pleading, "Take pity on me. I am hurt, and my life is in grave danger." He opened his eyes and saw the wolf kneeling in front of him. He noticed an arrowhead jutting out from the animal's buttocks each time it kowtowed to him.

"The hunters are after me," the wolf said. "If they catch me, they will definitely kill me. Please help me!" A few drops of tears rolled out of its squinted eyes, which effectively tugged at Mr. Dongguo's tender heartstrings.

"Well, you know the reputation of your fellow animals. If people know I've saved a wolf, what would they think of me?" asked Mr. Dongguo.

"I am a good wolf, and I am an herbivore. I swear I have never taken a life." Seeing Mr. Dongguo hesitate, the beast added, "Please! I beg you! I will repay your kindness if you save my life." The wolf's plea and its tattered condition further evoked Dongguo's sympathy. Finally, he asked, "But, how?"

"Hide me in your book sack!" Apparently the wolf had come up with that idea when it saw Mr. Dongguo's donkey dumping the sack before it sped away.

Mr. Dongguo emptied the books and hid them in the grass. Then he allowed the wolf into the sack. No sooner had Mr. Dongguo tucked the beast's big tail into the sack and tied it up than the hunters arrived on horseback.

"Sir, have you seen a wounded wolf coming this way?" the leader of the hunters asked.

"No! I am a stranger here myself. How do I know the whereabouts of a wicked, fleeing wolf?" answered Mr. Dongguo, blushing at the first lie he had ever told in his life. The change of his countenance would have betrayed him but for the veil of dust the hunters' horses had kicked up. Mr. Dongguo reconciled his guilt of lying with the thought of saving a life, be it a wolf or a human.

Mr. Dongguo's response deflected the hunters' suspicions. Thanking the scholar, they resumed their pursuit. When the dust had settled and the noise had dissipated, the wolf started to kick and scream in the sack, "Let me out! Let me out!" Mr. Dongguo released it at its command.

"Ouch, it really hurts. Can't you see the arrowhead is still in my butt?" the wolf yelled as it gingerly crawled out of the sack. Once in the open air, the wolf asked, pointing at the arrowhead with its paw, "Can you get the thing out?"

Mr. Dongguo confessed, "I've never even had the heart to pull out a splinter from my own finger. I don't think I can . . . ."

"Come on," the wolf interrupted, "there's no time to worry. The hunters may come back any time."

With his eyes closed, Mr. Dongguo yanked the arrowhead out of the wolf's buttocks. The wolf managed to muffle its howl of pain for fear that the pursuing hunters might hear it and return.

"You hurt me!" the wolf scolded Mr. Dongguo, without saying a word of thanks.

"Sorry," the baffled scholar apologized, and then reminded the beast, "but I've saved your life."

"You've saved my life? Nonsense!" the ungrateful wolf snarled. "No! You tortured me by stuffing me in that sack, cursed me in front of those hunters, hurt me when you touched my wound, and now," the wolf paused a second, "you're thinking of leaving me here to starve to death!"

"What?" Such an outrageous accusation rendered Mr. Dongguo speechless. Timidly he offered the wolf his bread. "You are kidding me!" growled the wolf. "Have you ever seen a wolf eating bread? Meat! I want meat! No, I want your flesh!" So saying, the wolf arched up its back, showed its teeth, and pounced at the scholar. Mr. Dongguo leaped back a few yards, turned around, and lo! he almost panicked because the donkey that he meant to hide behind was long gone. He had been unaware of its escape because he had been seized with terror when he first encountered the wolf.

Mr. Dongguo was a smart scholar, and in such an emergency, his brain worked harder than usual.

"Hold!" He commanded as he pulled himself together. "According to tradition, whenever we have a dispute that we can't settle, we have to find three elders for judgment. Let's go and find them. If they all agree that you can eat me, I'll be happy to be your meal. Otherwise, you have to let me go without complaint. What do you say?"

"Alright, alright," the impatient wolf consented reluctantly.

Mr. Dongguo and the wolf walked a few hundred feet without seeing a single soul. The wolf spotted an old maple tree on the roadside and urged Mr. Dongguo to put the question to it. The old maple had been amusing itself with the memory of its good old days. It was mumbling away without even raising its tangled eyebrows as Mr. Dongguo and the wolf approached it. Only after the wolf howled at it did the old tree mutter, "Of course, wolves always eat people. Wolves always eat people. . . ." Hearing this, the wolf turned to Mr. Dongguo, its mouth watering. Mr. Dongguo scampered behind the maple tree, crying, "Hey! You can't breach our gentleman's agreement. This is only the first of three elders. We need to find two more, and they must be humans." The wolf was accusing Mr. Dongguo of stalling when they heard an old cow mooing nearby. "Go and ask her," urged the wolf, too hungry to wait any longer.

"Just now you made me ask a tree, and it almost ruined me. What is the point of asking an old cow? We should find a human being."

"Well, I may gobble you up before you can find one," the wolf threatened. Mr. Dongguo had to relate the story again to the apparently unconcerned old cow and asked for her fair judgment.

To the scholar's dismay, the old cow muttered something to the effect that she did not care whatsoever who ate whom.

"Hold there!" Mr. Dongguo became desperate, trying all he could to keep the attacking wolf at bay. "We still have one more elder to consult!" It must have been Mr. Dongguo's lucky day, for as he was talking about an elder, an old man came up with big strides, a hoe on his stout shoulder. Despite his snow-white hair and whiskers, the old man seemed as agile as a youth. Mr. Dongguo hurried up, greeted the old man with a bow, and started to relate his encounter with the wolf. The old man was his last chance.

The wolf tried to make its own case. Painting itself as the victim of the scholar's persecution, the wolf added, "This murderous, glib-tongued pedant tried to kill me!" At this, Mr. Dongguo objected that he was only trying to save the beast's life, but it was repaying his kindness with ingratitude.

"Hmm, I can't trust either of you," the old man declared, "I have to know who's telling the truth and who's not."

"How?" Mr. Dongguo and the wolf said almost simultaneously.

"Show me how you put this big guy into that small sack of yours," the old man commanded Mr. Dongguo, who in turn invited the wolf into his sack. Eager to get a favorable verdict so that it could eat Mr. Dongguo, the wolf readily crawled into the sack. Mr. Dongguo tucked the rest of its body into it, as he had done before. The old man wasted no time tying up the sack. By now, the wolf had realized what the old man meant to do. It started to kick and howl frantically, but in vain. The old man began whacking the wriggling lump with his hoe. Thump, thump, thump . . . until the bundle gave neither movement nor sound.

PAINTED SKIN

This is one of several hundred tales originally collected and compiled by Pu Songling (1640–1715) in his 16-volume Liaozhai zhiyi (Strange Stories from a Make-do Study). *They are stories of spirits, immortals, foxes, and demons. Many of these characters assume the appearance of pretty young women. Some of them are good and some are bad, but their stories are all designed to teach a lesson—a lesson of friendship, love, betrayal, greed, lust, or treachery. In the stories, the boundaries between life and death, humans and other beings are blurred. A man may become a tiger because of his predatory nature, while a tiger may turn into a dutiful son owing to its kindness. As each story unfolds, the reader will realize that what the author dubbed a strange phenomenon may not be strange at all, for it is a reflection of human nature.*

"Huapi" ("The Painted Skin"), retold here, is one of Pu Songling's most popular tales; in fact, the term huapi *has become part of the Chinese vocabulary, meaning "the mask of an evildoer."*

Once upon a time there was a young man named Wang Sheng living in Taiyuan. He was an idler and a womanizer, although he had an able and virtuous wife. During an early morning walk, Wang Sheng ran into a pretty young woman, who was teetering along, a parcel under her arm. He walked up and tried to befriend her.

"Why are you traveling alone?" he asked in a phony tone of concern.

"What's the use of asking? I don't think you can help a stranger," the young woman answered, seemingly too shy to look at Wang Sheng.

"Well, I won't say no if you ask," responded Wang Sheng, who had already sensed her hidden desire for his aid.

"My parents loved money more than my well-being and sold me to a wealthy family as a concubine," the woman began her story, crying. "My husband's jealous, legal wife bullied me all the time. Because I could stand it no more, I am trying to run as far from them as I can."

"Do you have a place to go?" Wang Sheng showed more concern.

"No," the woman answered, gazing at the gallant young man with her beautiful, entreating eyes.

Her answer pleased Wang Sheng very much. Without hesitation, he said, "I have a dwelling not far from here. If you don't mind, I can put you up there."

The girl hesitated a second, but then happily accepted his invitation. Carrying her luggage, Wang Sheng led her to his study. Seeing no one in the room, the young woman asked whether he had a family. When she found out that this study was in a separate courtyard from his residence, she asked Wang Sheng to keep her presence a secret. Wang Sheng remained in his study with the young woman.

After not seeing her husband for days, Wang Sheng's wife became concerned. She went over to the study to find out what was happening. Polygamy was legal in China at that time, so when asked, Wang Sheng told his wife about his affair with the young woman. Pulling Wang Sheng aside, his wife quietly asked him to send the young woman away immediately. She said she did so not because she was jealous, but because she was worried about the family's safety.

"Let's assume what she said is true." she argued, "What if her husband traced her here. Since he is rich and powerful, don't you think you are inviting trouble?" However, Wang Sheng would not listen to his wife's admonition. He insisted on keeping the young woman as his concubine.

One morning Wang Sheng was taking a walk as usual when a Taoist priest accosted him, "You look like you are possessed," said the priest, "You must be seeing a stranger."

"No, I am not," Wang Sheng categorically denied.

"But I can see a mysterious air of evil shrouding you," the Taoist priest told him.

Wang Sheng did not argue with him. Instead, he turned and headed home, thinking that the priest must be a vagabond fortuneteller who desperately needed business.

"How could a young woman of such beauty be evil!" was his self-assuring statement, rather than a question.

When Wang Sheng reached the courtyard where his study was, he found its gate bolted from inside. He remembered the Taoist's warning and became alert. He slipped into the yard through a big hole in the wall, only to find the door of his study bolted as well. Quietly he maneuvered to the window and peeped in. Alas! What he saw almost knocked him out. At the desk, where he read with the young woman, was a ferocious demon. It was adding some touches of paint to a human skin spread on his desk. The skin looked like his concubine's. Wang Sheng would have thought that the demon had killed her but for what he saw and heard next. After it finished refurbishing the skin with paint, the demon shook it straight and put it on. In an instant, the demon changed into the concubine. It chuckled, "Hah, hah, the gullible Wang Sheng won't know who I really am until I take his heart away."

Horrified, Wang Sheng crept out of the courtyard and began to look for the Taoist priest. Finally he located him in an open field and begged him to save his life. The priest gave him a duster and told him to hang it over the door of his bedroom. Wang Sheng immediately returned to his wife and did as the priest had told him.

Late that night, it was deadly quiet. Wang Sheng and his wife could not get to sleep, apprehensive about what was in store for them. Suddenly they heard a rustling outside the bedroom. It was the demon. When it saw the duster, it faltered and then went away, cursing. In no time, the demon came back, grabbed the duster, and tore it into pieces.

"It must be the demon-busting Taoist that pursues me," said the demon with clenched teeth. "How can I cough up this delicacy already in my mouth? I'll finish up the womanizer before the Taoist comes after me." Emboldened by the thought, the demon smashed the door open, stormed into the room, and, knocking Wang Sheng's wife to the ground, seized the shivering Wang Sheng by the chest . . . .

When his wife came to, she found an empty hole in the chest of Wang Sheng's body. The demon had taken his heart away. While grieving over her husband, she remembered the Taoist priest and thought hopefully, "With his magic power, he may perhaps be able to bring my husband back to life."

The next morning she asked Wang Sheng's brother to go and look for the Taoist priest. When the brother told the Taoist about the tragedy, the Taoist said contritely, "I meant to drive the demon away without killing it. Apparently, I should not have been so lenient." He went to see Wang Sheng's wife and told her that he was there to get rid of the wicked demon.

Looking around, the Taoist gave a sigh of relief, "Luckily, the demon is still around." Then he asked, "Whose house is that over there?"

"Mine," answered Wang Sheng's brother.

"Have you taken in a stranger lately?" questioned the Taoist.

Wang Sheng's brother told him that his wife had just hired an elderly housekeeper that day. "You mean she is . . . ?" he asked with a shudder of terror.

"Yes, the housekeeper is the demon in disguise," the Taoist answered. He followed Wang Sheng's brother to his courtyard. There he wielded his magic wooden sword and challenged the demon to meet him. The demon bolted from the house in an attempt to escape. The Taoist priest dashed toward it and hit it with the sword. The demon fell to the ground; while it was falling, its painted skin came off. The demon twisted and turned in agony, begging the Taoist to spare its life. When the priest rejected its plea, it turned into a wisp of smoke, making another attempt to flee. The priest took out a bell gourd and set it on the ground. Immediately the gourd sucked the smoke into its belly. The priest capped the gourd and put it away. Rolling up the painted skin, he was ready to leave. Wang Sheng's wife dropped to her knees and implored him to bring her husband back to life

"I'm sorry, but I'm a mere exorciser. I'm not powerful enough to revive a human life," the Taoist confessed. "I can recommend someone to you, though. Remember the beggar in the street?"

"Yes, but are you sure the tramp . . . ?" both Wang Sheng's wife and brother asked with disbelief and hesitance. They knew the beggar too well. He was notorious for his filth and stink.

"Go and ask him. Trust me; only he can help," said the Taoist priest, "One thing you have to remember, though. Don't feel offended when he tries to humiliate you."

It did not take Wang Sheng's wife and brother long to find the tramp. From afar, they could see him wallowing in his feces. Wang Sheng's wife greeted him and asked for help. Nose running, the tramp slurred, "So you mean you love me? Hah, hah, hah . . . ."

"Sir, we're here to beg you to bring my husband back to life. Please don't tease me," Wang Sheng's wife said calmly, trying hard to repress her resentment and disgust at his foul odor and language.

"I'm not a savior. How can you expect me to make a dead man alive?" The beggar continued to jeer at her. And as if that were not enough, he hit her on the head with his walking stick and spat on the ground.

"Eat it," he demanded, pointing at the yellowish phlegm.

With the Taoist priest's advice in mind, Wang Sheng's wife obeyed. Immediately she felt a spasm of sickness swelling in her stomach when the phlegm got stuck in her chest. The beggar stood up and walked away laughing, "Hah, hah, hah! That woman really loves me." With the word, he vanished into thin air.

Deeply mortified, Wang Sheng's wife went back home. Seeing her husband's body, she could no longer keep her composure. Holding it in her arms, she began to wail. She cried and cried and then, all of a sudden, the phlegm stuck in her chest popped out of her mouth. Before she could catch it with her hands, it fell into the open wound in the chest of her husband's body. Looking closer, she was shocked to see that it was a pumping heart! Losing no time, she closed the open wound tight with her hands until she felt that it was healed.

When night came, Wang Sheng started breathing. The next day he woke up, stretched himself, and said to his wife, "I must have had a terrible dream. I felt a bit strange in my chest." So saying, he looked down and saw a scar as big as a coin on his bosom.

MONKEY KING STRIKES THE WHITE-BONE DEMON THREE TIMES

In the year 629, a Chinese monk of the Tang dynasty (618–906) named Xuan Zang, better known as Tang Seng (The Monk of Tang), traveled all the way to India on foot. He returned to China sixteen years later with 657 volumes of Buddhist scriptures. He spent the next decade translating them into Chinese, thus making a great contribution to the spread of Buddhism in China.

Journey to the West, *better known to Westerners as* Monkey King, *is an allegory of Tang Seng's pilgrimage. In the novel, fairy tales mingle with monster stories and Buddhism and Taoism blend with Chinese folk beliefs. The monk went through eighty-one calamities, encountering numerous devils and demons. In each encounter, he escaped with the help of three escorting disciples, whom Buddha had assigned him via Guanyin, Goddess of Mercy. The three disciples were Monkey King, Piggy, and a river monster called Sandy.*

Monkey King had learned from a Taoist master how to transform into seventy-two different forms. From the master he had also learned how to use clouds as his vehicle to travel 108,000 li (leagues) with a single somersault. His jingubang *(golden-ringed iron rod), which he had taken from the Dragon King of the East Sea, proved to be a formidable weapon, for it weighed a thousand pounds and could change size at its owner's bidding. After Monkey King wreaked havoc in Heaven in a failed rebellion, the Jade Emperor sentenced him to death. However, his magic power enabled him to survive all methods of execution. At his wit's end, the emperor ordered that the monkey be melted in a furnace. Instead of killing him, the furnace's smoke and fire only added exceptional sight to his eyes. Now Monkey King could see through monsters no matter how they disguised themselves. Finally, Buddha helped the Jade Emperor of Heaven by imprisoning Monkey King beneath a mountain. Five centuries later, Buddha made the monkey Tang Seng's disciple and bodyguard.*

Of all the calamities, or rather, the Monkey King's adventures, the story retold here is the most popular with the Chinese. The story, in which Monkey King makes good use of his perceptive eyes, teaches a lesson to those who are apt to judge a person only by appearance. From this story the term baigujing *(White-bone Demon) became part of the Chinese vocabulary, synonymous with "a sinister person," particularly if such a person appears to be an attractive young female.*

Tang Seng, or the Monk of Tang, was on his way to the west to get Buddhist scriptures. Escorting him were his three disciples. Foremost was the Monkey King, who had rebelled against the Jade Emperor of Heaven. To prevent him from rebelling against Tang Seng, Guanyin had given the monk a magic ring hat and asked him to put it on the monkey's head without telling him its purpose. She then taught Tang Seng a verbal charm.

"In case the monkey is disobedient," Guanyin told the monk, "you can use the charm to tighten the ring hat. It will cause an excruciating headache."

"Would that kill him?" asked Tang Seng, concerned.

"No. It just disables him for the moment," Guanyin answered with a smile. "Its purpose is to deter, not to hurt."

Another disciple was Piggy. Humorous and foolhardy, he liked food and women. He had been a general in the Imperial Palace of Heaven. For the offence of harassing Moon Goddess Chang'e, the Jade Emperor had banished him to Earth. By a freak accident, however, he found his soul reborn in the body of a pig. When Tang Seng and Monkey King came to recruit him, he had been pestering a country girl to become his wife. His departure for the westward journey came as a relief to the girl and her family.

The third disciple was a celestial general, condemned to spend the rest of his life as a monster in the River of Sand. Because of his strength and tenacity, he took the responsibility of carrying the pilgrims' luggage. The fourth and last disciple was Tang Seng's white horse, a condemned dragon prince. Like Monkey King and Piggy, Sandy and Dragon Horse were also atoning for their past misconduct by helping Tang Seng get the Buddhist scriptures. Buddha promised them sainthood if they succeeded in the mission.

After surviving a series of calamities, Tang Seng and his disciples arrived at the foot of a tall mountain. Tang Seng felt tired and hungry and wanted to stop to rest. They looked around, but could not see any sign of life for miles. Monkey King spotted something pinkish in the distance. "Master, I'll get you some peaches." While he made the offer, the monkey drew a big circle with his iron rod

---

around Tang Seng, Piggy, Sandy, and the Dragon Horse. He told them not to venture out of its boundaries and put themselves in harm's way. He said that the dark clouds cloaking the top of the mountain boded ill.

Monkey King was right. In a cave on the mountain there lived a demon of a skeleton. As she liked to wear a loose cape and appear in the form of a young woman, she preferred her soldier devils to call her Madam White Bone. They were a band of vampires, living on the blood of their victims, be they animals or humans. The White-bone Demon, as people in the region called her in horror, counted on fresh blood for her vitality. Nevertheless, living a vibrant life was not enough. She did not want her mortal life to end at all. There was a belief among the monsters that a mouthful of Tang Seng's flesh would let them live forever.

When a report came that the monk had arrived in her domain, the White-bone Demon was beside herself with joy. However, her elation quickly gave way to alarm. She remembered with a shudder that the monk had adopted Monkey King as his disciple and bodyguard. Demons everywhere knew what a formidable foe the monkey was. The mere thought of his thousand-pound iron rod sent a chill down her already cold spine. All the same, the temptation of never getting old was too strong to resist.

"If I can't win with might," the White-bone Demon said with clenched teeth, "I will defeat the monkey with my mind. I just can't let this long-awaited opportunity slip through my fingers."

Tang Seng, Piggy, and Sandy were anxiously waiting for Monkey King's return when Piggy spotted a pretty young woman approaching, food basket in hand. As she greeted Tang Seng and tried to get closer to him, something like an electric shock shoved her a few steps back.

"Amitabha!" prayed Tang Seng, his eyes shut and his palms closed before his nose. He apologized and, when asked, told the young woman that it was the magic circle that his disciple Monkey King had drawn to protect them. Then, looking at the young woman, he asked caringly, "Why are you walking alone in such an ominous place, young lady?"

"I am taking food to my husband, who is tilling the land a few miles away," the young woman replied. "Now that I've run into you, I'd like to donate the food to you." Now as *xingseng* (traveling monks or pilgrims), Tang Seng and his disciples lived on alms and donations from Buddhist followers.

"No, how can we eat the food your husband needs for his hard work?"

"Don't worry, if he sees no food brought to him, he'll come back home early. He won't go hungry. Besides, being a pious Buddhist like me, he'll be happy to know I've donated the food to you."

Piggy could not wait any longer. He was enthralled by the pretty face of the young woman and the delicious smell of the food. Ignoring the warnings of his "Brother Monkey," as he and Sandy called Monkey King, he jumped out of the magic circle, dragging Tang Seng with him.

The young woman was in fact the phantasm of the White-bone Demon. The plump and fair-complexioned monk would have made her mouth water, if she had any saliva. She was about to pounce on him when Monkey King landed in front of her. He had seen through the demon's disguise while in the air, and returned just in time. With a single blow, he knocked the demon to the ground. But having anticipated the blow, the spirit of the demon had already escaped, leaving behind only a vision to trick the monkey and his party.

The demon's ploy worked on Tang Seng, who, as a Buddhist, was an advocate of nonviolence. The slaying of a young woman under his nose was too much for him to take. He sat down, closed his palms, and began to chant the verbal charm, which made the magic ring on Monkey King's head tighter and tighter. Monkey King reeled and fell to the ground, writhing in agony. Only after Piggy and Sandy pleaded for mercy repeatedly did the angry monk relent. He told Monkey King not to kill again, or he would dismiss him.

The White-bone Demon dreaded Monkey King's magic perception and his might but saw some hope in the monk's gullibility. She came back in the form of an elderly woman, pretending to look for her missing daughter. When she saw the fake body of the young woman drenched in a pool of blood, she pretended to become distraught and went up to Tang Seng, grabbing him by the arm.

"Look what you've done to my poor daughter. You must go with me and tell her father what's happened," said the demon, trying to take Tang Seng with her.

"Amitabha! I'm terribly sorry for my disciple's criminal act," Tang Seng did not know what to say to allay the elderly woman's grief and anger.

The Monkey King, however, had seen through the demon from the beginning. He refrained from striking her for fear that Tang Seng would chant that headache-evoking charm. However, when the demon tried to seize Tang Seng, he determined to protect him at all cost. A single strike of his iron rod squashed the old woman. Feeling a puff of cold air whooshing by and into the distance, Monkey King knew that the demon had escaped again. Before he could leap up into the air to pursue her, his master had started to murmur the ring-tightening charm. Down plunged Monkey King to the ground and rolled about in anguish. After the corporal punishment, Tang Seng insisted that Monkey King leave him for good. Only after the monkey unwillingly apologized profusely did the monk agree to pardon him, saying that it would be the monkey's last chance.

Tang Seng and his disciples resumed their journey. But the White-bone Demon would not let Tang Seng go. She had to act fast or the monk would be out of her domain and become the food of her rival demons and monsters elsewhere. She went around Tang Seng and his party and waited for them a few hundred yards ahead. There she turned into a white-bearded old man in front of an illusionary cottage. He stood at the door supported by a cane, his hand cupped before his eyes, as if expecting someone.

"It must be the husband of the old woman and father of the girl!" said Piggy, already nursing a grudge against his Brother Monkey for slaying the pretty young woman. "Brother Monkey has killed both his daughter and his wife. What shall we do?"

"How do you know?" asked Sandy. "Aren't they visions of a demon, as Brother Monkey told us?"

"No. Remember the monkey's ability to transform himself? He must have conjured up both the women. He tricked our master because he feared his ring-tightening charm."

Hearing the conversation, Tang Seng felt extremely guilty about Monkey King's atrocity and did not know how to face the poor old man. As Tang Seng dreadfully anticipated, the old man asked if they had seen his wife and daughter. The honest and kindhearted monk had to tell him what had happened and apologized with profound remorse.

Flying into a rage, the old man raised his cane and charged at Tang Seng, yelling, "I want you to pay for their lives with yours!" Monkey King knew who the old man was from the start. Again, he balked at taking an action. If he struck the demon, his master would drive him away and never let him return. Nonetheless, when the demon began to attack Tang Seng, Monkey King had to act quickly. To make sure that the demon could not run off, as she had done before, Monkey King dispatched his spirit to summon all the gods of the surrounding lands and mountains, as well as a celestial army. He asked them to encircle the area to prevent the demon from escaping his blow—all this was done in a fraction of a second and was invisible to the demon and his comrades. Monkey King struck with all his might, and the demon fell and perished, revealing a heap of white bones.

Tang Seng would have believed what he saw and pardoned Monkey King for his necessary use of force but for Piggy, who claimed that the bones were but false visions created by his Brother Monkey. Piggy's argument convinced the gullible Tang Seng. He demanded that Monkey King leave him immediately.

"Trust me, Master," pleaded Monkey King, "The three people you saw were nothing but the visions created by this White-bone Demon. I didn't do anything to trick you."

"I can't trust you any more. You can never change your murderous nature. Since I've set you free from the mountain that imprisoned you for 500 years, I don't think I owe you anything now. You can go back to where you came from."

"Then you have to take this ring hat off me," Monkey King said, hoping that if Tang Seng did not know how to do it, he would have to keep him.

"I'm sorry that I don't know how, but believe me, I'll never chant the charm," his master said with determination.

Seeing no hope of changing Tang Seng's mind, Monkey King wanted to say thanks to him before his departure. Each time he dropped on his knees, Tang Seng turned away. Monkey King split himself into four images and knelt before his unforgiving master in all directions. Then he said goodbye to Sandy and Piggy, who was already regretting his mischief, which had gone too far. In tears, Monkey King soared into the sky and was instantly out of sight.

The next day, Tang Seng, Piggy, and Sandy encountered the Monster of Yellow Wind. Without Monkey King, Tang Seng and Sandy were easy prey. Piggy narrowly escaped captivity. Deeply remorseful for the folly that had caused Tang Seng to dismiss Brother Monkey, he decided to get Monkey King back. He wanted to apologize to him and ask him to come fight the monster.

Whether Monkey King forgave Piggy and went along with him to rescue their master is another fascinating episode of the Monkey King adventures. For the entire story of Monkey King, you may want to read Wu Ch'En-En, Monkey: A Journey to the West, *retold by David Kherdian (Boston: Shambhala Publications, 2000).*

Monkey King traveling on clouds with his formidable weapon, the iron rod.

A FOOLISH OLD MAN TRIES TO REMOVE TWO MOUNTAINS

A long time ago, to the south of Jizhou and north of Heyang, somewhere on the Great Plains of China, there stood two big mountains, one called Taihang and the other Wangwu. They were both thousands of feet high, and together they covered an area of 700 miles.

On the north side of the mountains and right beneath them there lived a family led by an old man in his nineties. Still robust and healthy, he went to work in the fields with his sons and grandsons every day. People did not know his real name but simply called him Yugong, or Mr. Foolish. They thought of him as foolish because they mistook his perseverance as stubbornness and his generosity as gullibility. Mr. Foolish and his family had a hard time making a living because all their farmland was on the other side of the mountains. Every day they had to spend a great amount of time traveling back and forth. One evening, Mr. Foolish called his family together.

"What do you think of removing the mountains in front of our house?" he asked. Before anyone in the family had time to answer, he continued, "If we work perseveringly, we will open up a road that will lead directly to our farmland on the Han River. What's your take?" Knowing him too well, none was surprised at his decision. Besides, they wanted to have easy access to their farmland themselves. Seeing that the patriarch had already made up his mind, they all showed their support. His wife, however, had some doubts.

"You are too old to level even a mound. How can you get rid of these mountains?" she asked. "Besides, where will we place the rocks and dirt we dig out?"

"We can dump them into the Bohai Sea," suggested their youngest son, rising and rolling up his sleeves in excitement.

The next day the entire family turned out with picks, chisels, shovels, and baskets in their hands and on their shoulders. Even some of the neighbors, including a seven-year-old child, joined them. They dug, dug, and dug. They carried, carried, and carried, dumping the rocks and dirt into the Bohai Sea. Because the mountains they were demolishing were hundreds of miles away from the sea, one round trip took them a year.

On the upper fork of the Han River on the other side of the mountains of Taihang and Wangwu there lived a Mr. Smart. He had this nickname because he took pride in his good judgment, claiming that he would never do anything he saw as useless. Curious about what was happening on the other side of the mountains, Mr. Smart came over to find out for himself. When he learned what Mr. Foolish was doing, he chuckled.

"What can I say? You are really worthy of the name Mr. Foolish! Don't you know how old you are? Do you think you can chisel away even a fraction of the mountains in your lifetime?" chided Mr. Smart.

"Well, I don't think you are really smart," Mr. Foolish retorted. "Why didn't you think of this fact: I will die alright, but my sons will continue working. When they die, their sons will do the same.

Their sons' sons will have their own sons and grandsons, so that the family line will never end. The mountains, however, will never grow. An inch chiseled away is an inch less. What say you?" At this, Mr. Smart was at a loss for words.

A *tudiye* (a local god of land) reported what Mr. Foolish had said and done to his superior Yuhuang Dadi (Jade Emperor of Heaven). Equally touched by the heroism and perseverance that Mr. Foolish and his family displayed, the emperor asked two giants to help them. The giants plucked up Taihang and placed it miles away on the east side of Mr. Foolish's house. Then, they plucked up Wangwu and placed it at an equal distance on the south. In consequence, from that time forward the family could see their farmland from the back windows of their house.

THE TWIN SISTERS AND THE MAGIC MALAN FLOWER

Long, long ago, there lived on top of Mt. Malan an immortal known as Ma Lang (Brother Ma). Young and handsome, he particularly loved the qualities of diligence and courage in people. To encourage them to make a living by honest labor while bravely standing up to any evildoing, he cultivated a species of flowers, which he called Malan, after the name of the mountain. He made it known that the magic flowers would bring happiness only to those who were hardworking and courageous. Since Mt. Malan was tall and steep, no one had ever been to its top and seen the flowers.

At the foot of Mt. Malan there lived an elderly couple with their twin daughters. Although the two young women looked exactly the same, their characters were as different as day and night. The one born first was Da Lan (Big Lan), and the one born after her was Xiao Lan (Younger Lan). Da Lan was fond of eating and averse to work, whereas her younger sister Xiao Lan was industrious. In fact, every day while Da Lan lounged at home munching, Xiao Lan worked with her father in the family orchard.

"Dad, have you ever seen a Malan flower?" Xiao Lan asked, as she was pruning an apple tree beside her father.

"No, I have only heard of it. Why?" responded her father.

"I want to see one very much," Xiao Lan told her father, "because I heard that a Malan flower will bring happiness to those who are hardworking and courageous."

"So you think you are hardworking and courageous?" her father jested good-humoredly.

"Dad, here you go again," Xiao Lan blushed as she pursed her pretty red lips.

"Xiao Lan, my dear," her father began, "I mean it. You're truly a good daughter, not like your sister Da Lan. I think your mom and I have pampered her too much." Then, after a brief pause, he continued with determination, "Tomorrow, when I go to the mountain to look for medicinal herbs, I'll try to get to the top and get you a Malan flower."

"No, Dad! Don't mind what I said. It is too dangerous to go up there. I don't want you to take the risk," Xiao Lan pleaded.

"Don't worry. I know how to take care of myself."

The next day Xiao Lan's father set out for the mountain. With great difficulty he reached the top of Mt. Malan and saw the beautiful Malan flowers. They danced in the breeze, throwing off bright and colorful sparkles, as if they had been heaps of sapphires and rubies, twinkling playfully in the sun. Xiao Lan's father was very excited. He was imagining how happy Xiao Lan would be to see the flower when, all of a sudden, the rock he stood on gave way. He reeled, and was about to fall into the deep valley below when Ma Lang caught him by the hand. Pulling him up to safety on top of the mountain, Ma Lang asked if he was hurt. The old man, collecting himself, thanked him and told him that he was alright.

"Sir, you're here for the Malan flowers, right?" Ma Lang asked amiably.

"I came because my daughter wants to see one," answered the old man.

"You mean Xiao Lan?" Ma Lang's eyes lit up, his face blushing.

"How do you know her?" questioned Xiao Lan's father, perplexed.

"Everyone knows she's a good girl, pretty, hardworking, and courageous. I love . . . I love people who are like her," said Ma Lang, stooping to pick a flower in the flower bed. It was the most beautiful of all—at least, that was what he thought. Then, he carefully handed it to Xiao Lan's father. "This is for Xiao Lan. I wish her happiness all her life!" Xiao Lan's father thanked Ma Lang and descended the mountain. Halfway down he began to feel tired. He leaned against an old tree to catch his breath.

"Hah, hah, hah . . . ."

"Who is it?" asked the startled old man. The sudden burst of chuckling took him by surprise.

"It's me. You are leaning against me," the old pine tree spoke.

"Hi, how are you doing?"

"I'm old, but I am happy," the old tree said with a contented smile, "I'm particularly happy that you are going to have Ma Lang as your son-in-law."

"What did you say? Ma Lang, the immortal, will be my son-in-law?"

"Didn't you see that he was in love with your daughter Xiao Lan? My sincere congratulations! They will make a good couple. Hah, hah, hah . . . ." replied the old pine tree.

Xiao Lan's father remembered Ma Lang's blushing and stammering. His fatigue instantly evaporated. He rushed back home without even knowing how he got there.

Xiao Lan was happy to see the flower and even happier to hear of Ma Lang's love for her. In fact, she had long felt drawn to Ma Lang, but she was too shy to reveal her affection to anyone.

The story would have ended happily but for a big, grey wolf. It had overheard the conversation between Xiao Lan's father and the old pine tree while hiding behind a big rock nearby. It dashed to the old man's home ahead of him. There, it ate his family cat and transformed into its feline form.

Initially, Da Lan did not care about the Malan flower and her sister Xiao Lan's marriage to Ma Lang because she did not like hard work in the first place and resented the prospect of toiling on top of a mountain with a "workaholic gardener," as she called Ma Lang. The wolf turned cat, however, coveted the Malan flower very much. Since it was by no means eligible for the magic plant, it decided to get it from Xiao Lan when she came back to visit her parents.

A week after her wedding, Xiao Lan was back home. Seeing her younger sister return empty-handed except for the Malan flower, Da Lan was disappointed. "You're poor alright, but how can you be so stingy that you don't even bring a cake or a candy home?" she complained.

At this, Xiao Lan burst into laughter, "I thought you would say so. Tell me what you want, and I'll get it for you."

"I want good things to eat and to wear," Da Lan demanded.

"Fine," responded Xiao Lan, as she held the Malan flower up and chanted quietly:

"Malan flower, Malan flower,

Fear you neither wind nor rain,

Asking you I am, a diligent person,

'Please show us your bloom now.' "

Suddenly the Malan flower bloomed. When the family rubbed their bedazzled eyes and opened them again, they saw spread on the table and the *kang* fabulous amounts of food, clothing, jewelry, and all the things that had gone through Da Lan's mind.

Instead of being happy, Dalan was at once seized with jealousy and regret. She had never anticipated the magic power of the Malan flower. She now realized that her sister's marriage to Ma Lang was not at all a hard life. Regretting not asking her father to get her a Malan flower, she wanted to get it from her sister.

Da Lan's change of mind provided the wolf turned cat with a perfect opportunity to get the Malan flower from Xiao Lan. That evening, when Da Lan was preparing to go to sleep, cuddling what she thought was her pussycat, it began to talk. The wolf turned cat hushed the startled Da Lan as it explained who it was. It asked Da Lan to see her sister off the next morning.

"If you cooperate with me," it said with a cunning look in its eyes, "we'll divide everything the flower may bring to us." When Da Lan heard this plot to use her to get the Malan flower from her sister, she was reluctant, saying, "No, after all, she is my sister. Why can't you do it yourself?"

"Well, think of the good things you'll enjoy all your life. You don't have to feel guilty at all because we are not going to hurt her. I only need you to pass for Xiao Lan. You two look so much alike that no one can tell who's who," the wolf coaxed.

The next morning, when Xiao Lan said good-bye to her parents, Da Lan insisted on seeing her off. The cat also tagged along. When they arrived at a fountain, Xiao Lan asked Da Lan and the cat to go back. Da Lan burst into tears, pretending that she could hardly tear herself away from Xiao Lan. She sobbed out, "I will miss you every minute of the day. How I wish I could have something that will make me feel close to you! It'll comfort me when you are not in my sight."

"I'll be back soon," Xiao Lan wiped the tears off Da Lan's cheeks with her slender fingers. "Tell me what you want from me, and I'd love to give it to you."

"I want to trade my earrings and clothes with you so that we both have a remembrance."

As soon as the sisters had traded their clothing and ornaments, the wolf grabbed the Malan flower and, to the horror of Da Lan, pushed Xiao Lan into the fountain. The wolf tried to make the flower bloom, but to its dismay, it did not remember exactly what the verbal charm was. He asked Da Lan if she knew it. Da Lan said "no". How could she? She had been concentrated so much on the good things the magic flower had conjured up that she had not heard a single word of what her sister had said. Looking at Da Lan in her sister's clothes and ornaments, the wolf had an idea. It ordered Da Lan to go to Ma Lang while in the guise of Xiao Lan and get the charm from him.

Ma Lang was very happy to see Xiao Lan back, particularly amused that she had also brought the family cat with her. Xiao Lan, however, did not look happy. When questioned, she said she was tired and needed some sleep. In fact, the cat had told Da Lan to stay as quiet as possible to prevent revealing her identity.

At bedtime, the remorseful Da Lan had to tell Ma Lang everything. When they went to catch the wicked wolf, it was nowhere to be found. It turned out that, never trusting Da Lan, the wolf had eavesdropped and overheard her confession and Ma Lang's vow to avenge Xiao Lan.

The next day, everyone in the village, except the old and young, turned out to help Ma Lang search for the wolf. Even the plants and animals on the mountain joined in the wolf hunt. A weed would sway violently for the birds scouting in the air to see and relay its findings. Eventually, Ma Lang and the villagers found the wolf at a cliff. Terrified, the wicked wolf lost its balance and fell into the deep valley below.

Led by Da Lan, Ma Lang rushed to the fountain where the wolf had drowned Xiao Lan. When Ma Lang fished out Xiao Lan's body, she looked as if she was only asleep. With the power of the Malan flower, Ma Lang brought Xiao Lan back to life. Holding Xiao Lan in her arms, Da Lan apologized and pledged to follow her example. "Sister," Xiao Lan said to Da Lan, "You are now the most courageous because you are brave enough to acknowledge your wrongdoing. So long as you form the habit of working, you will have a Malan flower for yourself."

Back in the village, Xiao Lan and Ma Lang chanted:

"Malan flower, Malan flower,

Fear you neither wind nor rain,

Asking you I am, a diligent person,

'Please show us your bloom now'."

Immediately, with the blooming of the flower, all kinds of food appeared. Xiao Lan and Ma Lang invited the entire village to a party to thank them for their help.

A MAN WITH A DOG'S LEG

Today, pet dogs are visible everywhere in Chinese cities and in the country. Pet shops and veterinary centers are mushrooming. Traditionally, however, the Chinese did not give dogs much respect. "No admittance by Chinese and Dogs," warned a sign on a foreign building in China at the turn of the twentieth century. This might seem to be no big deal to Westerners, but it has become a symbol of Chinese humiliation by foreigners. The reason is that things associated with dogs used to have a derogatory meaning in Chinese. This is evident in Chinese phrases like langxin-goufei *(wolf's heart and dog's lung). Someone with a* langxin-goufei *is cruel and unscrupulous. Someone with monstrous audacity is said to have a* goudan *(dog's gallbladder) "large enough to wrap the sky." A bad person is compared to a dog, and his or her loyal follower is referred to as* goutuizi *or "the leg of a dog." The following story, collected from a villager in North China, tells how the epithet* goutuizi *came about.*

Once upon a time there was an itinerant monk known for his humor and uprightness. He was also known for his unconventional behavior and lifestyle. Unlike other monks, he refused to have his head tonsured, or shaved. He drank alcohol and ate meat. With an old palm fan, he wandered from place to place wearing a dirty hat, a shredded gown, and a pair of worn shoes. Everywhere he went, he protected the oppressed from the oppressors. He could do so because he was no ordinary monk. He was believed to be a living bodhisattva, or *pusa*. Although his name was Dao Ji, people preferred calling him Ji Gong, or the Revered Ji.

One day Ji Gong arrived at a village and heard many complaints about a despotic landowner. He had a servant as mean as he was. Together they kept the farmhands working hard all day long, but gave them barely enough food to survive. The landowner and his servant also cheated many of the villagers of their land, which was vital to their livelihood. As a result, quite a few of the villagers had to leave home and go begging elsewhere. Neither the farmhands nor the villagers could do anything because the two villains had enough money to bribe the officials so that they could get away with anything. The worst thing was that, together with the officials, the two could easily send anyone who dared to defy them to jail or into exile. The farmhands and villagers could only protest secretly among themselves. Ji Gong overheard their complaints and decided to teach the vicious landowner and his servant a good lesson.

With his magic power, Ji Gong made the landowner suffer from a stroke and, as a result, hemiplegia, or paralysis affecting one side of his body. The landowner sent for a doctor. His servant encountered Ji Gong, who was in the guise of a country medicine man. Ji Gong had anticipated the landowner's solicitation for help and made sure that his servant could find him. He readily followed the servant to the landowner's mansion.

The landowner could only walk on one leg because his other leg was immobile. He asked Ji Gong to treat his leg. "Help me, Doc," entreated the landowner, his face distorted when he spoke due to his partial paralysis. "I'll give you whatever I have if you can make me walk on both legs."

"That's easy!" said Ji Gong. His words took the landowner and his servant by surprise. However, their joy quickly gave way to bewilderment and then fear because, after examining the landowner's leg, Ji Gong told him that he was suffering from a disease that neither medicine nor magic could cure. "This is because of what you have done to your farmhands and the villagers," Ji Gong added.

The despondent and frightened landowner vowed to amend his wrongdoings and begged Ji Gong to treat him. Ji Gong made him promise to treat his farmhands fairly and return all the properties to the villagers that he and his servant had cheated them of. The landowner did so readily.

"Since your leg is useless, I have to amputate it," said Ji Gong.

"Cut it off? Won't that be even worse than if I have the useless leg?" asked the landowner helplessly.

"Well, if you choose not to have any treatment, I don't care," said Ji Gong. "I'm afraid that if you don't, your other leg will be affected sooner or later."

"But can you find me a good leg after you cut off the bad one?" the landowner asked wistfully.

Ji Gong did not answer immediately, but his eyes wandered around the room and, in the end, focused on the legs of the servant. The servant gave a shudder because he seemed to have read what was in the monk's mind. The landowner looked as if he got the message, too, because he cast a demanding look at the servant.

"What can I say? If my master likes my leg, it can be his by all means," the clever and flattering servant said submissively, but he felt very sorry for himself at the bottom of his heart.

With his magic power, Ji Gong cut off the servant's leg painlessly and fixed it to the landowner. Since the servant's leg was shorter, the landowner became limp. Still, he was happy that he could walk on two legs again.

Before Ji Gong left the mansion, the servant begged him, "Please find me a leg, as you did for my master. How can I walk on one only?" Ji Gong looked around but found no one nearby. He said to the servant, "How can I help if there's no one to spare his leg?"

"How about getting a leg from one of the farmhands?" suggested the vicious servant.

"No!" the landowner cut in categorically because he remembered what he had promised Ji Gong.

Ji Gong smirked, "Since your master would not like you to have a leg from anyone in his mansion, I'll have to find it outside." As he said this, Ji Gong went out into the street, where he found a stray dog. He said to the dog, "I am so sorry, but I have to borrow a leg from you." He removed a hind leg from the dog. The animal did not feel any pain in the instantly healed wound. Ji Gong then went back to the mansion and added the dog's leg to the servant. Since then, the farmhands and villagers have called the servant *goutuizi* (a dog's leg).

The compassionate monk could not bear seeing the stray dog missing a leg. He found some mud and sculped a leg out of it. Then he fixed it to the dog. The clay leg looked and functioned like a real one. There was a catch, though: because the leg was made of clay, it was not waterproof. Water could soak and destroy it. Therefore, Ji Gong told the dog to raise the clay leg when it answered nature's call. That is why even today, male dogs still raise one of their hind legs when they urinate.

Tales of How Things Came to Be

Tales of origins not only satisfy people's curiosity about things they cannot scientifically explain but also serve as moral lessons. "The Origin of the World" teaches us how to become useful to others even after we cease to exist; "The Origin of Human Beings" teaches us to value lives, as did the goddess who devoted hers to their continuity; "The Origin of Chinese New Year and Its Customs" teaches us how to attack the enemy where it has a soft spot; "The Origin of the Mid-autumn Festival" teaches us not to trust someone readily; "The Origin of Kitchen God and the *Jizao* Festival" teaches us to be diligent; "The Origin of the *Duanwu* Festival" teaches us to love our parents for what they are; and "The Origin of the Twelve Zodiac Animals" teaches us to be truthful to our friends. Read them and you may find more.

Kids celebrating the Chinese New Year with a drum dance and firecrackers.

THE ORIGIN OF THE WORLD

Pangu, creator of the world in the eyes of the Han Chinese, did not become known until the Three Kingdoms period (A.D. 221–265). Historians and folklorists argue that Pangu was originally the ancestor of the Miao, one of the fifty-six ethnic groups in China today, and that some Miao wizards introduced the tale of Pangu to the Han Chinese later. Whatever the case may be, the accep-

tance of Pangu as one of the common ancestors of the Han Chinese testifies to the cultural benefits that China enjoys by being a multi-ethnic nation.

In the beginning, the universe was like a gigantic egg. Inside it was a mass of chaotic darkness. After a long, long time, a giant with a dragonhead and a human body was born in an egg-shaped space. His name was Pangu. Pangu slept for 18,000 years. He woke up and opened his eyes, but he could see nothing; he wanted to stretch, but his limbs hit the walls around him; he tried to stand up, but he bumped his head against the ceiling of the egg-shaped enclosure.

Pangu began to kick about and knock around until he broke the shell and stuck out his head and upper body. Looking around with wide-open eyes, he still saw nothing but darkness. Again he kicked and knocked, twisted and turned, until the yoke-like substance of darkness began to break up. As a result, the light and clear substance called *yang* started to float upward to form *tian* (the sky) and the dark and muddy substance called *yin* began to sink to the bottom to form *di* (the earth). Pangu was in between, his head against the sky and his feet upon the earth.

Fearing that *tian* and *di* would come together and form the chaotic darkness again, Pangu decided to stay in between until *tian* and *di* became permanently separate. His body began to grow at the speed of ten feet a day. As he grew taller and taller, *tian* and *di* were pushed farther and farther apart. Eventually Pangu became a giant 90,000 miles tall. Thus the sky and the earth were 90,000 miles apart. Pangu was sure that they would never have a chance to come together again.

By now, another 18,000 years had passed. Pangu was too exhausted to stand and grow anymore. One day he suddenly dropped to the ground and fell into a sleep from which he never woke. As he died, the parts of his body were transformed into the elements of nature. His head, torso, and limbs turned into five mountains, one in the center of the earth and one each in one of the four directions of the compass. The five mountains became the pillars of the tentlike sky. His left eye became the sun; his right eye, the moon; and his hair, the myriad stars in the night sky. His last breath became wind, fog, and clouds; his muscles, the soil; his blood and fluid, the rivers; his bones and teeth, the minerals and precious stones; his perspiration, the rain and dew; his body hair, the vegetation; and the parasites living in and on his body became the living creatures.

THE ORIGIN OF HUMAN BEINGS

The Chinese claim to be the offspring of several different ancestors: the legendary prehistoric Emperors Yan and Huang, the imaginary totem dragon, and the mythical creators known as Pangu and Nüwa. The diversity of ancestral origins may well indicate that today's Han Chinese came from people with diverse cultural backgrounds.

After Pangu created the universe, there appeared a goddess who had a human upper body and a snake lower body. Her name was Nüwa. She was infinitely resourceful, capable of changing into seventy different beings in a single day. All the same, she felt very lonely. She wanted to add something exciting to the earth. She began searching for that something, even though she had no idea what it was. While flying over a river, she looked down and happened to see the reflection of her face in the waters below. It was lively and beautiful. An idea dawned: "Why can't I create something that will look like me? Then, I will have companions." So thinking, she landed by the river and started to put her idea into practice.

Fishing some mud from the river, Nüwa kneaded it into a piece of dough. Then she molded a little figure after her human face and upper body. Instead of a snake lower body like hers, she gave it two limbs that she called *tui* (legs). The moment she placed the clay figure on the ground, it began to jump around with joy and called her "*Mama* (Mom)!" She happily named the little figurine *ren* (human). She then created more *ren* in the same fashion so that they could populate the world.

Nüwa worked day and night until she was too tired to go on. Leaning against a mound, she fell asleep. Waking up, she looked around and caught sight of a large pool of muddy water nearby. Something like a rope led her eyes from the edge of the muddy puddle up to the side of the mound. It was a vine. She suddenly had an idea. She dipped the vine in the puddle and whirled it around. As she swung the muddy vine round and round, pieces of mud flew off and soon covered a large area about her. In no time the larger pieces of mud had turned into human beings and the smaller ones into animals. The *ren* she had molded from the mud she fished from the river became the forebears of *guiren* (noble men and women), and the *ren* she created from the mud she slung were the ancestors of *pingmin* (the common people).

The earth now teamed with life, but Nüwa's joy did not last long. In time the humans began to die in great numbers. She realized that as mortals, they eventually would all perish, and she would have to create them all over again. The resourceful Nüwa never ran out of ideas, so she suggested to herself, "How about letting the humans regenerate themselves?" Acting on her thought, she blew a breath of *yang* into some of the humans so that they became men, and a breath of *yin* into others so that they turned into women. She then encouraged them to marry for the purpose of reproducing themselves. Since then, humanity has continued from generation to generation.

Humans lived a happy, peaceful life for years, until one day a great disaster struck them. Gonggong, a red-haired giant, started a war against the God of Zhuan Xu. Defeated, Gonggong became so furious that he banged his humongous head against Mt. Buzhou and caused it to crumble. The mountain was in fact one of the pillars of the four corners of the world, (north, south, east, and west), supporting the tent-like sky to prevent it from collapsing. Consequently a large chunk of the sky fell. Water gushed out from the big hole and poured onto the earth, which had been quaking violently in the wake of Mt. Buzhou's collapse. The seas swelled and began to submerge land after land. Dragons of fire and water and beasts of prey who were flushed out of their dens began to run wild and took a great number of lives.

Nüwa could not stand seeing the decimation of the humans and other creatures she had created. She was determined to rescue them. Facing such a large-scale calamity, Nüwa did not panic. Instead, she prioritized what she was going to do. She decided that the damage to the sky was the cause of everything, so took on the task of mending it. She collected a great number of multicolored stones from a riverbed, built a furnace in the Zhonghuang Mountain, and, after forty-nine days, melted the stones and created a huge piece of colorful slate. Embedding the slate in the hole, Nüwa managed to fix the leaking sky. Her action produced an unexpected side effect: the shining colors of the slate added to the sky a moon, a rainbow, and numerous stars.

Fearing that the sky might break loose again, Nüwa slew a giant turtle and propped the sky up with its legs in place of the fallen Mt Buzhou. Seeing that the sky was secure, she turned her attention to the other causes of the disaster. She slaughtered the dragons that had produced excessive fire and water and drove the beasts of prey into the depths of forests and mountains. With the ashes left in the furnace that had produced the colorful slate, she built dams and dikes to check the floods. In the end, when everything on earth returned to normal, Nüwa was too tired to get up. She fell into a peaceful sleep and never woke up.

Nüwa creating *ren*.

THE ORIGIN OF CHINESE NEW YEAR AND ITS CUSTOMS

It may sound strange, but it is true that few Chinese know when to celebrate their New Year without referring to a Chinese calendar. Such a calendar consists of both the Western and the Chinese calendric systems. The Chinese calendar divides a year into twelve months of twenty-nine or thirty days each, eleven days shorter than a Western calendar. To make up the difference, there is a leap month every two or three years. As a result, the Chinese New Year, which begins on the first day of the first Chinese month, falls on various days between the latter part of January and the first part of February. Here is a short list of when Chinese New Year will fall in the years to come:

2007	February 18
2008	February 7
2009	January 26
2010	February 14
2011	February 3
2012	January 23
2013	February 10
2014	January 31
2015	February 19
2016	February 8

A Chinese calendar also has twenty-four jieqi *(solar terms) of fifteen days each, designed to remind farmers when to plant, harvest, and rest. The first term,* lichun *(beginning of spring), constitutes the entire Chinese New Year season, which is as important a tradition to the Chinese as Christmas is to Westerners. Curiosity about the origin of the Chinese New Year has given rise to many beautiful folktales trying to explain how the tradition began.*

One tale goes that long, long ago, there lived in the deep sea a monster called *nian*. Larger than an elephant, it had two long horns and many sharp teeth. At sunset at the beginning of each year, *nian* would resurface from the depths of the sea and go on shore to prey on people and their beasts of burden. Each year people would flee their villages before the monster's arrival and take refuge in the surrounding mountains.

On one such afternoon, people were preparing to run when a white-bearded old man appeared in their village begging for food. Because the villagers were in flight from *nian*, none of them paid any attention to him. An elderly woman, however, gave him some bread and told him to run for his life.

"Run?" the old man chuckled, "No! I would rather stay."

"Aren't you afraid of the man-eating monster *nian*?" the startled elderly woman asked.

"No, not at all," answered the old beggar. "If you allow me to stay in your house tonight, I will drive the monster away."

Unable to persuade the crazy beggar to flee, the elderly woman left her house at his disposal and ran to the mountains with her fellow villagers. At midnight *nian* stormed into the village. Finding it vacated, the beast searched from door to door for animals and fowls left behind by the villagers. N*ian* was about to force his way into the elderly woman's courtyard when it suddenly bounced back with a scream of horror. It turned out that the doors were dazzling with red paper and the yard was bright with candlelight. Before *nian* could collect itself, the doors flew open and there appeared the white-bearded old beggar in a red cloak, bellowing amid loud crackling of burning bamboo sticks behind him. At this, *nian* took to its heels and dashed back to the sea.

At sunrise the villagers returned to their ransacked village. To their surprise, however, the elderly woman's residence was intact. When asked, the elderly woman thought of the old beggar and remembered what he had told her before her flight. Seeing the red paper pasted on the door, the bamboo sticks smoldering in the courtyard, and the candles burning their last drops of wax in the house, the villagers realized how the old beggar had driven the beast away.

"How could he know what the beast feared?" wondered the villagers.

"He must have been an immortal, coming here to teach us how to keep the monster at bay in the future," the wisest elder in the village concluded.

The tradition of pasting red paper on the doors, lighting candles all the night, and burning bamboo sticks to create crackling sounds soon spread everywhere. In the course of time, blank red paper began to have word of good wishes printed on it, and bamboo sticks gave way to firecrackers. (The written words *guonian*, which may have originally meant "survive *nian*," now stands for "celebrate the (New) Year" because the word *guo* has a double meaning of "passover" and "observe."

A different version of the story sheds light on more of the customs related to the observation of Chinese New Year. Long, long ago, the ferocious beast *nian* lived in the depths of a forest. It came out to prey on villagers and their livestock once a year. Eventually the villagers learned the pattern of its attack: On the last day of each year, *nian* would come out at sunset and leave the next day before sunrise, when a new year started. The villagers thus referred to that dangerous evening that bridged the past and the new years as *nianguan*, or "a crisis of a year."

Each year, before *nianguan* approached, all the villagers would try to come back to their homes no matter where they were. Every household would cook their meals early in the day. When evening set in, they would douse their kitchen fires, pen up their beasts of burden and domestic animals, and hole up behind closed doors. They would gather at a table spread with the good food they had fixed. They called the meal *nianyefan* (a dinner at the eve of the New Year), and treated it as their last get-together because no one knew what would be in store afterward. Neither did they know if they could get over the crisis and survive to see the next year. Before eating, they would pay tribute to their ancestors, who were symbolized by wood tablets with their names carved on them, which they called *lingwei* (places of souls). They prayed that their ancestors would protect them. After *nianyefan*, they would sit around chatting or playing board or card games in order to cheer one another up. None would dare to go to sleep.

When day broke, and *nian* retreated to the forest, people would turn out to congratulate each other on their survival. They would visit their neighbors and relatives and, shaking their own hands, exchange the greeting "*Gongxi facai* (Congratulations and wish you good fortune)!"

For years people managed to survive the attack of *nian*. By and by, they were no longer as vigilant. One year an entire village, except a newly married couple and a group of children, became the victims of *nian*. It turned out that the newlywed had decorated their house with red curtains, and they were dressed in red in accordance with wedding customs. The kids were playing around burning bamboo sticks, which gave out a series of loud, crackling noises. The red color, the fire, and the crackling had scared the beast away, thus preventing it from attacking them.

Since then people have learned to put up red-paper strips with words of good wishes on them, known as *duilian* (couplet), on their doorframes, hang red lanterns in and outside their houses, and dress themselves and their children in red as part of the New Year celebration. They have also learned to stay up the whole night during New Year's Eve and light firecrackers around *nianguan*.

However, not all the Chinese knew the customs. The vicious *nian* continued to kill. A goddess named Ziwei decided to eliminate *nian* once and for all. The next year, she came and hit *nian* with a big fire ball. After capturing *nian*, Ziwei imprisoned it by tying it to a stone column with iron chains. As a result, worship of Ziwei, now symbolized by a star, has also become part of the observation of the Chinese New Year in some regions of China.

A *duilian* (couplet) has been permanently engraved on the doorframes to bless the owner of this residence.

THE ORIGIN OF THE TWELVE ZODIAC ANIMALS

Ancient Chinese divided the space near the ecliptic—the imagined track of the sun's rotation in a year—into twelve equal parts. They gave each part a name, and the twelve different names put together constituted what we know as dizhi *(earthly branches). The Chinese combined each of the* dizhi *names with one of the ten* tiangan *(heavenly stems) symbols to designate a year. Altogether, there were sixty years in a cycle, and time progressed in a cyclic fashion. To remember the names of the* dizhi *easily, the ancient Chinese assigned an animal to each of them. The twelve animals— rat, ox, tiger, rabbit, dragon, snake, horse, sheep, monkey, rooster, dog, and boar—have since become* shuxiang, *known to Westerners as the Chinese Zodiac Animals. No one knows exactly why the animals are in that order and why animals like cats are not included in the list. A popular folktale, however, provides some interesting insights.*

Long, long ago, people did not know how old they were. Neither did they know the day, the month, and the year. One day, Yuhuang Dadi (the Jade Emperor of Heaven) got an idea. He wanted to use animals to help people count their years, believing that animals would be more interesting to people than anything else.

However, among the animals in the world, only twelve were needed. "How am I going to avoid offending the rest of the animals?" Yuhuang Dadi pondered. He thought that letting them compete would be a perfect solution. He decreed that all the animals in the world should report to him at the same time on the thirtieth day of the twelfth month that year. He would name the first twelve animals that first arrived in his presence the Zodiac Animals, and each would represent one of the twelve years on his calendar.

There lived on earth two good neighbors, a cat and a rat. The cat was in the habit of oversleeping, but he did not want to miss the opportunity of becoming a Zodiac Animal. The night before reporting to Yuhuang Dadi, the cat came to the rat and asked her to wake him up early next morning.

"No problem," said the friendly neighbor, "Go and take a hearty sleep. I will wake you up and we'll go to Yuhuang Dadi together." The cat thanked his rodent friend and went back to sleep. The next morning, however, the rat set out alone. In her rush to beat the other animals, she had totally forgotten her feline friend. Not only did she want to become one of the twelve Zodiac Animals, but she also desired to be in the first place.

Because she left very early, the rat was leading all the other animals in the race to the Jade Emperor despite her small body and short legs. Only an ox was hot on her heels. She knew that the ox would soon catch up with her due to his big strides. They ran and ran, when suddenly a river blocked their way. It was their last obstacle in the race, for on the other bank lay the Heavenly Palace, where Yuhuang Dadi was expecting their arrival.

It seemed that the ox would definitely win the race and become the leader of the Zodiac Animals. The little rat, however, did not despair. She tried to figure out a way to beat her big competitor.

"Yes, I'll use my brain so that I can use his strength!" the rat almost thought aloud, excited by her brilliant idea. When the ox approached the bank of the river, the waiting rat asked him to carry her on his neck so that she could cheer him up with her songs. Very tired, the ox found it hard to reject such a friendly and timely offer. Crossing the river, they arrived at the Heavenly Palace. Before the ox could step through the gate, the little rodent jumped to the ground and scampered toward the Jade Emperor. The ox had to take second place in the order of the Zodiac.

In the wake of the rat and ox came the tiger, the rabbit, the dragon, the snake, the horse, the sheep, the monkey, and the dog. The clumsy boar brought up the rear and became the last of the twelve Zodiac Animals.

The softhearted ox soon forgave the little rat's trickery, but the cat would never pardon the rat for her negligence, if not betrayal. He has since become her natural enemy and unleashes his vengeance whenever he gets a chance.

THE ORIGIN OF THE *DUANWU* FESTIVAL

The Duanwu *Festival, also known as the Dragon Boat or Double Fifth Festivals, falls on every fifth day of the fifth Chinese lunar month. It is popularly believed to commemorate Qu Yuan (339 B.C.–277 B.C.), a great poet of the state of Chu during the Warring States Period (403 B.C.–221 B.C.) in Chinese history. The people of Chu loved him for his uprightness and patriotism, while his peer courtiers discriminated against him for his different political opinions. As a result, he went into exile. In May 278 B.C., Chu fell into the hands of the expanding state of Qin—a tragedy that he had predicted and tried to prevent. In despair over the corruption and inability of the Chu Court, he drowned himself in the Miluo River on the fifth day of the fifth lunar month, a month after the fall of his beloved state.*

According to popular Southern Chinese folklore, after Qu Yuan's death, people threw all kinds of food into the river to feed the fish that would otherwise nibble at Qu Yuan's body. However, whatever they threw into the water would float onto the surface. Finally, at the suggestion of Qu Yuan's spirit, they made what they called zongzi, *rice dumplings wrapped in bamboo leaves, and cast them into the river from their boats. Because* zongzi *were very heavy, they sank without difficulty. From this comes the tradition of the* Duanwu *Festival, characterized by eating* zongzi *and racing boats.*

However, in Geng Village at the outskirts of Gaocheng City, Hebei Province, in North China, a different version of the story was found. As you will see, it has nothing to do with history and politics.

A long, long time ago, a man named Qu Yuan lived in the Yellow River basin. He was the first man to discover firestones, which were used to start a fire as matches do today. Firestones were available only on *Xishan* (East Mountain) at the upper fork of the Yellow River in Shannxi Province. So that everyone could have firestones, Qu Yuan decided to go to *Xishan* to get them. Because there were no other means of transportation, he went there on foot. The Yellow River rushed down above *Xishan* and formed a waterfall. Firestones existed on the side of the mountain behind the falls. So Qu Yuan had to build a boat and steer it against the torrent to reach the firestones. He also made a pickaxe to pick firestones from the mountain. While he picked, the firestones kept dropping into the boat, where he stood steadfastly.

Thinking that it would take him twelve years to make a round trip, Qu Yuan wanted to get as many firestones as the boat could carry. Pick after pick, he worked incessantly. While he was picking the last batch of firestones, he used so much force that his pickaxe got caught in a crevice in the cliff. When he tried to yank the pickaxe out of the crevice, he was pulled out of the boat where he had been standing, and the violent current of the Yellow River washed the boat downstream.

Qu Yuan managed to settle himself at the foot of the mountain behind the waterfall. Now that his boat was gone, he had to resign himself to a lonely life trying to survive on the mountain. He built himself a hut and searched for whatever food he could find. He knew that when people found out that he was missing, they would send another person to get the firestones. He figured that it would be about twelve years before he would get a chance to return to his homeland and his people.

Soon Qu Yuan found that he was not alone on the mountain; a female savage lived in a cave there. Eventually the savage discovered Qu Yuan. When she saw him, she felt drawn to his handsomeness. She took him to her cave and made him her husband, against his will. Every morning she would place a large piece of stone at the entrance of the cave before she went out to search for food. She did not want Qu Yuan to escape. She made sure that the stone was heavy enough so that Qu Yuan could not move it.

The next year, they had a son. Qu Yuan named him Hairui. Every day Qu Yuan was forced to stay with his son in the cave while his savage wife went out for food. When Hairui was seven, Qu Yuan thought that he was old enough to help. Each day, while the boy's savage mother was away, he trained his son to move the stone. Then they tried to move the stone together. They tried and tried. Finally, on the eleventh birthday of Hairui, they were able to move the stone. With extraordinary effort, they pushed the stone out inch by inch until it opened enough for them to squeeze out of the cave, one after the other. Once they were out, it took a while for Qu Yuan and his son to adapt to the sunlight. Fearing that the female savage would come back at any time, they ran toward the Yellow River in the hope of finding the person picking firestones. When they reached the foot of Xishan at the waterfall, they were relieved to see a boat loaded with firestones. Before it departed, they jumped onto it and left with the boatman.

When the female savage came back and found the cave empty, she looked everywhere for her husband and son. She rushed to the Yellow River, but her husband and son were already a mile or so downstream. She called dolefully at the top of her voice, but to no avail. She was so grieved and depressed that she jumped into the river and drowned herself, to the great remorse of Qu Yuan and his young son, Hairui.

When Qu Yuan died, the orphaned grown-up Hairui began to miss his mother, savage as she had been. After all, she had brought him into this world. Hairui decided to commemorate his mother on the day of her death each year, namely, the fifth day of the fifth Chinese lunar month. He would go to the Yellow River and throw all kinds of food into it, hoping that his mother's spirit would be able to enjoy it. To his dismay, however, whatever food he cast into the river would float to the surface and be swept away by the current. He tried to find a way to keep the food from resurfacing. He tried and tried. Finally, he found a solution: he wrapped glutinous rice, dates, and sugar with reed leaves and made them into four-angled dumplings. He called the weighty food *zongzi*. He boiled them until they were well done. From a boat, he threw them into the Yellow River. To his satisfaction, all the *zongzi* sank into the water. The practice soon spread everywhere and has since become the tradition of *Duanwu* Festival, of which the eating of *zongzi* and the racing of boats are the most prominent features.

THE ORIGIN OF THE MID-AUTUMN FESTIVAL

For some reason, the Han Chinese have a stronger emotional attachment to the moon than to the sun. A full moon, comparable to completeness and, therefore, family reunion, tends to make Chinese travelers homesick. As Su Shi, a famous ci poet of the Song Dynasty, wrote, "May we live forever so that we can share the beauty of chanjuan though a thousand li apart." Chanjuan (pretty woman) referred to the Moon Goddess called Chang'e, whose tale appears below.

A long, long time ago, there were altogether ten suns, each riding on the back of a black raven. They took turns shedding light on the earth. When one was away on duty, the rest would perch on a big, tall tree called *fusang*. One day, however, they made a whimsical decision to appear together in the sky. Terrible disasters happened in consequence: seas sizzled, mountains cracked, vegetation withered, and humans and other living creatures died in droves.

Humans prayed to Yuhuang Dadi (the Jade Emperor of Heaven) for help, and he sent a young god of archery named Hou Yi to shoot down the suns. Each fiery bird he shot down brought some relief to the sufferings of the earthlings. He shot and shot until one was left. As Hou Yi prepared to shoot down the last one, people asked to keep it. They said that without a sun, they would have no daylight and, therefore, no yield of crops. Hou Yi stopped. He had become a hero of the humans he had saved.

Back in heaven, Hou Yi accidentally killed a son of the Jade Emperor of Heaven. Considering what he had done to save the world, the emperor spared his life. He banished Hou Yi and his beautiful wife Chang'e to earth, where they were to live a life of mortality like the humans. The humans welcomed Hou Yi and Chang'e. They made Hou Yi their leader after the death of their former ruler. Hou Yi and Chang'e lived a happy life on earth with their people, but the idea of death loomed larger with each passing year.

One day, Hou Yi remembered what he had heard when in heaven about the Goddess of Life and Death, called *Xiwangmu* (the Queen Mother of the West). It was said that she had pills that gave perpetual life. Hou Yi said good-bye to Chang'e and set out for Mt. Kunlun, the residence of *Xiwangmu*. Crossing big rivers and climbing over high mountains, Hou Yi finally arrived at Mt. Kunlun. With the tail of a leopard and teeth of a tiger, the goddess was resting with her maidservants on a terrace at the top of the mountain. Hou Yi's arrival did not surprise her; she seemed to have anticipated his coming. She told him that she admired him for his heroic deed and would grant his request. When Hou Yi asked her for pills of immortality, she gave him two, one for him and the other for his wife Chang'e. Hou Yi was very grateful. He thanked the Queen Mother of the West and returned to his wife.

Traditionally, Chinese liked to pick a *jiri* (a lucky day) for doing something important in their lives. Hou Yi and Chang'e decided to take the pills of immortality in about a month, on the fifteenth day of the eighth moon.

Hou Yi liked hunting. Each time before he left, he would ask Chang'e to keep her eyes on the pills. Chang'e would hide them in her jewelry box. Pengmeng, a cunning lieutenant who had gained Hou Yi's trust, learned their secret by eavesdropping. A few days before their lucky day, Hou Yi went hunting again. Before he left, Hou Yi promised his wife that he would not go too far and be back home in time. All his attendants went on the hunting trip with him except Pengmeng. He asked to stay behind on the pretense that he was sick. In fact, he was going to steal the pills of immortality from Chang'e.

The night before the lucky day when Hou Yi would return, Pengmeng stole into Chang'e's bedroom. As he was fumbling around, he accidentally knocked against a vase and sent it crashing to the ground. The noise awakened Chang'e from her sleep. She was startled to see Pengmeng in her chamber. She wanted to shout, but Pengmeng shushed her. He told her that he was not there to attack her; he just wanted a pill of immortality, enough to make him live forever. Chang'e knew that was the pill for her husband, whom she loved so much. She could not bear the thought of his dying and her living, possibly, together with this scoundrel, against her will.

Realizing that she was no match for Pengmeng, Chang'e panicked. At a loss for what to do, she put the pills into her mouth to protect them. What happened next was totally out of her control. In a struggle with Pengmeng, the pills slipped down her throat. Two pills for one person proved to be too much of a dose. All of a sudden, Chang'e felt weightless. She flew off the ground, out of the window, and into the air. As Chang'e soared higher and higher, her fear gradually gave way to grief. She knew there was no turning back and that she would never have a chance to see her husband: in addition to the distance between them, her husband would eventually die as a mortal.

Chang'e did not want to return to where she and her husband had come from, namely, the Heavenly Palace. She did not know how to explain to her fellow celestial beings what had happened. Therefore she steered her course away from it and veered toward the moon, which she thought was unpopulated. However, the moon was not absolutely desolate. When she landed there, much to her surprise Chang'e was greeted by a middle-aged man named Wu Gang, a toad, and a rabbit. It was to some extent a relief as well. At least she would not be lonely.

Courtsey of Baihua Literature and Art Publishing House.

Chang'e learned from Wu Gang that he had been a woodcutter on earth. Unhappy with his poor life, he had dreamed of becoming an immortal. He left home for a Taoist temple to look for the pills of immortality, leaving his wife and two children behind. During his absence, King Yan's son took his wife as a concubine. When Wu Gang came back, he killed the king's son. The king was so angry that he had Wu Gang sent to the moon to live a life of perpetual torture: He had to cut a sweet-scented osmanthus tree that would heal itself and never fall. After the death of his wife, his two sons came to keep him company. One turned into the toad and the other the rabbit. The rabbit soon became Chang'e's pet.

On the evening of the fifteenth day of the eighth month, the lucky day that Hou Yi and Chang'e had picked to take the pills of immortality, Hou Yi came home. He was horrified to find that both his beloved wife and the pills were gone. "Oh, Jade Emperor of Heaven!" Hou Yi looked into the sky and pleaded, "Tell me where my wife is and what she has done to me." When he caught sight of the big, full moon, he found the answer: the shadow on the surface of the moon bore a resemblance to his wife.

"How could she betray me? How could she take both the pills herself?" He wanted to ask Pengmeng what had happened but could not find him. Frustrated, Hou Yi ordered several guards to look for Pengmeng. They caught him fleeing. When Hou Yi learned what had happened to Chang'e, he put Pengmeng to death. The confirmation that the shadow on the moon was indeed his faithful wife gave Hou Yi great solace. He laid a table outside the house and spread on it all the fruits and snacks that Chang'e had favored. He wished that his beloved wife could see them and know that he was still deeply in love with her.

Hou Yi's people ever since have followed the same practice every year, and it has become a tradition known as *zhongqiujie* (the Mid-Autumn Festival). This traditional festival is second only to the Chinese New Year in importance. Some of the snacks gradually took the shape of the full moon and came to be called *yuebing* (moon cake). There is a recipe in Part 2 that shows how to make *yuebing*.

THE ORIGIN OF KITCHEN GOD AND THE *JIZAO* FESTIVAL

China has a long history of worshipping fire. After zao *(kitchen stove) was invented, the belief in* Zao Wangye *(Kitchen God) began. Kitchen God is supposed to watch the household where he resides and report its deeds or misdeeds to* Yuhuang Dadi *(Jade Emperor of Heaven) on the day of the* Jizao *Festival, namely, the twenty-third of the twelfth lunar month, a week before the eve of the Chinese New Year. Around the* Jizao *Festival, people would try to bribe Kitchen God with maltose candy so that, with his sweetened mouth, he would put in a good word for them to Jade Emperor. There are different versions of the Kitchen God story. The following story was collected from a villager in Hebei, China.*

Kitchen God was originally a member of a rich family. His name was Zhang Kui. He was a good-for-nothing. Gambling was the only thing he could do. He often gambled with Uncle Wudao, who later became a god in charge of the treasury of the King of the Netherworld.

Zhang Kui's first wife, Guo Dingxiang, tried to stop him from gambling, and for that reason he divorced her. Soon he went bankrupt. To pay his debt of honor, he sold his second wife, Liu Haitang.

Without any means of living, Zhang Kui went begging. One day he wandered into the household to which he had sold his wife, Liu Haitang. She worked in the household's kitchen. The sight of her bedraggled ex-husband aroused Liu Haitang's compassion. After all, they had been husband and wife for more than a decade. She let Zhang Kui into the mansion and hid him in the kitchen where she worked.

"He must have gone hungry for a long time," thought Liu Haitang. So, every day she cooked some extra food and secretly gave it to Zhang Kui after everyone else was fed. For days she provided for Zhang Kui in the kitchen without mentioning a word about him to the rest of the household. She did not want them to find out that she was keeping a beggar without their knowledge and consent. Besides, it would be difficult to explain what had been going on between her and her ex-husband.

One day Liu Haitang wanted to give her ex-husband a treat. She fixed him a chicken. However, before it was fully cooked, the anxious and greedy Zhang Kui fished it out of the steaming pot and ate it. He was in such a hurry that he did not take care to debone the bird. As a result, a wishbone became stuck in his throat. He could neither swallow it nor spit it out. Liu Haitang panicked. In a short time, Zhang Kui stopped breathing, his face as purple as an eggplant. Liu Haitang had more to fear than the sight of Zhang Kui's face. She was afraid to imagine how the master of the house would react when he saw a dead beggar with her in the kitchen. "What am I going to tell him?" She tried all possible explanations, but none seemed satisfactory.

Finally she made a decision: She had to make the body disappear before anyone in the household knew what had happened in the kitchen. A desperate person usually shows extraordinary resourcefulness in an emergency, and this was true of Liu Haitang. She knew that there was enough space in the hearth of the *zao* to hide Zhang Kui's body. So she managed to yank the big pot off the *zao* and place Zhang Kui in the hearth. Then she covered the body with a large amount of fuel ash.

After she "buried" Zhang Kui in this unconventional manner, sorrow seized her. She blamed herself for his death. She would never have thought that she would kill her ex-husband by trying to save him from starvation. She wanted to commemorate him with a customary ritual. She burned some incense and joss paper (money for the dead) in front of the *zao*. While she was doing so, the master of the house happened to come to inspect the kitchen.

"What are you doing?" the bewildered patriarch asked.

"I was burning incense and paper to honor the kitchen stove so that it will guarantee that the household will always have enough to eat!" answered the quick-witted Liu Haitang.

The unsuspecting patriarch was very satisfied with the answer and appreciated what Liu Haitang was doing for the family. He said, "I like your idea. Why can't we make it a yearly event? We'll burn incense and paper to honor the stove on this day every year." This started the tradition of worshipping Kitchen God. Because the day of Zhang Kui's death was on the twenty-third of the twelfth lunar month, that day has since become the *Jizao* Festival.

A traditional house museum. A *zao* in its living room connects to the *kang* (dried-mud clay brick bed) in the bedroom next door (The fence was erected by curators to deter museum visitors). On the wall and above the stove is an altar to *Zao Wangye* (Kitchen God).

Proverbial Tales

In addition to Chinese tales, Chinese proverbs also open a window onto Chinese culture. Some proverbs are summaries of prior experiences; some are excerpts from famous ancient philosophers; others are tales themselves, such as the ones retold below.

In its 4,000-year civilized history, the Chinese have generated innumerable proverbs. There can be a proverb for almost any situation. Judicious use of proverbs in Chinese writing is regarded as a sign of good education rather than pedantry or showing off one's knowledge of clichés.

Chinese proverbs can be split into *chengyu* (accepted phrases), *yanyu* (familiar sayings), *suyu* (popular sayings), and *xiehouyu* (two-part allegorical sayings). Unique to the Chinese language, *xiehouyu* proverbs are vivid with images and dramatic results. However, as many of them achieve dramatic results by using puns, or by playing on words with similar pronunciations but different meanings, they are barely translatable. Guess what this *xiehouyu* proverb means: "Da po shaguo: wen dao di"? Translated literally, it means, "When a clay pot is broken, the crack would run from its top to the bottom." However, you cannot take it literally. It is actually either a criticism of or compliment to someone who is very inquisitive. The key is the last part of the proverb "wen dao di ("a crack runs from top to bottom") . It is a pun, the sound of which also carries the meaning of "ask questions in order to know the top and bottom of something." The connotation is what the proverb really means. The proverbs collected in appendix A include *xiehouyu* only when they are explainable by themselves.

打破沙锅璺到底

Chinese characters for the *xiehouyu* "Da po shaguo: wen dao di."

A STEED LOST IS MORE HORSES GAINED

A long time ago, China had a hostile neighbor in the north known as the Huns, or Xiongnus. They constantly harassed the Chinese at the borders and threatened an all-out invasion. The Chinese army had to fight a protracted war against them. Because most of the nomadic Hun troops were cavalrymen, the Chinese army had to fight them on horseback as well. Therefore, breeding warhorses became a very profitable business on the frontier.

There was a veteran breeder whose horses were in great demand. One wintry morning, his son found that a prized steed was missing from the stable. He tracked its hoofprints in the snow to the border. Apparently the horse had fled to the Huns. The breeder's son had to give up the chase. When he got back home, he found the place filled with neighbors; all had come to comfort his father for the loss of the prized horse. To the surprise of the son and the neighbors, the veteran horse breeder, puffing smoke from a tobacco pipe, seemed completely undisturbed, as if nothing had happened.

"Aren't you worried about your horse? Losing such a good steed must have cost you dearly," one of the neighbors finally could not help asking.

"Well," blowing a puff of smoke, the horse breeder began slowly, "I don't see how the missing horse is a loss."

"Why?" still another neighbor asked, "It's worth a lot of money!"

"Because you never know what will happen in the future. The lost horse may bring me good luck some day," said the old breeder behind a thin veil of smoke. Seeing no need to comfort him, the neighbors left, amused by his blind optimism.

Amazingly, a few months later, not only did the missing horse return, but it also brought along an equally good steed from the other side of the border. Hearing the good news, neighbors came over to congratulate the horse breeder on his windfall. However, they were puzzled to find the old man as unruffled as usual.

"You are really lucky!" exclaimed the neighbors. "You've made a good fortune without even lifting a finger." Frowning, the old horse breeder said flatly, "Well, instead of good fortune, this free horse may bring us bad luck."

His neighbors departed, thinking the veteran horse breeder was crazy. Soon, however, they changed their minds. A few days later, while the breeder's son was trying out the horse that had come from the Huns, the beast bucked him off and he broke his leg.

When the neighbors showed their concern for his son's injury, the father responded indifferently, "Thank you for your concern, but my son's broken legs could be a blessing in disguise."

"He must be out of his mind," one of the neighbors said as they stepped out of his house.

"The mishap must have proved too much for him to bear!" another offered as a reason for his odd attitude.

A few days later, the Huns launched an all-out attack across the border. All the young people had to join the resistance army to fight the aggressors. The war was so brutal that nine out of ten of the young people drafted were either wounded or killed. The horse breeder's son, however, escaped the conscription due to his broken leg and consequently survived the war intact.

This story gave rise to the proverb saiweng-shima *(an old man on a frontier lost his horse). It means "An apparent loss may be a blessing in disguise."*

A PROFESSED DRAGON LOVER

Long ago, a scholar known as Lord Ye proclaimed that he loved dragons. Not only did he talk about his fondness for dragons, but he also put his affection into practice, and in a big way. He had his clothes embroidered with dragons, his ornaments carved with dragons, and even the shield of his favorite sword engraved with dragons. Dragon patterns were present everywhere in his house—on the beams, the columns, the walls, the doors, the windows, the curtains, and the bedding. Every piece of his furniture was also a lavish show of dragon art. He read nothing but stories about dragons, wrote nothing but dragon tales, and painted nothing but dragons.

Eventually a heavenly dragon heard of Lord Ye's predilection for its kind. Very touched, the dragon decided to pay Lord Ye a visit to express its appreciation and make friends with him. One sunny afternoon, Lord Ye was painting a dragon in his dragon-adorned study when the bright daylight suddenly dimmed, as if a colossal, black veil had fallen from nowhere and shrouded the entire world. Gusts of wind brought wave after wave of dark clouds, which, churning and swelling, began to permeate the air. Then dazzling streaks of lightning temporarily tore the dark veil open, and from the zigzagging crevasse in the clouds came a crashing thunderbolt, followed closely by a long-drawn-out rumbling.

Before Lord Ye had a chance to shut the windows, which were flapping and banging in the wind, whooshing out from behind the dark clouds came a gigantic dragon, its eyes shining like daggers on its mammoth, long-antlered head, brandishing eaglelike claws from its wriggling, scaly, serpentine body. Opening its camel-like, blood-red, fanged mouth in an attempt to smile, the dragon tried to explain its surprise appearance. However, it could not find Lord Ye, whom it had spotted just a few seconds before. It turned out that the sight of the real dragon had frightened Lord Ye so much that he collapsed and was now lying unconscious beneath his desk.

This story gave rise to the proverb yegong-haolong *(Lord Ye claimed to be fond of dragons). It is a derisive remark about those who profess to love something that they actually fear.*

NUMBER IS SECURITY

In the state of Qi, one of the ancient kingdoms of China, there was an idler known as Mr. Nanguo. One day, as Mr. Nanguo was loafing around, he heard that the emperor, who was a fan of *yu* (a traditional Chinese musical instrument) and loved to listen to it played in chorus, was hiring *yu* players. The emperor was going to form a band of 300 players and pay handsomely for their performances.

Yu has a dozen bamboo pipes lying side by side on top of a bowl-like copper base. To produce a sound, a player must inhale and exhale from a mouthpiece on the base. To play a tune, the player must cover and uncover the holes on the pipes with his fingers. In fact, *yu* was the only musical instrument at the time that could play different notes simultaneously. No wonder the emperor fell in love with it, so much so that he wanted to keep a band in his palace to be at his disposal at any moment. He argued, "It would be too inconvenient to call up so many musicians on short notice."

Boy playing a *sheng*, a cultural symbol of fertility homophonic to "giving birth"; a musical instrument similar to the ancient *yu*. Courtesy of Baihua Literature and Art Publishing House.

Mr. Nanguo coveted the money to be paid to the musicians, but unfortunately he was not a *yu* piper. In fact, he could not play any musical instrument. All the same, he did not want to let slip this lucrative opportunity. He tried to figure out a way to get himself into the band. After all, he was not entirely worthless; everyone knew that he was a good mimicker. When he learned that one of the interviewers was as greedy for money as he was, Mr. Nanguo bribed him into recruiting him. The little money he spent on the corrupt official was, in his opinion, merely a small fish with which he had baited his hook in order to catch a larger fish, namely, a position in the band.

Soon the band took shape and prepared for its debut performance. Three hundred *yu* musicians sat in a square formation in the spacious court. Mr. Nanguo managed to pick a position in a corner at the back. He held a *yu* to his mouth and mimicked every movement of the other pipers as they played. He wagged his head left and right when they did theirs; he rocked his upper body back and forth the same way they swayed. Even though he did not produce a single note, the pipers around him were too involved with their own performance to notice him faking. In a short time, Mr. Nanguo had made a lot of money by passing for a *yu* musician.

However, his good fortune did not last long. The next year the emperor died, and his son succeeded to the throne. The new emperor was also fond of *yu* music, but he liked the pipers to play solo. That is, he wanted the pipers to play individually in front of him. Upon hearing this, Mr. Nanguo had to flee the country, and so did the corrupt official. They knew that deceiving an emperor was a capital crime, and the new emperor would certainly have their heads chopped off for fooling his father.

This story gave birth to the proverb lanyu-chongshu *(pass oneself off as a* yu *player just to make the number). The proverb satirizes someone who holds a position without adequate training.*

FORGOT HOW TO WALK BACK HOME

Long ago there lived a youth in Shouling, a town in the state of Yan. He hated the way he walked. In fact, he found that no one in his state had an acceptable gait. The youth of Shouling tried a different way of walking each day despite his neighbors' laughter. Even his wife would jeer at him, calling him a fool. Nonetheless, he persisted in the experiment.

One day a friend who had been to the state of Zhao told him that people in that state carried themselves in the most graceful manner he had ever seen. At this, the youth of Shouling made up his mind to visit the state of Zhao and learn from its residents how they took their steps. The next morning he bade farewell to his family and set out for Handan, the capital of the state of Zhao.

After a month's travel, the youth of Shouling finally arrived in Handan. Sure enough, everyone he saw walked elegantly. He followed them and observed their movement. However, his strange behavior began to bring him trouble. On one occasion, a young woman mistook him for a stalker. Only after much apology and explanation did he calm the woman down and prevent her from complaining to the authorities. This incident did not deter the youth from tagging along behind the pedestrians of Handan. He set his heart on acquiring the walking style of the Zhao people. In order to prevent any more trouble, he distanced himself from the people he followed. This, however, aroused the suspicion of an elderly man, who thought him as a spy. The elderly man hastened to get an ally and ambushed the youth. The commotion drew a big crowd. When the youth of Shaoling told them what he was doing, they all bent over with laughter. They had never heard such absurdity in their whole lives.

"What?" one of them asked with amazement, "You have come all the way just to see how we walk?"

"I heard that you all walked gracefully. Now that I am here, I find it to be true. I just want to learn how you pace the street, and I really mean no harm to you," the youth of Shaoling said in one breath.

The crowd guffawed, and one of them finally stopped laughing and said, "We actually like the way you walk." At this, the youth of Shaoling merely shook his head and went away, thinking that the people of Handan did not appreciate what they had.

Day after day, month after month, the youth of Shouling practiced walking like the people of Handan, but he could not get it. Racking his brains, he tried to figure out why. Finally, he realized that he still had the legacy of his own way of walking!

"I must forget my way of walking before I can learn a new one," he vowed.

A month passed and still he did not know how to walk like the people of Handan. As he was running out of traveling money, he had to return to his hometown. The problem now was that he did not know how to walk at all, for not only had he failed to learn how the people of Zhao walked, he had also forgotten his original way of walking. Consequently he had to crawl back to his hometown in the state of Yan, and he became a laughingstock to the people in both the states of Zhao and Yan.

This story gave birth to the proverb handan-xuebu *(learning how residents of Handan walk). It derides those who imitate others slavishly and thus lose their own individuality.*

WAITING FOR A RABBIT TO BUMP INTO A TREE

Long ago there was a farmer in the state of Song. Toiling on a few acres of land, he lived a modest life. He often dreamed of a windfall that could spare him the backbreaking labor.

One day he was tilling the fields when, all of a sudden, a rabbit darted by. The rabbit was in a great hurry as if it were fleeing from a beast of prey. Before the farmer could see where the rabbit was going, the animal had accidentally bumped into the trunk of a big tree growing in the corner of the farmer's fields and killed itself, blood oozing from a wound in its head. The farmer had not tasted any meat for months. He had never imagined that a fat rabbit would be so readily available.

The next day, when he returned to his farmland, instead of farming, he settled himself down beneath the big tree and waited. He was expecting another rabbit to come and slam into it. Then he would have another supply of meat without making any effort. Day after day and month after month, he waited and waited, until the weeds grew even taller than the sparsely sprawling crops. Still not a single rabbit showed up in his fields.

"How can you expect an incident that happens once in a million years to take place again?" a villager commented as he tried to persuade the farmer to give up his useless watching.

"How do you know that it won't happen?" retorted the stubborn, silly farmer.

Every day he went to his farmland and did nothing but wait for a rabbit to kill itself by running into the tree trunk. Soon winter set in. The farmer finally understood that an accident was an accident, and he should not bet his livelihood on it. Unfortunately this revelation came too late; he did not harvest a single grain that season. He really had no idea how to live during the winter without food and straws of wheat and stalks of corn to use as fuel.

This story gave rise to the proverb shouzhu-daitu *(waiting beneath a tree for a rabbit to bump into it). It is a lesson for those who do not work hard but rely on the repetition of unlikely events.*

FISHING FOR A SWORD DROPPED INTO A RIVER FROM A MOVING BOAT

Long ago, a man from the state of Chu dropped his sword into a river while he was traveling on a ferry. Immediately he asked a fellow traveler for a knife and began to carve the side of the boat where his sword had fallen into the water.

"Hey there, what are you doing to my boat?" yelled the boatman, half angry and half bewildered. The strange behavior of the man of Chu also baffled the rest of the people on the ferry.

"I am making a mark to remind me of where I dropped my sword," the man of Chu answered, pointing to the cut he had just made on the side of the boat. At this, the others looked at one another, dumfounded. Finally they seemed to have figured out the reason for his weird conduct.

"The loss of that priceless sword of his must have driven him crazy!" one of his fellow travelers whispered.

"He may be doing it just for fun—a way to comfort himself after his loss," speculated another in a hushed voice.

Still another came up to the man of Chu and, patting him on the shoulder, said with a broad smile, "As the old saying goes, 'you can't get a new thing if you don't lose the old one.'" He was apparently trying to cheer him up with a proverb that sounded logical.

The man of Chu wondered what his fellow travelers were doing, laughing secretly at their foolishness. When the boat approached the riverbank, the man of Chu climbed overboard on the side where he had left the mark, and jumped into the knee-deep water. The bemused fellow travelers on the boat and people gathering on the bank held their breath and watched him fumbling in the water with his extended arms.

"What the world is he doing?" people in the crowd queried one another. Finally, one of them could not contain his curiosity and shouted out, "What are you doing there in the water?"

"I am fishing for my sword," answered the man of Chu in a high-pitched voice.

"But how?" one of his fellow travelers asked, as he had seen the sword dropped while they were in the middle of the river a couple of miles away.

"Don't you see the mark I cut? This is where my sword slipped into the water. Give me a second and I will find it."

At this, everyone on the boat burst into laughter, which instantaneously spread to the spectators on the bank. A scholarly looking man on the ferry asked, "Don't you know that your sword is still where you dropped it, far away from here in the middle of this river? How are you going to find your sword when the boat has moved so far from the location where you dropped it?"

This story gave birth to the proverb kezhou-qiujian *(mark a boat to get the sword dropped into the river). It is a spoof on those who take action without regard to changes in circumstances.*

NO SYCEE BURIED HERE BUT THREE HUNDRED *LIANG*

Long, long ago, there lived in a village a bachelor named Zhang San. Orphaned at an early age, he did not have much except for the rickety house his parents left him. He worked hard and lived a thrifty life. Years later, he had finally scraped up 300 *liang* of sycee, which are lumps of pure silver used as money in ancient China. It was a lot of money at that time, particularly for Zhang San, who had never owned a single silver nugget in his life. He had big plans for spending the money. First and foremost, he would find himself a wife. He was in his early thirties, while other men in his village had married in their late teens or early twenties. He wanted to have a lot of children and share the wealth with them. The more he thought of the happy prospect lying ahead of him, the happier he became. Merrily he went to sleep . . . .

In his dream he found himself married with the prettiest girl in his neighborhood, whom he had coveted all along. He wanted to show her the money he had accumulated all these years, but wherever he looked, he could not find it! His panic was beyond words . . . . When he opened his eyes, sweating all over, he realized that it had been a nightmare. To his great relief, the box of silver was still sitting securely on the table at his bedside.

Nevertheless, his joy soon gave way to anxiety. "The dream must be a warning," the superstitious Zhang San thought. "I have to find a safe place for the silver. I can't let thieves or robbers take my hard-earned money away from me." For days he tried to figure out where to hide the money. He looked everywhere in his house but could not find a safe hiding place. He thought of a hundred options for stowing away the money but gave them all up in the end because none seemed safe enough. He began to lose his appetite and was unable to sleep. Whenever he closed his eyes, the same nightmare would recur.

Finally he decided to bury the silver money in the ground at the back of his house, thinking that no thieves would ever imagine that his money was outside his house! He would have patted himself on the back if he could have for coming up with such a brilliant idea.

Deep in the night, Zhang San sneaked out to the backyard and began digging quietly in the ground close to his house. He did not want his neighbors to know what he was doing, but digging a hole without making noise was a great challenge. Just before dawn, Zhang San finally accomplished the task. He buried the box of silver and covered the hole carefully so that no one would be able to find a trace.

He was about to leave the site when fear seized him: "What if I forgot where I buried my money? That would be as bad as if someone took it!" As he was trying to figure out a solution, gazing indifferently at the dark shades on the moon, he remembered that they were marks of a palace where a fairy was residing. A mark! Yes, making a mark! "Wait a minute," he said to himself, almost aloud, "If I mark where I buried the money, people will know it." He mulled over the idea of doing something on the marking to warn potential thieves.

He went back to his house, found a pen and a piece of paper, and wrote: "No silver buried here but 300 *liang*!" He liked the poster because, he thought, it would serve dual purposes: telling potential thieves to go elsewhere for their fortune while at the same time reminding him of the location and amount of the buried money. Zhang San was proud of this, the best idea he had ever had. After posting the warning at the location where he had buried his money, Zhang San finally heaved a sigh of relief. He wanted to recover the sleep he had lost ever since he got the money.

Zhang San had a neighbor called Wang Er, who loved money as much as Zhang San, but hated to work or practice frugality. Every day he lounged or loitered, dreaming of a windfall. When he saw Zhang San's poster in the early morning, his eyes lit up! He rejoiced at his good luck and laughed at Zhang San's stupidity. Seeing that there was no one around, he quickly and quietly dug open the hole, took the silver with him, and . . . .

Zhang San had a good sleep and got up later than usual. As soon as he awoke, he remembered his money and got up to inspect the location where he had buried it. To his relief, the sign was still there. When he took a closer look, however, he did not know whether to cry or laugh. The sign read, "Your neighbor Wang Er did not steal the 300 *liang* of sycee!"

This story gave rise to the proverb ci di wu yin sanbai liang *(no sycee buried here but three hundred* liang*). It describes a guilty person who gives himself away by consciously protesting his innocence.*

THE INVINCIBLE SPEAR VERSUS THE IMPENETRABLE SHIELD

In the state of Chu, a weapon monger was hawking a spear and a shield in a market. Brandishing the spear, he called out, "There, everybody! Take a close look at this spear. Made of a special alloy, it is as sharp as can be. I am not bragging: It is so sharp that it can penetrate any shield, be it metal, rattan, or leather!"

People in the market began to gather around him, curious to see the all-conquering spear. Encouraged by his marketing stunt, the monger began to promote his shield in the same manner. He held it above his head and flaunted it at the growing crowd. "Look at this shield," he hollered proudly. "It is made of the best leather in the world. It is so tough that nothing can ever pierce it!" Throngs of onlookers were vying for a better look at the invulnerable shield, when someone in the crowd shouted, "Hey, you just said you had a spear that could pierce anything in the world, and now you told us that this shield could resist any penetration. What do you mean?"

"I mean they are both good weapons," the monger answered without thinking.

"Well, try your spear on your shield and see what happens!" the same person in the crowd challenged. The crowd also echoed his demand with a bellow. At this, the weapon monger became speechless. Blushing with shame, he fled the jeering crowd in the market, dragging his spear and shield.

This story gave rise to the proverb: zixiang-maodun *(one's spear versus one's own shield). It is used to criticize one who contradicts himself during an argument. The proverb also gaves birth to the word* maodun *(contradiction), which literally means "a spear and a shield."*

A SMILE WORTH A THOUSAND OUNCES OF GOLD

Many monarchs in Chinese history let their states perish because of their immoral lifestyle. However, in a male-dominated society, women usually took the blame for corrupting the monarchs, as is evident in the following proverbial story.

One day in 1600 B.C., two dragons landed in the state of Zhou and drooled on the floor of the royal court. Fortunetellers told the King of Zhou that the dragons' saliva was a good omen. The king ordered the dragon's saliva to be collected and stored in a treasure box.

King Li of Zhou succeeded to the throne and inherited the treasure box. Overwhelmed by curiosity, King Li opened the box. As he held the box, he accidentally jerked it and spilled the dragon's saliva. Instantly the sticky fluid that dropped to the floor turned into a black turtle, crawling into the king's chamber. One of the king's maids of honor spotted the turtle and consequently became mysteriously pregnant. She did not give birth until forty years later. It was a chubby girl. However, when the new king, Xuan, learned about the newborn's background, he ordered the mother to be thrown into jail and the baby girl cast into a river, for he thought of them as demons. Whoever was given the task of throwing away the baby girl must have taken pity on her, for when a peddler of bows and arrows happened to stop to drink at the lower fork of the river, he found the baby floating in a small wooden tub. He picked her up and adopted her. Too poor to raise her, he later gave her up to a wealthy family named Bao. The new parents named her Bao Si and brought her up. When she was sixteen, Bao Si was already an extremely beautiful young woman.

About 782 B.C., King Xuan died, and his son succeeded to the throne as King You. The new king loved to be with his concubines so much that for three months he refused to hold his court. His ministers were deeply worried about his neglect of state affairs. A minister named Bao Xiang tried to admonish him, but the corrupt king put him in jail. In order to rescue Bao Xiang, his son purchased Bao Si from her adoptive parents and traded her for his father's freedom.

Bao Si became King You's favorite concubine and the focus of his attention. However, King You soon found that the beauty had a shortcoming: she had a poker face. When he asked if there was anything wrong with her, she would always say, "I'm fine. I was born quiet." King You would not settle with a beauty who did not smile. He believed that if she did, she would be even more attractive. Determined to see her look happy, King You announced that whoever could make Bao Si smile would receive a reward of a thousand ounces of gold. Responses were overwhelming. People flooded the capital, bringing with them all kinds of tricks and jokes. None, however, was able to change Bao Si's gloomy countenance.

Guo Shifu, a flattering minister, came up with an idea that appalled the entire court. He suggested activating the beacon towers on top of Mt. Black Stallion. The beacon towers were normally used to summon troops from vassal states to the king's rescue when they saw the smoke from the signal fires. They were a military communication system, enabling troops in the far distance to know that the king was in imminent danger. Therefore, lighting the beacons was a serious business, but the desperate king cared for nothing but a smile from Bao Si.

When the troops found out that it was a joke, they were at a loss, wondering whether the king's practical joke was funny or annoying. Watching the contorted faces of the officers and soldiers, Bao Si broke into a smile. The troops left, frustrated and resentful. Nevertheless, King You was exceedingly happy that Bao Si had smiled at long last. He rewarded the flattering minister Guo Shifu with the gold, as he had promised.

King You liked Bao Si so much that the following year, he made her the queen, replacing his wife Shen. He also disowned his eldest son Yi Jiu and made Bao Si's newborn Bo Fu the heir to his throne. Adding insult to injury, the king also deprived the former queen's father, Lord Shen, of his rank of nobility and threatened to attack his dukedom. This was too much for Lord Shen to endure. He began to plan a preemptive strike against King You. Short of military men, Lord Shen went to Quanrong, a nomadic tribe state in the north, for help. The Quanrongs had yet to be assimilated into the Chinese nation, and they readily accepted Lord Shen's invitation to invade the state of Zhou.

In 771 B.C., Lord Shen led the Quanrong army in the attack. Terrified, King You immediately ordered the beacons to be lit so that his vassal states would come to his rescue. Thinking that the king was joking again, the vassal states did not send a single soldier. Consequently, the Quanrong invaders ransacked the capital, killed both King You and his heir Bo Fu, and captured Bao Si as their trophy.

Having avenged his daughter, the dethroned Queen Shen, and himself, Lord Shen began to regret inviting the Quanrong army because they started pillaging the state as conquerors. Stealthily he sent for the vassal armies, who came and drove the Quanrongs away. Together with the vassal states, he made Yi Jiu, the eldest son of King You and Lord Shen's daughter, the new king, known in history as King Ping of Zhou. Angry at Lord Shen's betrayal, the Quanrong army began harassing the state of Zhou incessantly. King Ping had to relocate the capital of Zhou to Luo Yiang, in the east. Historically, this move marked the end of the West Zhou dynasty and the beginning of the East Zhou.

This story gave rise to the proverb qianjin-maixiao *(a smile purchased with a thousand ounces of gold). Said in a sarcastic tone, it implies that something may be unwelcome even though heavy investment of money, time, energy, or emotion has been made.*

REDUCING AN IRON ROD
TO A SEWING NEEDLE

Li Bai (A.D. 701–762), better known to Westerners as Li Bo (or Li Po), is one of China's greatest poets. More than 900 of his poems have survived. He is as respected in the Chinese-speaking world as Shakespeare is in the English-speaking world. However, when he was young, Li Bai was not very fond of going to school. He particularly disliked the books of classics and history that his teacher made him read. He thought they were difficult and boring.

One day young Li Bai managed to slip out of his classroom while his teacher was taking a nap next door. On a sunny spring day, the outside world looked fascinating and relaxing. Young Li Bai loitered here and there, and before he knew it, he had arrived at a little brook. It gurgled and giggled as if to say, "Hello, hello" to him, which made the little guilt Li Bai felt about playing truant evaporate instantly. Lighthearted and carefree, he was sauntering along the bubbling brook when he ran into an elderly woman honing a thick iron rod by the water. She was so focused on what she was doing that she did not notice the presence of Li Bai until he spoke to her.

"What are you doing, Grandma?" asked Li Bai. Like all polite Chinese children, he spoke to strangers the way he did to his own family members.

"I am making a sewing needle," answered the elderly woman, a little startled at first but quickly collecting herself at the sight of a gentle boy.

"Making a needle?" Li Bai asked in bewilderment, for he did not understand how the grandma could possibly reduce the thick iron rod to a tiny sewing needle. "Grandma, what you have in your hand is an iron rod, not a needle!" the puzzled young Li Bai pointed out.

"You are right, son," said the elderly woman. She rubbed the beads of sweat off her forehead with the back of her gnarled hand as she raised her head and looked at Li Bai's chubby face. Then she continued, her amiable smile reminding Li Bai of his own grandma, "I am honing the iron rod because I want to reduce its size and make a needle out of it."

"But since the iron rod is so thick, when do you think you can make it as small as a needle?" asked Li Bai, apparently unprepared for the grandma's surprising answer.

"It's true that the rod is big and thick, and it is very difficult to make it thinner." The elderly woman paused and said to Li Bai in a significant tone, "But I will never stop working at it. If I persist, I will get the result sooner or later." She patted Li Bai on his little shoulder and went on, "Remember this, son: As long as you work hard, you can reduce an iron rod to a sewing needle."

"I understand now, Grandma!" exclaimed Li Bai, who had a sudden revelation, "that no pains, no gains! What you said is true also with my studies. So long as I don't give up, I will be able to overcome any difficulty down the road." Li Bai said thanks to the elderly woman and hurried back to the school. He apologized to his teacher and classmates, told them about his encounter with the elderly woman, and promised to study hard every day.

This story gave birth to the proverb tiechu-chengzhen *(an iron rod can be reduced to a sewing needle). It is often used to encourage people to persevere in what they are doing. Its moral is that so long as one does not give up, one will accomplish what seems to be a "mission impossible."*

AN UNFOLDED MAP REVEALS A DAGGER

From 770 B.C. to about 475 B.C., China split into many kingdoms. Eventually, after decades of war and annexation, only the states of Qi, Chu, Yan, Han, Zhao, Wei, and Qin survived. Finally, the state of Qin emerged as the superpower. Its invincible army swept through one state after another under the command of the King of Qin, who was bent on establishing a unified country.

The King of Qin's bloody conquest sowed great hatred among the peoples of the other states. For instance, in a battle with the state of Zhao, a Qin general named Bai Qi ordered 400,000 surrendered Zhao soldiers to be buried alive. The King of Qin became a public enemy of the weaker states and the target of many assassination attempts.

The King of Yan set his mind on getting rid of this tyrant. He tried to recruit assassins from all over China. A young man from the state of Han named Jing Ke answered his call. The King of Yan was very happy to have Jing Ke and asked him to stay for some time so that they could work out a perfect plan and wait until the right moment came to make their move.

When the day came for Jing Ke to set out, the King of Yan saw him off at the Yi Shui River. They both wept, knowing clearly that this would be a suicide mission. In order for Jing Ke to win the trust of the King of Qin, Fan Yuqi, a former Qin general who had defected to the state of Yan, offered to die so that Jing Ke could bring his head as a gift to the King of Qin, who would give anything in the world to get at the traitor, dead or alive. Another gift was from the King of Yan—a map of a prefecture that he offered the King of Qin. Jing Ke knew how significant these two gifts were and vowed to accomplish his task. In the cold wind, Jing Ke bade farewell to the King of Yan and other people who came to say good-bye to him.

The King of Qin seldom received guests in his court for fear of a possible assassination. However, the traitor's head and a map of a surrendered land helped Jing Ke win the king's trust. Jing Ke stepped up close to him and offered to show him the map, folded up in a scroll. He unfolded the map inch by inch, and at the end of it there was a chilling dagger. Jing Ke had hidden it in the map so that he could bring the dagger close to the King of Qin unsuspected. Jing Ke grabbed the dagger and charged at the king. Unfortunately, he missed his target. In panic, the King of Qin did not know what to do, dodging the attack by leaping left and right. Because he had forbidden his ministers and guards to bear arms in the court lest they might assassinate him, they could only watch helplessly.

"Use your sword, Your Majesty!" reminded one of the ministers, who had just collected himself enough to think clearly. With great effort, the king drew out the long sword he had on his waist and tried to fend off Jing Ke's repeated attacks.

"Please give the order to bring in the guards!" another minister begged at the top of his voice. The King of Qin gave the order, which he had forgotten to issue in his desperate struggle with the assassin.

The guards arrived and caught Jing Ke. At last the King of Qin plunged his sword into the bosom of Jing Ke. Before dying, Jing Ke said, "I may have failed to kill you in this world, but I will keep haunting you from the other!"

For all the efforts of the other states to kill him, King of Qin survived and eventually united the country of China. He proclaimed himself *Qin Shihuang* (the First Emperor of Qin). But his House of Qin lasted only fourteen years before the Han dynasty replaced it in 206 B.C.

This story gave rise to the proverb tuqiong bishou xian *(when a map is unfolded, there appears a dagger), which means, "As events unfold, one's true intent begins to reveal itself." (If the story sounds familiar, you must have seen the Chinese movie* Hero, *which is a liberal adaptation of this story.)*

A KING WHO "EATS BITTER"

In 494 B.C., King Fu Chai of the state of Wu launched an attack against the state of Yue. He wanted to avenge himself on King Gou Jian of Yue for killing his father in a previous battle. The army of Wu took the capital of Yue and captured King Gou Jian.

King Fu Chai of Wu had an ambition to make his state the leader of its neighbors. For better publicity, he decided not to kill King Gou Jian of Yue. Instead, he chose to humiliate him by making him his horse keeper. Together with his wife and his Prime Ministers Fan Li and Wen Zhong, King Gou Jian began a life of disgrace in captivity.

In order to get free so that he could stage a comeback, King Gou Jian suffered the humiliation stoically. Pretending to be submissive, he tried every means to gain King Fu Chai's trust. When King Fu Chai was sick, he went to great lengths to take care of him, even to the point of tasting his stool every day as a means of checking his vital signs. This effectively lowered King Fu Chai's guard. After his recovery, he set King Gou Jian free, against the advice of his ministers, particularly his loyal, intelligent, outspoken Prime Minister Wu Zixu.

After his release King Gou Jian was obsessed with avenging his humiliation and restoring his state's dignity. However, the financial and military strengths of the state of Yue were no match for those of Wu. They would remain so in the near future. Prime Ministers Fan Li and Wen Zhong recommended that King Gou Jian be fully prepared before attempting to retaliate. For now, they told him, the state of Yue had to lay low while renewing its strength.

At their suggestion, King Gou Jian had the ransacked capital rebuilt, and then issued a series of new policies to prompt increases in the birth rate and agricultural production. He also rebuilt his army. As the preparation would take at least a decade, King Gou Jian feared that he might slip back into his old extravagant lifestyle, which would whittle away his will to accomplish his goal. To constantly remind himself of the hardships, he replaced his comfortable bedding with a straw mattress. He also hung a hog's gallbladder above his dinner table so that he could taste the bile before each meal. (The Chinese word for "endure hardships" is *chiku,* meaning to "eat bitterness.")

One day, King Gou Jian complained to one of his prime ministers, Wen Zhong, "How long will it take before we can avenge ourselves on King Fu Chai for what he did to us?"

"You can speed up the preparation for a counterattack if you take my advice," Wen Zhong answered.

A King Who "Eats Bitter"

"Tell me. I will do whatever you say to the letter of the word," said King Gou Jian in earnest, for he trusted Wen Zhong's loyalty and judgment.

Wen Zhong then told him seven stratagems: bribe King Fu Chai of Wu; purchase as much of his grain as possible so as to deplete his granaries; send him the best building materials to encourage him to waste his resources on large-scale construction projects; plant spies in his court; and spread rumors and slanders among his people about his faithful ministers in order to alienate them from King Fu Chai.

"And at the same time," Wen Zhong paused to take a breath, "we'll store as much grain as we can . . . ."

"Okay, that's stratagem 6, but what is the seventh stratagem?" King Gou Jian cut in before Wen Zhong could finish.

"The seventh and last stratagem is to send him some beauties so that he will become self-indulgent and less concerned about his state affairs."

King Gou Jian began to implement each of the stratagems that Wen Zhong had proposed. He commissioned Prime Ministers Wen Zhong and Fan Li to find ten beautiful women. He would have them trained and two of the best would be chosen for the mission. In training classes, the girls learned all the court etiquette, such as the manner of eating, how to walk, and the various ways of entertaining a monarch. They literally became the earliest women spies in Chinese military history. In the end, a girl named Xi Shi and her neighbor and friend Zheng Dan were selected and were sent to King Fu Chai.

When Xi Shi and Zheng Dan arrived at the imperial court of Wu, their beauty literally added brilliance to the palace's splendor and, as had been expected, enthralled King Fu Chai. Prime Minister Wu Zixu tried to warn the king against a possible conspiracy. However, his judgment muddled by his lust, King Fu Chai said, "The gift of these two beauties is a testimony of Gou Jian's gratitude for the favor I piled upon him." So saying, he took Xi Shi and Zheng Dan by their hands and retreated to his chamber. From that moment on, his ministers rarely saw him in the court. When Prime Minister Wu Zixu admonished King Fu Chai for his self-indulgence and neglect of state affairs, Xi Shi and Zheng Dan managed to turn the king against him and eventually had him executed for his "questionable loyalty."

Without Wu Zixu's wise advice, King Fu Chai's irrational behavior went unchecked, while the strength of his state diminished dramatically. However, King Fu Chai still cherished the hope of building up his state's supremacy. Encouraged by Xi Shi and Zheng Dan, he embarked on a campaign to conquer his neighbor, the state of Qi.

Wen Zhong and Fan Li, Prime Ministers of the state of Yue, came to see King Gou Jian and told him, "Your Majesty, now that the already weakened Wu has started a war against Qi, the time for revenge has come." King Gou Jian recruited Sun Wu (known to Westerners as Sun Tzu), the military strategist who had written the famed *Art of War*, and made him the commander-in-chief. Sun Wu led the Yue army in an all-out attack against the state of Wu. Together with the state of Qi, the army of Yue routed King Fu Chai's troops. King Fu Chai killed himself before King Gou Jian could get hold of him.

This story gave rise to the proverb woxin-changdan *(sleep on straw mattress and taste hog's gallbladder), which means "undergo self-imposed hardships so as to strengthen one's resolve to do something great."*

APPENDIX A: CHINESE PROVERBS

Following is a selection of Chinese proverbs, some of which are self-explanatory, so literal translation (denotation) is sufficient. The majority, however, may be difficult for readers of other cultures to understand without further explanation. Where that happens, the underlying meanings, or connotations, of the proverbs are given to complement the denotation.

Chinese: *Hao ma bu chi huitoucao*
   Denotation: A good horse never returns to feed in the stable it has left.
   Connotation: Don't look back once you have made the decision to move on.

Chinese: *Jinshang-tianhua*
   Denotation: Add flowers to a bouquet.
   Connotation: Make improvements on something that is already good, to aim at perfection.

Chinese: *Xueshang-jiashuang*
   Denotation: Add frost to snow.
   Connotation: Add insult to injury.

Chinese: *Huashe-tianzu*
   Denotation: Add legs to a painted snake as a finishing touch.
   Connotation: If it's not broken, don't fix it.

Chinese: *Huoshang-jiaoyou*
   Denotation: Pour oil on the flame.
   Connotation: Add fuel to the fire.

Chinese: *Jiang shi lao de la*
   Denotation: Aged ginger is more pungent.
   Connotation: Older people are more experienced or cunning.

Chinese: *Qian li zhi di, kui yu yixue*
   Denotation: A thousand-mile dam may collapse due to an ant.

   Connotation: Overlook a small problem, and you will have big trouble.

Chinese: *Kaijuan-youyi*
   Denotation: Any book you open will benefit your mind.

Chinese: *Yu bang xiang zheng, yuweng de li*
   Denotation: When a snipe and a clam are locked in a fight, a fisherman catches them both.
   Connotation: Two parties locked in a dispute may fall victim to a third party.

Chinese: *Yu ren fangbian, ziji fangbian*
   Denotation: Giving convenience to others is to give it to yourself.

Chinese: *Linke-juejing*
   Denotation: Dig a well only when you feel thirsty.
   Connotation: Don't wait until it is too late.

Chinese: *Shu zhong zi you huang jin wu*
   Denotation: A book holds a house of gold.
   Connotation: If you study hard, you will be able to make big money.

Chinese: *Ban ping cu: luan huang dang*
   Denotation: A bottle half filled with vinegar tends to rock.
   Connotation: Still waters run deep.

Chinese: *Fen lin er tian, jie ze er yu*
   Denotation: Burn a forest to farm and drain a pond to fish.

Connotation: Solve a problem at the sacrifice of 'your fundamental interests.

Chinese: *Xiemo-shalü*
Denotation: Butcher the donkey after it finishes working at the mill.
Connotation: (Don't be) ungrateful to those who have just helped you.

Chinese: *Yangqun libian chu luotuo*
Denotation: A camel amid a flock of sheep.
Connotation: (Behavior) too much out of the ordinary.

Chinese: *Yu jun yi xi tan, sheng du shi nian shu*
Denotation: A chat with a friend is worth ten years of schooling.

Chinese: *Niren pa yu, huangyan pa li*
Denotation: A clay figure fears rain; a lie fears truth.

Chinese: *Ben niao xian fei*
Denotation: A clumsy bird must start off first.
Connotation: A "less able" person must act before others.

Chinese: *Tianxia wuya yi ban hei*
Denotation: Crows are equally black everywhere.
Connotation: Bad people are the same everywhere because human nature never changes.

Chinese: *Xiaoli-cangdao*
Denotation: A smile may conceal a dagger.
Connotation: Velvet paws hide sharp claws.

Chinese: *Yi dong bu ru yi jing*
Denotation: A deliberate inaction is better than a blind action.
Connotation: Think before you leap.

Chinese: *Shushan wu lu qin wei jing, xuehai wu ya ku zuo zhou*
Denotation: Diligence is the path on the mountain of books; endurance is the boat across the endless sea of learning.
Connotation: There is no shortcut in the matter of reading and learning.

Chinese: *Huo bu dan xing*
Denotation: Disasters never come alone.
Connotation: Misery loves company.

Chinese: *Luobo kuai le bu xi ni*
Denotation: A turnip cooked hastily may still have soil residue.
Connotation: When hurrying through a job, one finds it impossible to attend to details.

Chinese: *Banmen-nongfu*
Denotation: Display one's skill in chiseling before Lu Ban, the master of carpentry.

Connotation: Show off one's elementary skills before an expert.

Chinese: *Yuanshui jiu bu liao jinhuo*
Denotation: Distant water won't help extinguish a fire close by.
Connotation: A slow remedy cannot deal with an emergency.

Chinese: *Gouji-tiaoqiang*
Denotation: A dog will jump over a wall when cornered.
Connotation: A cornered person will become desperate.

Chinese: *Daren bu da lian, chifan bu duo wan*
Denotation: Don't hit one on the face; don't grab one's bowl at dinner.
Connotation: Don't disclose one's shortcomings in public because it would mortally hurt him.

Chinese: *Yong ren bu yi, yi ren bu yong*
Denotation: Don't suspect one you trust; don't trust one you suspect.

Chinese: *Yao xiang ren bu zhi, chufei ji mo wei*
Denotation: Don't do what you don't want others to know.
Connotation: The evil that you do in secret will eventually reveal itself.

Chinese: *Long you qianshui zao xia xi, hu luo pingyang bei quan qi*
Denotation: Dragons can be teased by shrimps in a creek; tigers can be bullied by dogs on a plain.
Connotation: A capable person may become an underdog in an alien environment.

Chinese: *Yi long sheng jiu zhong, zhong zhong bu tong*
Denotation: A dragon has nine sons, each different from the others.
Connotation: Rarely do siblings have the same personalities.

Chinese: *Huabing-chongji*
Denotation: Draw a cake to satisfy your hunger.
Connotation: Finding an unrealistic solution to a problem is as good as self-deception.

Chinese: *Dishui-chuanshi*
Denotation: Dripping water can eat through a stone.
Connotation: Perseverance leads to success.

Chinese: *Gou bu xian jia pin, er bu xian niang chou*
Denotation: A dog won't forsake a poor master; a son never dislikes a homely mother.

Connotation: Filial duty ought to be one's instinct.

Chinese: *Jiu feng zhiji qian bei shao, hua bu touji ban ju duo*

Denotation: Drinking with a bosom friend, a thousand shots are too few; talking with a disagreeable person, half a sentence is too many.

Chinese: *Tongchuang-yimeng*

Denotation: Dream different dreams on the same bed.

Connotation: Hide different purposes behind the semblance of accord.

Chinese: *Chi shui bu wang jue jing ren*

Denotation: When drawing water from a well, never forget the well diggers.

Connotation: Always be grateful to those who helped you.

Chinese: *Tou ji bu cheng fan shi yi ba mi*

Denotation: Lose one's rice bait to the chickens that one wants to steal.

Connotation: Start out to hurt others but end up getting hurt.

Chinese: *Chi yi qian, zhang yi zhi*

Denotation: A fall into a ditch is a gain in one's wit.

Connotation: People learn from their mistakes.

Chinese: *Yidu-gongdu*

Denotation: Fight poison with poison.

Connotation: Fight fire with fire.

Chinese: *Magan da lang: liangtou pa*

Denotation: Fighting a wolf with a flex stalk; either party is afraid of the other.

Connotation: Neither party knows the real potency of the other.

Chinese: *Dahai-laozhen*

Denotation: Fishing for a needle from the sea.

Connotation: Looking for a needle in a haystack.

Chinese: *Shui zhi qing ze wu yu*

Denotation: Fish cannot survive in pure water.

Connotation: There is no absolute perfection.

Chinese: *Hunshui-moyu*

Denotation: Fishing in muddled water.

Connotation: Take advantage of a chaotic situation.

Chinese: *Cangying bu ding wu feng dan*

Denotation: Flies never infest eggs without cracks.

Connotation: People with frailties are more vulnerable to bad influences.

Chinese: *You xin zaihua hua bu kai, wuyi chaliu liu cheng yin*

Denotation: A flower deliberately grown may not bloom; but a sapling planted accidentally may grow into a tree.

Connotation: Things may happen independent of one's will.

Chinese: *Liu shui bu fu, hu shu bu du*

Denotation: Running water does not go bad; a door hub gathers no termites.

Connotation: Things that move do not decay.

Chinese: *Jiao ge pengyou duo tiao lu, shu ge diren duo du qiang*

Denotation: A friend made is a road paved; an enemy created is a wall built.

Chinese: *Shanmen nan kai, shanmen nan bi*

Denotation: The door of charity is hard to open; but once open, it is even harder to close.

Connotation: It is difficult to say yes, but it is more difficult to say no.

Chinese: *Shou ren yi yu zhi jiu yishi zhi ji, shou ren yi yu ze jie yisheng zhi xu*

Denotation: Giving one fish helps one only temporarily; teaching one the skill of fishing helps him all his life.

Connotation: God helps those who help themselves.

Chinese: *Huo xi fu suo yi, fu xi huo suo yi*

Denotation: Good fortune may forebode bad luck, or vice versa.

Connotation: Do not rejoice over good fortune and despair over a mishap.

Chinese: *Zhi xu zhouguan fang huo, bu xu baixing dian deng*

Denotation: A governor, who may commit arson, does not allow his people to light a lamp.

Connotation: One who commits a big crime won't tolerate a minor offence by others.

Chinese: *De chong si ru, an ju si wei*

Denotation: Guard against disgrace when favored; guard against danger in times of security.

Connotation: One must always prepare for the worst.

Chinese: *Ning dang jitou, bu zuo fengwei*

Denotation: Rather be the head of a chicken than the tail of a phoenix.

Connotation: Better to be a big fish in a small pond than a small fish in a big one.

Chinese: *Daozizui-doufuxin*
> Denotation: A mouth of a dagger but a heart of tofu.
> Connotation: Harsh words may have good intentions.

Chinese: *Wanhuo-zifen*
> Denotation: He who plays with fire may become its victim.
> Connotation: An evil doer will eventually end up being punished.

Chinese: *Jin zhu zhe chi, jin mo zhe hei*
> Denotation: He who stays near vermilion is stained red; he who stays near ink is stained black.
> Connotation: One may pick up the good or bad habits of his company.

Chinese: *Jiu ji bu jiu qiong*
> Denotation: Help the needy but not the poor.

Chinese: *Koumi-fujian*
> Denotation: honey-mouthed and dagger-hearted
> Connotation: kiss of death

Chinese: *Canglong-wohu*
> Denotation: Hidden dragons, crouching tigers.
> Connotation: Able people in low profile.

Chinese: *Mo dao bu wu kanchai gong*
> Denotation: Honing the hatchet will not delay woodcutting.
> Connotation: Good preparation may take some time, but it can speed up a task.

Chinese: *Shaoxiao bu nuli, laoda tu shangbei*
> Denotation: One who does not study hard when young will regret it when old.

Chinese: *Lin yuan mu yu, bu ru tui er jie wang*
> Denotation: It is better to start weaving a fishing net than yearning for fish at the seaside.
> Connotation: Act immediately instead of daydreaming.

Chinese: *Yi cun guangyin yi cun jin; cun jin nan mai cun guangyin*
> Denotation: A second is worth an ounce of gold, but an ounce of gold cannot purchase a second.
> Connotation: Time that is gone will never come back

Chinese: *Yu bu zhuo bu cheng qi, ren bu jiao nan cheng cai*
> Denotation: A jade is useless before it is carved; a man is good-for-nothing until he is educated.

Chinese: *Sha ji gei hou kan*
> Denotation: Kill a chicken before a monkey.
> Connotation: Warn many by punishing a few.

Chinese: *Yijian-shuangdiao*
> Denotation: Kill two vultures with one arrow.
> Connotation: Kill two birds with one stone.

Chinese: *Yuhou-chunsun*
> Denotation: bamboo shoots after a spring rain
> Connotation: (Things or events) grow or develop as fast as mushrooms after rain.

Chinese: *Qian li zhi xing shi yu zu xia*
> Denotation: A thousand-mile journey starts from the first step.
> Connotation: Success comes from concrete hard work.

Chinese: *Aiwu-jiwu*
> Denotation: Love my house, love the raven on it.
> Connotation: Love me, love my dog.

Chinese: *Diaohu-lishan*
> Denotation: Lure a tiger out of a mountain.
> Connotation: Lure an enemy out of its well-defended fortress.

Chinese: *Renxin ge dupi*
> Denotation: A man's heart is indiscernible behind his chest.
> Connotation: One cannot read others' mind.

Chinese: *Tanglang bu chan, huangque zai hou*
> Denotation: A mantis stalking a cicada is unaware of an oriole behind it.
> Connotation: While coveting a gain ahead, be aware of the danger behind.

Chinese: *Qiang niu de gua bu tian*
> Denotation: A melon forced off its vine is not sweet.
> Connotation: You can lead a horse to water, but you can't make it drink.

Chinese: *Wang yang bu lao, you wei wei wan*
> Denotation: It is not too late to mend the fold after a sheep is lost.
> Connotation: It is never too late to mend one's ways.

Chinese: *Cha zhi haoli, miu yi qian li*
> Denotation: An iota of a distance at the start leads to a thousand-mile difference in the distance.
> Connotation: A small error at present can lead to a serious mistake in the long run.

Chinese: *Hai ren zhi xin bu ke you, fang ren zhi xin bu ke wu*
> Denotation: Never harbor the intent to victimize others; but always guard against being victimized.

Appendix A: Chinese Proverbs

Chinese: *Tianxia meiyou bu san de yanxi*
Denotation: No banquet in the world ever lasts.
Connotation: Friendship, relations, and life—nothing is eternal.

Chinese: *Chouming-yuanyang*
Denotation: Notoriety travels farther.

Chinese: *Wu feng bu qi lang*
Denotation: There are no waves without wind.
Connotation: There is no smoke without a fire.

Chinese: *San shi liu ji, zou wei shangce*
Denotation: Of the thirty-six stratagems, running away is the best.
Connotation: Retreating or quitting may sometimes be the best option in some situations.

Chinese: *Yi nian zao she yao, shi nian pa jing Sheng*
Denotation: Once bitten by a snake, one fears a rope for a decade.
Connotation: Once bitten, twice shy.

Chinese: *Qihu-nanxia*
Denotation: Riding on a tiger, one may find it hard to get off its back.
Connotation: A catch-22 situation.

Chinese: *Yinye-feishi*
Denotation: Refuse to eat for fear of being choked.
Connotation: (One can't) stop trying just because there is a possibility of failure.

Chinese: *Yi ge heshang tiao shui he, liang ge heshang tai shui he, san ge heshang mei shui he*
Denotation: One monk fetches water, two monks share the labor, and three go thirsty.
Connotation: Lack of individual initiative could breed dependence upon one other.

Chinese: *Yi ge bazhang pai bu xiang*
Denotation: One palm makes no applause.
Connotation: Both parties in a dispute are to blame.

Chinese: *Zhizuzhe chang le*
Denotation: One who knows the limit knows true happiness.
Connotation: Insatiability is the source of unhappiness.

Chinese: *Chang zai hebian zou, na neng bu shi xie*
Denotation: How can one who often walks along a river avoid getting his shoes wet?
Connotation: One that does the most work is apt to make more mistakes.

Chinese: *Zhi li bao bu zhu huo*
Denotation: Paper cannot wrap fire.
Connotation: Truth will eventually come out.

Chinese: *Jian le zhi ma, diu le xi gua*
Denotation: Pick up a sesame seed only to lose a watermelon.
Connotation: Concentrate too much on trivialities at the expense of important matters.

Chinese: *Duiniu-tanqin*
Denotation: Play a harp before a cow.
Connotation: Cast pearls before swine.

Chinese: *Zhisang-mahuai*
Denotation: Point at a mulberry while abusing the pagoda tree.
Connotation: Accusations directed at A are actually meant for B.

Chinese: *Jiehua-xianfo*
Denotation: Borrow a flower to give to Buddha.
Connotation: When regifting, you get away easily from the embarrassment as you compare the recipient complimentarily to a Buddha.

Chinese: *Xuezu-shilü*
Denotation: Reshape one's feet to fit into new shoes.
Connotation: In real life there are indeed people who sacrifice the important for the trivial.

Chinese: *Yuanmu-qiuyu*
Denotation: Climb a tree to catch fish.
Connotation: Make a fruitless effort.

Chinese: *Bai wen bu ru yi jian*
Denotation: Seeing once is better than hearing a hundred times.
Connotation: Seeing is believing.

Chinese: *Xueli-songtan*
Denotation: Send charcoal in a snowstorm.
Connotation: Give help to someone badly in need. It is the opposite of *jin shang tian hua*.

Chinese: *Dumu bu cheng lin, danxian bu cheng yin*
Denotation: A single tree makes no forest; one string makes no music.
Connotation: This proverb illustrates the significance of teamwork.

Chinese: *Jiaotu-sanku*
Denotation: A wily rabbit has three burrows.
Connotation: One must make elaborate precautions for self-protection.

Chinese: *Liu de qingshan zai, bu pa mei chai shao*
> Denotation: So long as the mountains are green, there will be no shortage of firewood.
> Connotation: Don't overtax non-replenishable resources such as the environment and your health.

Chinese: *Xiabuyanyu*
> Denotation: A speck on a jade stone does not obscure its radiance.
> Connotation: A shortcoming will not write off one's merits.

Chinese: *Dangjuzhemi*
> Denotation: A spectator sees more than a player in a game.
> Connotation: A third party usually has a better perspective than those deeply involved.

Chinese: *Yaner-daoling*
> Denotation: Steal a bell with one's ears plugged.
> Connotation: Bury one's head in the sand.

Chinese: *Dacao-jingshe*
> Denotation: Beat the grass and scare away the snake.
> Connotation: Act rashly to alert the enemy.

Chinese: *Yan lei jiu bu liao huo*
> Denotation: Tears cannot put out a fire.
> Connotation: Weakness will lead nowhere.

Chinese: *Geqiang-youer*
> Denotation: There are always ears on the other side of the wall.
> Connotation: Little pitchers have big ears.

Chinese: *Zeihanzhuozei*
> Denotation: A thief cries, "Stop thief!"
> Connotation: Criminals often use a ploy to divert the attention of investigators.

Chinese: *Wujibifan*
> Denotation: Things will develop in the opposite direction when they become extreme.
> Connotation: The pendulum swings back and forth.

Chinese: *Paozhuan-yinyu*
> Denotation: Throw out a brick to attract a jade stone.
> Connotation: Offer a few commonplace remarks by way of introduction so that others may come up with valuable opinions.

Chinese: *Hu du bu shi zi*
> Denotation: Fierce as a tigress can be, she never eats her own cubs.
> Connotation: Those parents who hurt their children are worse than beasts of prey.

Chinese: *Ren wu yuan lü, bi you jin you*
> Denotation: Short of a long-term plan will lead to imminent trouble.

Chinese: *Fushui-nanshou*
> Denotation: Water spilled is irretrievable.
> Connotation: Things have developed to a degree that there is no point of return.

Chinese: *Min bu wei si, nai he yi si ju zhi*
> Denotation: When people don't fear death, there is no use threatening to kill them.

Chinese: *Pin ju naoshi wu ren wen, fu zai shenshan you yuanqin*
> Denotation: The poor living in a city may have no visitors, but the rich residing in the remotest mountain can be called upon by distant relatives.
> Connotation: The proverb criticizes snobbishness.

Chinese: *Qiaofu nan wei wu mi zhi chui*
> Denotation: Without rice, even the cleverest housewife cannot fix a meal.
> Connotation: If you have no hand you can't make a fist.

Chinese: *Lijian shang ren you ke yu, eyu shang ren hen nan xiao*
> Denotation: A sword wound may be healable, but damage caused by word of mouth is irreparable.

Chinese: *Bu ru huxue, yan de huzi*
> Denotation: You can't catch a cub without venturing into the tigress's den.
> Connotation: No pain, no gain.

Chinese: *Bu dangjia bu zhi chaimi gui, bu yang er bu zhi fumu en*
> Denotation: You don't know the cost of food and fuel without being the head of a household; you will not appreciate the love of your parents without becoming a parent yourself.

Chinese: *Zhi ji zhi bi, bai zhan bu dai*
> Denotation: Knowing one's own situation and that of the enemy will make one invincible.

APPENDIX B: MOTIFS AND TALE SOURCES

Prepared by Haiwang Yuan

Monkeys Fishing the Moon. The tale is *Type AT1335A Rescuing the Moon.* A group of monkeys formed a chain to rescue the moon in a pond but fell into it: This motif is a variant of *J2133.5. Men hang down in a chain until top man spits on his hands. They all fall.* They found the moon still in the sky: This motif is a variant of *J1791.2. Rescuing the moon. A numskull sees the moon in the water and throws a rope in to rescue it, but falls in himself. He sees the moon in the sky. At least the moon was saved!*

> **Source**: This tale was first recorded by Dao Shi (618–906) in his *Fa Yuan Zhu Lin* (*Buddhist Garden and Beautiful Woods*); Qu Yang, ed., *Zhongguo Yuyan* (*Chinese Fables*), Beijing: Beiyue Wenyi Chubanshe, 1996; *Chengshi Ban Zhongguo Shaonian Bao*, (*Chinese Young Adult Daily, City Edition*), Vol.187, 2004.

A Frog in a Well. This is a variant of *Type AT278B The Frog's Small World.* A frog in a well thought it was the entire world: The motif is a variant of *T617. Boy reared in ignorance of the world.*

> **Source:** Zhuang Zi (475–221 B.C.) *Qiu Shui* (*Autumn Water*); Qu Yang, *Zhuangguo Yuyan* (*Chinese Fable*), Beiyue Wenxue Chubanshe, 1996; *Zhongguo Ertong Wenxue Wang* (*Chinese Children's Literature Net*), www.61w.cn/2004-7/2004719185042.htm, 2004.

A Fox and a Tiger—Who Is the Real King of the Jungle? This is a variant of *Type AT101* The Dog Wants to Imitate the Wolf.* Threatened by a tiger, a fox challenged the tiger to follow her and see who the real king was: This motif is a variant of *K547.9. Threatening tiger challenged to strength contest.* The tiger thought that the running animals were afraid of the fox instead of him: This motif is a variant of *K1715.1. Weak animal shows strong his own reflection and frightens him. Tells him that this animal is threatening to kill him. J1706.1. Tiger as stupid beast.*

> **Source:** Liu Xiang (77 B.C.–6 B.C.) , *Zhanguoce: Chuce* (*Stratagems of the Warring States: Stratagems of State of Chu*); Lin Zhiman, *Zhonghua diangu* (*Chinese Literary Quotations*), Zhongguo Xiju Chubanshe, 2002; Qu Yang, ed., *Zhongguo Yuyan* (*Chinese Fables*), Beijing: Beiyue Wenyi Chubanshe, 1996.

A Tiger That First Sees a Donkey. The tale is *Type AT 125E* Ass Frightens Other Animals by Braying*. A tiger who first saw a donkey thought of it as a supernatural being: This motif is a variant of *J1785.3. Ass thought to be the devil*. The tiger felt scared when the donkey brayed and kicked: *K2324.1. Ferocious animal frightened by ass braying*. The tiger ate the donkey after learning its limited ability: *J50. Wisdom (knowledge) acquired from observation*.

> **Source:** Liu Zongyuan (773–819), *Sanjie (Three Commandments)*; Lin Zhiman, *Zhonghua diangu (Chinese Literary Quotations)*, Zhongguo Xiju Chubanshe, 2002; Qu Yang, ed., *Zhongguo Yuyan (Chinese Fables)*, Beijing: Beiyue Wenyi Chubanshe, 1996.

Wolf "Mother." The tale is a variant of *Type F913. Victims rescued from swallower's belly*. Two sisters lived with their mother: *P252.1. Two sisters*. A wolf ate the mother on her way back for a home visit and entered the sisters' house by passing for the mother: This motif is a variant of *K2011.1. Wolf poses as mother and kills child. K1822. Animal disguises as human being*. The sisters found out the wolf's identity by querying its furry appearance: This motif is a variant of *K2011.2. Tiger-ogress pretends to be girls' mother: explains tail as boil*. They killed the wolf with a trick: *J1510. The cheater cheated. J1111. Clever girl*. The sisters cooked the wolf and the soup they poured transformed into a cabbage, which turned into their mother: *D431. Transformation: vegetable form to person. D431.6.1. Woman emerges from plant*.

> **Source:** Wang Bingru, the author's mother, retold the story on June 30, 2005, in Tianjin, China. She had told the story to the author when he was young.

A Monkey and a Tiger. This tale is *Type 78B The Monkey is tied to the Tiger by rope*. Two friends, Tiger and Monkey mistook a couple's fear of something or someone stronger than they were: *A2493.14.1. Friendship between monkey and tiger. J1750. One animal (thing) mistaken for another*. Before their flight, a human thief with the same fear accidentally jumped off the roof and onto the tiger's back. It ran for its life, carrying him: This motif is a variant of *N392. Robber attempting to steal cow at night seizes thieving tiger*. It is also a variant of *N392.1. Escaping prisoner falls by accident onto tiger's back and is carried away*. To chase the human down a tree where he had escaped, Monkey improvised a way to escape possible danger but got itself killed in the end: *N330. Accidental killing or death. K1600. Deceiver falls into own trap*.

> **Source:** The author collected this tale from an oral tradition from Wang Liansuo, farmer and storyteller of Geng Village, Gaocheng City, Hebei Province, China, on June 14, 2005.

Nezha Fights Sea Dragons. This tale is *Type AT300 The Dragon Slayer*. Prolonged conception gave birth to a flesh ball, which turned to a mighty boy: *T574. Long pregnancy*. The motif is also a variant of *A1266.1. Man made from meat-ball*. With a magic weapons that an immortal gave him, the boy killed a sea monster who was trying to seize children for the dragon king as sacrifices: *D811. Magic object received from God (a god). F628.0.1. Precocious strong hero as mighty slayer. B11.10.3. Dragon devours children*. The boy then killed the dragon's son who wanted to avenge the sea monster: *B11.11. Fight with dragon*. The dragon king called in his dragon brothers to demand the boy's life, or would flood his hometown: *B11.7.1. Dragon controls water-supply*. This motif is also a variant of *B11.11.8. Dragon doubles his demand after men's rebellion*. The boy killed himself: *W28. Self-sacrifice*. The immortal sent for his soul and rebuilt his body with lotus flowers: *A185.12.1. God resuscitates man. A1310.2. Assembling the body. D975.1. Magic lotus-flower*.

> **Source:** Wu Cheng'en (1510–1582), *Xi You Ji (Journey to the West)*; Xu Zhonglin (1573 - 1620), *Feng Shen Yanyi (Romance of Gods and Heroes)*; *Kecheng biaozhun shiyan jiaocai zidu keben, 8-nianji xia-ce, (Experimental Self-teaching Textbook II Compatible with Curriculum Standards for the 8th Grade)*, Renmin Jiaoyu Chubanshe, 2004.

A Beauty on a Painting Scroll. *This tale is Type AT400B Girl-in-Painting as Wife or Paramour.* A beautiful young woman and an honest young man fell in love at first sight: *F575. Remarkable beauty. T15. Love at first sight.* An emperor, who learned of her beauty, wanted her to be his concubine: *T11.1.1 Beauty of woman reported to king causes quest for her as his bride.* The young woman jumped off a cliff: *T311.2.1. Girl commits suicide rather than marry man she does not love.* A goddess saved her and hid her on a painting scroll: This motif is a variant of *K521.3. Disguise by painting (covering with soot, etc.) so as to escape.* Disguised as a poor woman, the goddess sold the painting to the young man: *K1811. Gods (saints) in disguise visit mortals.* The emperor's men killed him and took the young woman: *P19.2.1. King abducts woman to be his paramour.* The goddess resuscitated him and helped the young woman to mend the emperor's gown: *A185.12.1. God resuscitates man. H900. Task imposed. H975.1. Tasks performed by aid of goddess.* The embroidered sea on the emperor's gown drowned the emperor and his men: *D1402.0.2.2. Magic spell causes person to be drowned.*

> **Source:** The origin of this popular tale is unknown. The first written record appeared in the early seventeenth century as a drama script written by Wu Bing (1595–1648). A movie with the same name was produced by Changchun Dianying Zhipian Chang in 1958.

The Field-snail Fairy. The tale is *Type AT400C Snail Wife.* An orphaned youth was too poor to marry: *L111.4. Orphan hero.* After acquiring a field snail, he found his meals secretly cooked: *F365.7. Fairies steal cooking. F346. Fairy helps mortal with labor.* Curious, he hid near home and watched: *H1554. Test of curiosity.* When he found a young woman emerged from the snail, he hid its shell: *F225 Fairy lives in a shell. D398 Transformation: snail to person.* He surprised her and proposed to marry her: This motif is a variant of *F302.4.4. Man binds fairy and forced her to marry him.* Unable to return to the snail, the fairy became his wife: *T111. Marriage of mortal and supernatural being.*

> **Source:** *Taiping guang ji: jixianji (Extensive Record of Peace and Tranquility: Collection of Fairytales)*, vol. 62, A.D. 977; *Tianluo guniang (Field-snail Girl)*, a teleplay by Yu Shengchun and Su Lisheng, 1988; You Zhuoyu, reteller, *Tianluo guniang (Field-snail Fairy)*, Zhongguo Minjian Gushi Net, www.6mj.com/2004-4/2004426201155.htm, 2004.

Dragon Princess. This tale is a variant of *Type AT555* The Grateful Dragon Princess.* Having a grudge against people, a dragon king withheld water and caused a drought: *B11.7.1. Dragon controls water-supply.* Sympathized with people, the dragon princess stole her father's dragon pearl and brought rain to people: *A185.16 God pities mortal. B11.6.2.3. Dragon's pearl stolen. B11.7. Dragon as rain-spirit.* Her action offended her father, who banished her in shackles: This motif is a variant of *C501. Tabu: contact with things belonging to a king.* A scholar passed her message to her uncle, a dragon king of a lake, who persuaded her father to relent: *A189.1. Mortal as ally of gods. B11.3.1.1 Dragon lives in lake.* The father consented to her daughter's marriage and gave the dragon pearl to the newlywed: *D812.7. Magic object received from dragon king.*

> **Source:** Gan Bao (618–906), *Soushenji (Record of Searching for Supernatural Beings)*; Li Chaowei (d. 741), *Liu Yi zhuan (Legend of Liu Yi)*; Shang Zhongxian (1280–1368), *Liu Yi chuanshu (Liu Yi, the Messenger)*, *script of a zaju drama*; Lu Yanguang, reteller, *Longnü muyang (Dragon Princess, a Shepherd)*, Lingnan Meishu Chubanshe, 1983.

The Magic Lotus Lantern. The tale is a variant of *Type 960B1 Revenge Delayed until the Son Grows up.* A scholar and a healing goddess fell in love: *F344. Fairies heal mortal. T91.3. Love of mortal and supernatural person.* While the scholar was away, the goddess gave birth to their demigod son: *A122. God half mortal, half immortal.* Her brother coerced her to give up the relationship, *K2211. Treacherous brother. Usually elder brother.* When rejected, he had her protective magic lotus lantern stolen and imprisoned her in a mountain: *D1385.29. Magic lamp protects against demons. D838. Magic object acquired by stealing. R45. Captivity in mound (cave, hollow hill). Q255. Punishment of woman who prefers mortal lover to gods.* An immortal adopted her son and trained him: *A185.3. Deity teaches mortal.* The immortal tested him with a dragon transformed out of his walking stick, which, in turn, turned to a magic axe: *A185.13. God puts mortal to test.* The motif is a variant of *D441.7.1. Transformation: rod to serpent. D451.6.3. Transformation: stick to weapon.* D1097. *Magic battle-axe.* After retrieving the magic lantern guarded by his uncle's dog, he cleaved the mountain open with his axe: *H1236.2. Quest on path guarded by dangerous animals. D1561.2. Magic object confers miraculous powers.* The immortal and the goddess' maidservant help reunite the family: *T96. Lovers reunited after many adventures.* The goddess gave up her goddess nature to be with her husband and son: *F302.6.2.2. Fairy gives up her fairy nature and becomes mortal to be able to return to her mortal husband.*

> **Source:** It is part of an oral tradition, the origin of which is unknown. First written record was a script for *zaju* (poetic drama set to music) titled *Chen Xiang taizi pi huashan* (*Prince Chen Xiang Opens Mt. Hua*) 1280–1368, and its author is unknown; Jiao Xun (1644–1911), *Chen Xiang taizi pi shan jiu mu* (*Prince Chen Xiang Opens the Mountain to Rescue His Mother*); Li Zhonglin (adapted), *Baoliandeng* (*Magic Lotus Lantern*), a *wuju* (drama dance), 1957; Wang Changyan (adapted), *Baoliandeng*, a Heibei opera, 1957.

Monkey King and the Iron Fan Princess. A mountain of fire blocked Tang Seng and his disciples on their journey west: *F753. Mountain of fire.* Only a magic fan can put out the fire with rain and wind it produced: *D1542.1.4. Magic fan produces rain. D1543.3. Magic fan produces wind. D1566.2.2. Magic fan quenches fire.* The fan's owner would not lend it to Monkey King, so he sneaked into her belly to torment her: This motif is a variant of *K952.2. Man transforms self to gadfly to enter giant's stomach and kill him.* She gave the monkey a fake fan, which intensified the fire and burned Monkey King's buttocks: *A2362.1. Why monkey's buttocks are red.* Monkey King obtained the real fan from its owner in the guise of her husband: *K1840. Deception by substitution.* To retrieve the fan, the husband started a fight, in which each combatant tried to outsmart the other by transforming into forms of different animals: *D101. Transformation: god to animal.* Monkey King triumphed with the help of other gods: *A528. Culture hero has supernatural helpers.*

> **Source:** The author collected this tale from an oral tradition from Zhang Caicai, farmer and storyteller from Geng Village, Gaocheng City, Hebei Province, China, on June 14, 2005. Zhang based his story on Wu Cheng'en (ca. 1500–ca. 1582), *Xi You Ji* (*Journey to the West*), chapters 59–61, Shanghai Guji Chubanshe, 1990.

A Cricket Boy. The tale is a variant of *Type AT 1960M–The great insect.* A magistrate catering to the emperor's love for cricket exacted crickets from villagers as levy: a variant motif of *J814.2. Flatterer always agrees with king even in opposite opinions.* A villager found a qualified cricket, but his curious young son wanted to look at the cricket in a jar: *H1554. Test of curiosity.* The cricket fled, and the boy killed it while trying to catch it: *N170. The capriciousness of luck.* The boy went into a coma after committing an unsuccessful suicide, but his spirit became a cricket and was sent to entertain the emperor: *D183.2. Transformation: man to cricket. K200. Deception in payment of debt.* The little cricket could dance for the emperor: a variant motif of *B293.0.1. Animals dance for king.* In so doing, the son prevented his father from being punished: *R154.2. Son rescues father. B486.2. Helpful cricket.*

> **Source:** Pu Songling (1640–1715), *Liaozhai zhiyi* (*Strange Tales of a Make-do Studio*); Chen Guoying, ed., *Jing xuan lianhuanhua liaozhai zhiyi* (*Picture Book of Selected Tales from Strange Tales of a*

Make-do Studio), Tianjin Renmin Meishu Chubanshe, 1988; Pu Songling, *Strange Tales from Make-Do Studio*, translated by Denis C. Mair and Victor H. Mair, Beijing Foreign Languages Press, 2003.

The Butterfly Lovers. The tale is *Type AT885B Suicide of Loyal Lovers.* The end of the story is a variant of *Type 970A Inseparable Pairs of Birds, Butterflies, Flowers, Fish and Other Animals.* A girl persuaded her father to allow her to go to school dressed like a boy: *K1837. Disguise of woman in man's clothes.* She met a classmate and fell in love with him: *N710. Accidental meeting of hero and heroine.* Upon graduation, the girl tried to hint at her love but in vain: *T55. Girl as wooer.* She then told him to propose marriage to her "twin sister": *D1905. Means of inducing love. J1111. Clever girl.* Thinking of the boy as poor, the girl's parents married her to a rich family against her will: *T91. Unequals in love. T131.1.2.1. Girl must marry father's choice.* The boy fell ill and died brokenhearted: *F1041.21.1. Illness from excessive grief. F1041.1.1. Death from broken heart.* The girl joined him in his grave: *T311.2.1. Girl commits suicide rather than marry man she does not love.* Their spirits became a pair of butterflies: a variant of *D186.1. Transformation: man to butterfly. E616.2. Reincarnation as butterfly.*

> **Source:** Its oral tradition traces back to A.D. 400; written record became available from the beginning of the Tang dynasty (618–907); Bai Pu (1280–1368), *Zhu Yingtai sijia Liang Shanbo* (*Zhu Yingtai Married Liang Shanbo in Death*); Yuan Xuefen and Fan Ruijuan (retold), *Xin Liang-Zhu ai shi* (*New Tragic Story of Liang and Zhu*), ed. by Xu Jin, produced by Huadong Yueju Shiyan Jutuan, 1951.

A Forsaken Wife and Her Unfaithful Husband. The tale is a variant of *Type AT884 The Forsaken Fiancée.* A scholar abandoned his family and left them in poverty: a variant motif of *Outcast wife and her son live in* poverty. *S62. Cruel husband. S11. Cruel father.* The scholar married a princess: *T145. Polygamous marriage.* His wife and children went to look for him: a variant motif of *H1385.4. Quest for vanished husband.* When the scholar rejected them, the prime minister let the wife tell her story in the scholar's presence, hoping that he might repent: a variant motif of *H1573.7.1. Test of repentance: culprit exposed to situation identical to that in which he sinned.* The scholar hired someone to kill his wife and children: This is a variant motif of *S11.3.7. Father orders son assassinated.* The assassin killed himself to spare their lives: a variant motif of *K512.0.1. Compassionate executioners.* A judge executed the scholar for murder and lying to the emperor despite royal intervention: *Q211. Murder punished. Q236. Punishment for deceiving (divine) emperor.*

> **Source:** The tale first appeared as a drama titled "Sai piba" ("Better Than Piba") in *Huabu nongtan* (*The Flower Section of Nongtan*) by Jiao Xun (1763–1820). The tale later appeared as a Hebei bangzi opera titled *Minggong duan* (*A Wise Judge's Case*); Xu Suling (directed), *Qin Xianglian* (movie), Changchun Dianying Zhipian Chang, 1955.

A Peacock Flying Southeast. The tale is a variant of *Type AT885B Suicide of Loyal Lovers.* The husband's mother mistreated his wife and, accusing her of disobedience, forced him to divorce her: *S51. Cruel mother-in-law. K2218.1. Treacherous mother-in-law accuses innocent wife.* Back to her parents' home, the young woman's elder brother forced her to remarry when a rich suitor sent his emissaries to propose: *T131.1.1. Brother's consent for sister's marriage needed. K2211. Treacherous brother. Usually elder brother. T51. Wooing by emissary.* She refused, but in vain: *J482.1.1. Woman refuses a second marriage.* The couple pledged to be together in another world and committed suicide: *T211.3. Husband and wife kill themselves so as not to be separated.*

> **Source:** Gan Bao (A.D. 317–A.D. 420), "Han Ping qi," in *Soushenji* ("Han Ping's Wife," in *Record of Searching for Supernatural Beings*); Xu Ling (507–583), "Gushi wei Jiao Zhongqing zhi qi zuo" ("An Ancient Poem Written for Jiao Zhongqing's Wife"), *Yutai xin yong* (*New Songs of Yutai*); Guo Maojing (960–1126), *Yuefu shi ji* (*Anthology of Yuefu Verses*).

Cowherd and Weaving Girl. This tale is a variant of *Type AT400* The Swan Maiden* and part of it is a variant of *Type AT511A The Little Red Ox*. An orphaned cowherd was driven out of home by his wicked elder brother: *L111.4. Orphan hero. K2211. Treacherous brother. Usually elder brother*. A celestial weaving fairy fell in love with and married him: *A451.3.1. Goddess of weaving and spinning. T91.3.2. Love of goddess for mortal. T111. Marriage of mortal and supernatural being*. The fairy's parents threatened to kill her family if she refused to return to heaven: *Q255. Punishment of woman who prefers mortal lover to gods*. The cowherd's dying cow began to speak: *B211.1.5. Speaking cow*. It told the boy to use its hide as a vehicle to catch up with his wife: *B560. Animals advise men. F300.2. Husband pursues fairy wife to heaven*. With her hairpin, the fairy's mother created Milky Way to stop him: *A778. Origin of the Milky Way*. Magpies formed a bridge for the couple to reunite once a year: *B451.6. Helpful magpie*. The cowherd with his children became the Aquila constellations: *A779.2. Origin of Aquila*. The fairy with her weaving shuttle became the Lyra constellation: *A776. Origin of constellation Lyra*.

> **Source:** Xiaoya: dadong of *Shi Jing* (*The Book of Poems*) compiled between 11 B.C. and 625 B.C.; Gan Bao (A.D. 317–420), "Dong Yong," *Soushenji* (*Record of Searching for Supernatural Beings*); Hu Yuting (retold), *Tianxian pei* (*A Fairy's Marriage with a Mortal*) edited by Lu Hongfei (Huangmei Opera), 1953.

Meng Jiang Wails at the Great Wall. This tale is a variant of *Type AT888C* Faithful Wife Revenges Husband's Death*. A childless, old couple harvested a gourd only to find a little girl in it: *D965.2. Magic calabash (gourd)*. This motif is also a variant of *D1380.2.1. Calabash as guardian of girl*. They raised her up: *N825.1. Childless old couple adopt hero*. When grown up, she married a young man who found refuge in her house to escape official recruiters of laborers: *N710. Accidental meeting of hero and heroine. A511.2.3. Culture hero is hidden in order to escape enemies*. The young woman went on a tough quest for her husband after his capture only to fine him dead and buried in the Great Wall: *H1385.4. Quest for vanished husband*. The motif is also a variant of *E431.10.1. Corpse buried under stones*. She wept until a section of the wall collapsed revealing skeletons: *Z49.11.1. Wall in construction collapses*. She found her husband's bones with blood drops: This is a variant motif of *D1610.16.1. Speaking blood drops*. She then drowned herself in the sea: *T311.2.1. Girl commits suicide rather than marry man she does not love*.

> **Source:** Zuo Qiuming (770 B.C.–476 B.C.), "Qi Liang zhi qi," in *Zuoshizhuan: xiang gong er-shi-san nian* ("Qi Liang's Wife," in *Biographies by Zuo: The 23rd Year of Duke Xiang*); *Tongxianji* (*Record of the Same Virtues*) written by an unknown author during the Tang dynasty (618–906); Liu Xiang, ed. (A.D. 25–220), *Lienü zhuan* (*Legend of a Woman Who Died in Defense of her Chastity*).

A Romance of Zhang Gong and Cui Yingying. Part of the tale is a variant of *Type AT 910 B The servant's good counsels*. Besieged by bandits who demanded the hands of her daughter, the wife of a deceased prime minister offered her daughter to whoever could rescue them: *N765. Meeting with robber band. T68.1. Princess offered as prize to rescuer*. A scholar invited friend's troops and routed the bandits: *R111.1.9. Princess rescued from undesired suitor*. The mother rescinded her promise: *T50.1.1. Girl carefully guarded by mother*. The daughter's maid helped the young couple in their tryst: *N831. Girl as helper. T131.1.3. Marriage against will of parents*. When discovered, the maid managed to put the blame on the mother for parental negligence: *J1250. Clever verbal retorts—general*. The mother had to consent to the union but demanded that the young man improve his social status before consummating the marriage: a variant motif of *Bridal couple must never see each other before wedding. L161.1. Marriage of poor boy and rich girl. T134.1*. When the couple finally reunited, the maid became a member of their family: *T133.1. Faithful servant accompanies bride to new home*.

Source: Yuan Zhen (779–831), *Yingying zhuan* (*Legend of Yingying*); Wang Shipu (ca. 1260–1336), *Xixiangji* (*Romantic Story in the West-wing Chamber*); Wang Zhaoshan (adapted) *Hongniang* (movie), directed by Huang Jianzhong, Beijing Dianying Zhipian Chang, 1998.

Xu Xuan and His White-snake Wife. This tale is a variant of *Type AT411 The King and the Lamia.* A young druggist encountered two snake spirits in the form of a young lady and maid: *F234.1.7 Fairy in form of worm (snake, serpent).* The druggist and the young lady fell in love and were married: *T15. Love at first sight. T111. Marriage of mortal and supernatural being.* An abbot gave the husband a formula to reveal his wife's serpentine identity: This is a variant motif of *K2280. Treacherous churchmen.* And *D1410.5. Serpent charmed into helplessness by magic formula.* The sight of a serpent scared the druggist to near death: This is a variant motif of *C31.1.2. Tabu: looking at supernatural wife on certain occasion.* His wife stole a magic herb at great risks and revived him: *F365. Fairies steal. E105. Resuscitation by herbs (leaves).* Spellbound by the abbot, the ungrateful husband abandoned his wife: *D5. Enchanted person. W154. Ingratitude.* His wife and maid went to rescue him, only to be beaten by the abbot: *A162.8. Rebellion of lesser gods against chief.* When the druggist returned, the couple reconciled: *T298. Reconciliation of separated couple.* The abbot imprisoned the fairy beneath a tower: a variant motif of *R41. Captivity in tower (castle, prison).* The maid defeated the abbot and rescued her mistress: *P361. Faithful servant.* The couple reunited: *T96. Lovers reunited after many adventures.* The abbot was condemned to encasement in a crab: This is a variant motif of *Q551.3.2. Punishment: Transformation into animal.*

Source: "Xihu santa ji" ("Legend of Three Towers at West Lake") written by an unknown author during 1127–1279. The original was nowhere to be found, but mentioned in the Ming (1368–1644) writer Hong Pian's *Qingping shantang huaben* (*Script for Storytelling from the Serenity and Peace Mountain Hall*); Feng Menglong (1574–1646), ed. "Bai niangzi yong zhen leifengta," ("White Lady Permanently Imprisoned Under Leifeng Tower"), *Jingshi tongyan* (*Words as Warnings to the World*); Tian Han (adapted) *Baishe zhuan* (*Legend of White Snake*) (Beijing Opera) 1945–1953.

Guanyin, Goddess of Mercy. Guanyin was an incarnation of a devout Buddhist's son condemned for unwittingly causing a massacre: *D12. Transformation: man to woman. D661. Transformation as punishment.* Her royal father had been denied an heir for his bloody conquest: *Q553.3.1. God refuses king a son on account of his many wars.* As a young woman, Guanyin refused to marry and became a nun: *M131. Vow of chastity.* A similar motif is *Q431.3. Banishment because of disobedience. Maiden wants to become nun and not marry.* The angry father tried to burn the nunnery down: *C927. Burning as punishment for breaking tabu.* Jade Emperor cast red light to protect the nunnery: *D1382. Magic object protects against cold or burning.* Before her suffocation, a white tiger carried her to the underworld: *S113.2. Murder by suffocation.* This motif is similar to one from India: *F98.1. Trip to lower world on tiger.* There her prayer freed the shackled dead, and the King of Hell had to send her back to this world: *D1766.1. Magic results produced by prayer. E481.9. King of world of dead.* Buddha took her as his disciple and made her bodhisattva: *E600. Reincarnation. Return from the dead in another form.* She began to help both mortals and immortals: *N817.0.2. Goddess as helper.* One that Guanyin helped was a dragon princess: *B11.2.0.1. She-dragon.* The princess went to a festival celebration in human form: *K1811. Gods (saints) in disguise visit mortals.* An accidental splash of water forced her to transform into a fish: *D562.1. Transformation by application of water. B11.2.1.3. Dragon as modified fish.* Guanyin sent her assistant to rescue the fish: *A185. Deity cares for favorite individuals.* The assistant did so with incense ashes that he passed for money: *D475.1.1.1. Transformation: ashes to gold.* The dragon princess had since become Guanyin's disciple: *A192.2.1. Deity departs for heaven (skies).*

Source: Gan Bao (618–906), *Soushenji* (*Record of Searching for Supernatural Beings*), chapter 20; Zhu Dingchen of Ming dynasty (1368–1644), ed. *Nanhai Guanyin Pusa chushen xiuxing zhuan* (*Birth and Self-cultivation of the South Sea Guanyin Bodhisattva*); Men Jihua, *Guanyin Pusa chuanqi* (*Legend of Bodhisattva Guanyin*), Beijing: Zongjiao Wenhua Chubanshe, 2003.

Mazu, Mother Goddess of the Sea. Mazu is a Chinese goddess of sailors: *A456.1. Goddess of sailors.* Her mother conceived her after dreaming of a goddess giving her a pill: *T516. Conception through dream. D812.8. Magic object received from lady in dream.* Mazu acquired magic powers from immortals: *A185.3. Deity teaches mortal. D1710. Possession of magic powers.* At meditation, she could see things in a distance: *D1732. Magic power obtained by meditation.* After she received bronze tablets from a deity of a well, she was able to heal sick people and exorcise evil spirits: *V134.1. Oracles and auguries from holy well. D811. Magic object received from God (a god). D2161. Magic healing power. A1459.3. Acquisition of sorcery.* With a magic scarf, she subdued two demons: *D1400.1.4. Magic weapon conquers enemy.* They became her helpers in her subsequent deeds: *H1233.4.4. Demon as helper on quest.* She went to a mountain top and ascended to heaven: *A117.4. Mortal transfigured to god on mountain top. A192.2.1. Deity departs for heaven (skies).* After her deification, there have been a dozen reported divine manifestations: *V222. Miraculous manifestation acclaims saint.*

> **Source:** Liao Pengfei, *Shengdun zumiao chongjian shunjimiao ji* (*Record of Reconstructing the Shunji Temple on the Site of the Ancient Shendun Temple*), A.D. 1150; Cheng Ruixue (1271–1368), *Lingci miao ji* (*Record of Lingci Temple*); Shi Wanshou, *Taiwan de Mazu xin yang* (*Taiwan's Belief in Mazu*), Taiwan Taiyuan Chubanshe, 2000.

A Dancing Crane. This tale is a variant of *Type AT75D1 Hospitality Rewarded with Inexhaustible Wine.* An immortal looked for an honest man in need of help: *K1811. Gods (saints) in disguise visit mortals. A185. Deity cares for favorite individuals.* He frequented a restaurant in the guise of a beggar: a similar motif is *K1982. Ubiquitous beggar. In disguise obtains alms three times from the same person.* When the restaurant owner treated him well, he painted a magic crane on his wall to help with his business: *D817 Magic object received from grateful person. A182.3.4.2. God promises mortal prosperity for man and offspring.* The crane brought large number of customers to the restaurant before it disappeared years later: *B463.3. Helpful crane. Q40. Kindness rewarded.*

> **Source:** Wu Yuantai of Ming dynasty (1368–1644), *Dong you ji* (*Journey to the East*); Zhu Yueming, *Baxian de chuanshuo: Lü Dongbin he huanghelou* (*Stories of the Eight Immortals: Lü Dongbin and the Crane Pavilion*), www.zhongguohun.com/fairyism/003.html, 2005; Kerstin Chen (retold), *Lord of the Cranes*, North-South Books, 2002.

Eight Immortals Crossing the Sea. Part of the tale is *Type AT592A1*e The Magic Object that Dries Up (Boils) the Sea.* Eight immortals decided to cross the East Sea, each with his or her special tool: *F1057. Hero (giants) wades across sea. D1524.1. magic object permits man to walk on water.* Their move caught the attention of the sea dragon: *B11.3.1. Dragon's home in bottom of sea.* His elder son captured one of the immortals: *B11.9. Dragon as power of evil.* To rescue the captive, an immortal killed the arrogant elder dragon prince: *B11.11. Fight with dragon.* A female immortal helped mortally wound the dragon's younger son: *B11.11.7. Woman as dragon slayer.* The Dragon King fought the immortals himself: *A162.1. Fight of the gods and giants.* The immortals burned the sea dry with their magic gourds: *D1592. Magic object heats or cools water.* The Dragon King tried to flood the immortals: *A1018.3. Flood brought as revenge for injury.* The immortals retaliated by pushing a mountain into the sea: *A901. Topographical features caused by experiences of primitive hero (giant, demigod, deity).* Before a bigger confrontation began, Guanyin intervened: *A172 Gods intervene in battle.* She restored the sea to normal and placed the mountain where it had been: *D2136.3. Mountain (hills) magically transported.*

> **Source:** Wu Yuantai of Ming dynasty (1368–1644), *Dong you ji* (*Journey to the East*); Wolfram Eberhard, *A Dictionary of Chinese Symbols: Hidden Symbols in Chinese Life and Thought*, translated by G. L. Campbell, New York: Routledge, 2001; Lin Zhiman, *Zhonghua diangu* (*Chinese Literary Quotations*), Zhongguo Xiju Chubanshe, 2002.

Bao Zheng and the Fox Fairy. Bao Zheng was born a meatball, and his second sister-in-law persuaded his father to abandon him: *A1266.1. Man made from meat-ball. K2212.2. Treacherous sister-in-law.* A tigress suckled him until his eldest brother adopted him: *B535. Animal nurse. Animal nourishes abandoned child.* His father reinstated him when he found him still alive, but banished him at the request of the second sister-in-law: *N731.3. Father unexpectedly meets abandoned son and reinstates him.* Part of this motif is a variant of *S11.5. Father banishes son at request of fairy wife.* While herding the family cow, Bao Zheng saved a fox fairy, who escaped the scourge of the god of thunder under his clothes: This motif is a variant of *G303.6.2.12. Devil hides in clothes of people running from storm. A522.1.4. Fox as culture hero.* The motif is also a variant of *Q552.1. Death by thunderbolt as punishment.* The fox fairy helped Bao Zheng evade several murderous attempts through her prophetic power: *B142.1. Prophetic fox. B350. Grateful animals.* Later, the fox appeared in Bao Zheng's dream as a young woman to offer him help: *D313.1. Fox transforms to person.*

> **Source:** The author collected this tale from an oral tradition from Wang Liansuo, farmer of Geng Village, Gaocheng City, Hebei Province, China, on June 14, 2005.

Mulan Fights in the Guise of a Male Soldier. This is another variant of *Type AT884B The Girl as Soldier.* When an invalid reserve was drafted, his younger daughter disguised as a soldier to fight in his place: *P234. Father and daughter. K1837.6. Disguise of woman as a soldier. L54. Compassionate youngest daughter.* She pretended to surrender, went to the enemy's camp and caught the enemy's commander: *K2350. Military strategy. H961. Tasks performed by cleverness.* The war over, the emperor wanted to award her with riches and a high-ranking position for her courage and her filial duty: *Q111. Riches as reward. Q113.0.1. High honors as reward. Q82. Reward for fearlessness. Q65. Filial duty rewarded.* Declining all, she asked to be allowed to return home with some camels and gifts: *L220. Modest request best.* Her former comrades visiting her were surprised to find their former commander a pretty woman: This is a variant motif of *D12. Transformation: man to woman.*

> **Source:** A Serbi (one of the Xiongnu tribes) song orally spread among Han Chinese; first recorded by Wu Jing (670–749) in his lost *Gu yuefu* (*Ancient Yuefu Poems*); Mei Lanfang (adapted) *Mulan congjun* (*Mulan Joins the Army*) (Beijing Opera), 1912.

Women Generals of the Yang Family and Commander-in-Chief Mu Guiying. This tale is a variant of *Type AT884B The Girl as Soldier.* The Song army, led mostly by the widows of fallen generals, won many battles: a variant motif of *L160. Success of the unpromising hero (heroine).* The enemy deployed an invulnerable formation and challenged the Song army to break it: *P556. Challenge to battle.* The Song commander sent his son to ask a rebel women warrior for help because only she knew its countermeasure: *A515.2. Father and son as cultural heroes. F565.1. Women warriors.* The woman warrior forced the young general to stay and marry her: *T55. Girl as wooer.* The Song commander sentenced his son to death for returning the next day: *H1245. Quest to be accomplished in one day.* The woman warrior came to his rescue: *R152. Wife rescues husband.* The father made her the commander so that she could break the enemies' deployment: a variant motif of *H1135. Task: Annihilating (overcoming) army sin-*

gle-handed. She led the Song army in winning the decisive battle: a variant motif of *H217.1. Decision of victory by single combat between army leaders.*

> **Source:** Qin-Huai Mo Ke (aka) of Song dynasty (1606), *Yangjiajiang yanyi* (*Romance of the Yang Family Generals*); Wang Zengyi (retold) *Yangjiajiang quanzhuan* (*Complete Biography of the Yang Family Generals*), adapted by Liu Lanfang, Wanfang Shuju Dianzi Chubanshe, 2004.

Gun and Yu Conquer the Deluge. The Water God caused great flood: *A420. God of water. A1010. Deluge. Inundation of whole world or section.* A god that pitied humans stole magic earth to save them: *A185.16. God pities mortal. D838. Magic object acquired by stealing.* The heavenly king sent God of Fire to kill him: a variant motif of *Q552.13. Death by fire from heaven as punishment.* His body gave birth to a demigod Great Yu: a variant motif of *E474.1. Offspring of living and dead person. A515.2. Father and son as culture heroes.* Yu fought God of Water: *A162.1. Fight of the gods and giants.* A flying dragon marked the land so that Yu could dig water-diverting canals: *B11.4.1. Flying dragon. B498 Helpful mythical animal.* A merman gave him a plan for water control, and a phantom of a god gave him a magic, land-measuring ruler: *B82. Merman. D812.4. Magic object received from ghost.* Yu transformed into a bear to speed up his work: a variant motif of *D113.2. Transformation: man to bear.* It scared his wife into becoming a rock, which gave birth to their son: a variant motif of *D231. Transformation: man to stone. T544.1. Birth from rock.* Places that the demigod worked upon became landmarks: *A901. Topographical features caused by experience of primitive hero (giant, demigod, deity).* He finally defeated God of Water: *A531. Culture hero overcomes monsters.* When Yu died, birds visited his tomb twice annually: *B251.2.9. Birds lament saint's departure.*

> **Source:** *Shangshu: yugong* (*Book of Shang: Chinese Historical Geography*) (around 551 B.C.–479 B.C.); Liu Xiang and Liu Xin of Western Han (206 B.C.–A.D. 9), ed., *Shanjing: shanjing* (*Book of Mountains and Seas: Book of Mountains*); Zi Niu, ed., *Zhuyin jinghuaben: shenhua gushi* (*Best Selected Folktales with Phonetic Notation*), Xi'an: Weilai Chubanshe, 1993.

Laozi's Prophecy. This tale is *Type 930 The Prophecy* and a variant of *Type AT910 Wise through Experience.* The deified Laozi visited Magistrate Xi on his way to the west: *K1811.2. Deity disguised as old man (woman) visits mortals. A561. Divinity's departure to the west.* Magistrate Xi wanted to learn from Laozi which of his twin sons would provide for him in his old age: *A515.1.1.2. Twin culture heroes—one foolish, one clever. J152. Wisdom (knowledge) from sage. J761. Old age must be planned for.* Laozi tested the twins with gold: *H1555. Test of fidelity.* He found that Older Brother refused hitting father for the gold: *J247. Goodness preferred to wealth.* Younger Brother was the opposite: *P251.5.4. Two brothers as contrasts.* Laozi predicted that Older Brother would take care of Xi: *J701. Provision for the future.* He repudiated Xi's blind confidence in Younger Brother who looked smarter: *U110. Appearance deceive.* Decades later, Older Brother took care of the old Xi, but Younger Brother was nonchalant: *P233.5. Oldest son responsible for the welfare of others.* He even refused to see Xi in his deathbed: *P.236. Undutiful children. S140.1 Abandonment of aged.* Only then did Xi realize the truth of Laozi's prophecy: *J21. Councils proved wise by experience.*

> **Source:** Chen Xi (retold), Laozi de yuyan (Laozi's Prophecy) *Gushi pindao*, www.qiwa.net/gspd/ShowArticle.asp?ArticleID; 322), 2004; Zhongguo Minjian Gushi Wang, www.6mj.com/, 2004; K–12 Zhongguo Zhong-xiao Xue Jiaoyu Wang, www.k12soso.com/ resinfo.php/K12SYS100000005-0000000000076969, 2005.

A Compassionate Scholar and an Ungrateful Wolf. The tale is a variant of *Type 155 The Ungrateful Serpent Returned to Captivity.* A fugitive wolf begged a scholar to save its life from pursuing hunters: *B251.4.1.1. Wild beast seeks protection of saint against hunter.* The scholar hid the wolf in his book bag and misdirected the hunters: *K515. Escape by hiding. K646. Fugitive's confederate misdirects pursuer.* The hunters gone, the wolf threatened to eat the scholar: *W154.2.1. Rescued animal threatens rescuer.* Neither a tree nor a buffalo that the scholar consulted helped him: *D1311.4.1. Tree appealed to as arbitrator. B211.1.5.2. Speaking buffalo.* An old man tricked the wolf into the bag and killed it: *N825. Old person as helper. J1172.3. Ungrateful animal returned to captivity. Q281. Ingratitude punished.*

> **Source:** Ma Zhongxi (1446–1512), *Dongtianji: zhongshanlang zhuan* (*Collection of Dongtian: Tale of the Zhongshan Wolf*); Lin Zhiman, *Zhonghua diangu* (*Chinese Literary Quotations*), Zhongguo Xiju Chubanshe, 2002; *Jiu-nian yiwu jiaoyu 6-nian zhi xiaoxue shiyong keben 2-nian ji yuwen keben* (*Trial Version of Textbook for Grade 2 of 6-year Elementary School Education in a 9-year Compulsory Education Program*), Renmin Jiaoyu Chubanshe, 2004.

Painted Skin. Part of the tale is *Type AT 1350—The loving wife.* A womanizing scholar befriended a seductive young woman and took her as a concubine against the warnings of his wife and a Taoist exorcist: *K2016. Friendship pretended to obtain access to girl. K1310. Seduction by disguise or substitution. E474. Cohabitation of living person and ghost.* When the scholar found that the girl was a demon wearing a human skin, he went back to the Taoist for help: *D531. Transformation by putting on skin.* The Taoist gave him a horsetail whisk to ward off the demon: *D1385. Magic object protects from evil spirits.* The demon ignored it and took the scholar's heart: a variant motif of *F585.1. Fatal enticement of phantom woman.* With his magic gourd, the immortal captured the demon transformed into a wisp of smoke: a variant motif of *G303.17.2.1. Devil detected, goes up chimney in smoke. D2177.1.1. Demons imprisoned by magic.* The scholar's wife asked a beggar to save her husband's life: *N826. Help from beggar.* The beggar humiliated her by forcing her to eat his spittle: *H923.1. Task assigned before wife may rescue husband from supernatural power.* When the spittle she threw up fell into the wound of her husband, it became his new heart and brought him back to life: *E114. Resuscitation by spittle.*

> **Source:** Pu Songling (1640–1715). *Liaozhai zhiyi* (*Strange Tales of a Make-do Studio*); Huang Buyi and Baofang (adapted), *Hua Pi* (*The Painted Skin*) (a movie), Kong Kong: Fenghuang Changcheng, 1966; Chen Guoying, ed., *Jingxuan Lianghuanhua liaozhai zhiyi* (*Picture Book of Selected Tales from Strange Tales of a Make-do Studio*), Tianjin Renmin Meishu Chubanshe, 1988.

Monkey King Strikes the White-bone Demon Three Times. A monk went to seek true Buddhist scripts with three potent disciples: *F12.4. Journey to heaven to see Buddha.* This motif is a variant of *F601. Extraordinary companions: A group of men with extraordinary powers travel together.* One disciple was the Monkey King, born of a mountain stone: *A132.2. Monkey as god.* The motif is a variant of *A1245.5. Man born from mountains.* A fiery punishment for his rebellion had unexpectedly enabled him to see through any disguise: *D1787. Magic results from burning.* A white-bone demon wanted to eat the monk, believing that his flesh could perpetuate its life: *E422.1.11.4. Revenant as skeleton.* The motif is a variant of *D551.3. Transformation by eating flesh.* Fearful of Monkey King's lethal weapon that changed sizes at his will, the demon disguised itself as a beautiful young girl to appear before the monk: A variant motif of *D631.3.3. Sword large or small at will. G303.3.1.12.2. Devil as a beautiful young woman seduces man.* She could not get near the monks as the monkey had drawn a magic circle to protect them: *D1380. Magic object protects.* Monkey King saw through the demon's identity: *F640. Extraordinary powers of perception.* He killed only the demon's illusion: *K500. Escape from death or danger by deception.* The gullible monk, incited by Piggy, thought that Monkey King had murdered an innocent person: *J2300 Gullible fools. A132.7. Swine-god.* The monk punished the monkey by causing him a headache with a charm: *D1502.1.1. Charm for headache.*

When Monkey King finally finished the demon: the monk banished the monkey. *Q431.9. Banishment for murder.*

> **Source:** Wu Cheng'en (ca. 1500–ca. 1582.), *Xi You Ji* (chapter 27, *Journey to the West*), Shanghai Guji Chubanshe, 1990; Gu Xidong and Bei Geng (adapted), *Sun wukong san da baigujing* (*Monkey King Strikes the White-bone Demon Three Times*) (movie), Tianma Dianying Zhipian Chang, 1960; Guo Fengming, *Xi you ji: poyuedong* (*Journey to the West: The Poyue Cave*), Hebei Yishu Chubanshe, 2001.

A Foolish Old Man Tries to Remove Two Mountains. This tale is *Type AT911* *The Old Man and the Mountain.* An old man wanted to remove two mountains in front of his house: *H1010. Impossible tasks.* A man who thought himself as smart jeered at him, saying that he was being foolish: *A515.1.1.2. Twin culture heroes—one foolish, one clever. Z253. Fool as hero.* In retort, the old man said that his family and his future generations would work ceaselessly at the mountains: *J156. Wisdom from fools. H945. Tasks voluntarily undertaken.* The old man's deed moved the deity, who sent two giants to carry the mountains elsewhere: *Q81. Reward for perseverance. D2136.3. Mountain (hills) magically transported.*

> **Source:** Lie Yukou (compiled), *Liezi: tangwen*, about A.D.200; Mao Zedong, *Mao zedong xuanji* (*Selected Readings from the Works of Mao Zedong*), Beijing: Waiyu Chubanshe, 1971; Qi Yusheng, ed. *Zhonghua chengyu diangu* (*Chinese Dictionary of Literary Quotations*), Jilin Sheying Chubanshe, 2002.

The Twin Sisters and the Magic Malan Flower. The tale is a variant of *Type AT 711 The beautiful and the ugly twins.* A young god grew magic flowers on top of a mountain: *F759.1. Mountain with marvelous objects at top.* Twin sisters lived below, the elder lazy and the younger industrious: *A525. Good and bad culture heroes.* The young god gave the younger sister a flower through her father: *D810. Magic object a gift.* A tree revealed to the father the young god's love for his daughter: *D1316.5.1. Voice comes forth from tree, revealing truth.* His younger daughter and the young god were married: *T111.1. Marriage of a mortal and a god.* The elder sister was jealous, and so was the family cat, transformed from a wolf that had eaten it: *G303.3.3.1.2. Devil in form of a cat.* They drowned the younger sister and tried to get the charm from the young god: *K2212. Treacherous sister. Usually elder sister.* The young god revived the younger sister with magic flower: *D1390. Magic object rescues person.* Saying the charm to the flower, the young god and the younger sister prepared a feast to celebrate: *D1472.2.4. Charm prepares feast. D1472. Food and drink from magic object.*

> **Source:** Part of an ancient oral tradition, its origin is untraceable; Ren Deyao (adapted), *Malan hua* (*The Malan Flower*), (a musical), 1956; Pan Wenzhan and Meng Yuan (directed) *Malan hua* (*Malan Flower*), (movie), produced by Haiyan Dianying Zhipian Chang, 1960; Huan Lu (retold) *Malan hua* (*Malan Flower*), illustrated by Duan Weijun, Renmin Yishu Chubanshe, 1979.

A Man with a Dog's Leg. A deity in the guise of a medicine man punished a despotic landowner by causing him partially paralyzed and then replaced one of his legs with that of his servant: *D42. God in guise of mortal. Q551.6. Magic sickness as punishment. E782.4.1. Substituted leg. Injured leg replaced by another.* The deity then gave the servant a dog's leg and thereby the nickname for a henchman. *Q401. Chain of punishments.* The deity then made the dog a clay leg and asked it to avoid wetting it when it urinated: *A2200. Cause of animal characteristics.*

> **Source:** The author collected this tale from an oral tradition from Zhang Caicai, farmer and storyteller of Geng Village, Gaocheng City, Hebei Province, China, on June 14, 2005.

The Origin of the World. From an egg of chaos, Pan Gu, the creator, came into being: *A605. Primeval chaos. A20 Origin of the creator. A22. Creator comes out of chaos. A27. Creator born from egg.* He grew until he separated earth from the sky: *A701. Creation of the sky. A801. Earth born of Chaos.* After his death, his breath, fluid and body parts became the objects of the universe and the earth: *A192.1. Death of the gods. A710 Creation of the sun.* A740 *Creation of the moon.* A940 *Origin of other bodies of water. A950: Origin of the land. A960 Creation of mountains. A1180 Establishment of present order—miscellaneous motifs.*

> **Source:** Xu Zheng (A.D. 220–265), *San-wu li ji* (*Three and Five Historical Records*); Ren Fang (907–923), *Shuyi ji: juan yi* (*Record of Strange Accounts, vol. 1*); Yuan Ke, ed., *Zhongguo shenhua gushi daquan jingbian lianhuanhua* (*The Complete Collection of Chinese Marchen—A Picture Book Series*), Zhejiang Shaonian Ertong Chubanshe, 1994.

The Origin of Human Beings. A goddess half human and half snake created humans with mud in her image: *A15.1. Female creator. A13.4.1. Snake as creator. A123.1.2. God with two joined bodies. A1241. Man made from clay (earth). A1212. Man created in creator's image.* She made them men and women with her breaths and let them regenerate: *D1005. Magic breath. A1271. Origin of first parents.* A conflict of two giants broke a sky-supporting mountain and tore the sky: *A665.3. Mountain supports sky.* Calamities such as deluge and fire ensued: a variant motif of *A1015.1. Flood from conflict of gods. A1030. World-fire.* Sometimes (as with the flood legends). Devastating beasts ran rampant: *B16. Devastating animals.* The goddess set about mending the sky by melting colorful stones: *A669.2. Sky of solid substance.* The stone slate added stars to the sky: This is a variant motif of *A763. Stars from objects thrown into sky.* She slaughtered a giant turtle and used its legs to prop up the sky: *B875.3. Giant turtle.* the motif is also a variant of *A815. Earth from turtle's back. A665.2.1. Four sky-columns.* She controlled the flood with ashes: *A1028. Bringing deluge to end. D931.1.2. Magic ashes.* She died of fatigue: *A192.1. Death of the gods.*

> **Source:** The earliest mention of the goddess was in *Shan hai jing: da huang xi jing* (*Book of Mountains and Seas: Book of the Uncultivated West Land*), written between 770 B.C. and 221 B.C.; the goddess' sky-mending motif first appeared in Qu Yuan (ca. 335 B.C. –296 B.C.), *Chu ci: Tian wen* (*Song of Chu: Enquiring the Heaven*); Liu An (206 B.C.–A.D. 24), *Huainanzi: lan ming xun* (*Huainanzi: Lecture on Viewing the Darkness*); Wen Zebai, "Nüwa zao ren" ("Nüwa Creates Humans"), *Zhongguo shenhua gushi daquan jingbian lianhuanhua* (*The Complete Collection of Chinese Märchen—A Picture Book Series*), Zhejiang Shaonian Ertong Chubanshe, 1994.

The Origin of Chinese New Year and Its Customs. A man-eating sea monster attacked people annually: *B16.5.1.2. Devastating (man-eating) sea-monster (serpent).* An old immortal came to their rescue: *N819.1. Immortal as helper. N825.2. Old man helper.* He scared the monster away with red-colored decorations: *D1385.26. Red color protects against demons.* He then taught the people how to do the same: *A185.3. Deity teaches mortal. A545. Culture hero establishes customs.* Another tale tells of a man-eating monster from the woods prey on people on the eve of a new year: *G303.8.13. Devil in the woods. G303.6.1.1. Devil appears at midnight.* Uncertain of their fate, people got together, had a feast, and spent the night awake: *A1510. Origin of eating customs. C735.1. Tabu: sleeping during certain time.* Only after the monster destroyed a whole village did people learn how to deal with it: *A1502. All customs for the year established.*

> **Source:** It is from an oral tradition, the origin of which is unknown; Feng, Chih-ting, *The Chinese New Year Festival: The Long History of the Lunar Calendar: Origin of Present Customs*, Peking : Peking Leader Press, 1929; Li Lulu, *Zhongguo jie: Tu shuo minjian chuantong jieri* (*Chinese Festivals: An Illustrated Account of Chinese Traditional Festivals*), Fujian: Fujian Renmin Chubanshe, 2004; Chinese Language Program, Department of East Asian Languages & Cultures, University of Southern California, *Chunjie de gushi—nianshou* (*Story of Chinese New Year—The Beast of Nian*), www.usc.edu/dept/ealc/chinese/clp/cls/festivals/year_monster.htm, 2005.

The Origin of the Twelve Zodiac Animals. Jade Emperor of Heaven helped people to count years with animals: *E755.1.1. Heavenly hierarchy. A1485. How people learned about calculating time and the seasons.* He asked all the animals to race to him, and he would make the first twelve the Chinese Zodiac Animals: *A796. Origin of the signs of the zodiac.* The mouse and the cat had been friends, but they turned out to be sworn enemies: *A2493.9. Friendship of cat and mouse. A2494.1.1. Enmity between cat and mouse.* The mouse pretended to sing for the good-hearted ox on its neck, but jumped off to reach the Emperor first: *B214.1.9. Singing mouse. K98. contest won by deception.* It became the leader of the Zodiac Animals: *L114.4. Cheater as hero.*

Source: Wei Chengsi, *Fengwu hua yuan* (*Origins of Social Customs*), Zhongyang Minzu Xueyuan Chubanshe, 1989; Monica Chang, *Shi-er shengxiao de gushi* (*Story of the Twelve Chinese Zodiac Animals*), Taiwan: Yuanliu Chubangongsi, 1994; Zhongguo qingnian yuedu wang (China Youth Readings Net), www.cnread.net/cnread1/etwx/index.html, 2005.

The Origin of the *Duanwu* Festival. The first man to get flint from a mountain at the upper stream of Yellow River on a boat found himself stuck in the mountain: This motif is a variant of *A1415. Theft of fire. Mankind is without fire. A culture hero steals it from the owner. A513.2. Culture hero arrives (and departs) in boat.* A giantess kept him captive in a cave with a stone at its entrance and gave birth to his son: This motif is a variant of *R45.3.1. Bear keeps human wife captive in cave with stone at entrance. F531.0.4. Giant woman. R18. Abduction by rejected suitor. F531.5.7.1. Mortal son of giant.* The man and his son eventually escaped: *A515.2 Father and son as culture heroes.* The giantess drowned herself in despair: *T93.3. Disappointed lover kills self. M451.2. Death by drowning.* To commemorate his mother, the son invented a special food and cast it into the river from a boat, thus giving rise to a traditional festival featured by the food and boat racing: *A1510. Origin of eating customs. A1541.4.2. Origin of dragon festival.*

Source: The author collected this tale from an oral tradition from Wang Liansuo, farmer and storyteller of Geng Village, Gaocheng City, Hebei Province, China, on June 14, 2005.

The Origin of the Mid-Autumn Festival. Ten suns rode on ravens to give light in turn: a variant motif of *A739.3. Each of sun brothers works for a month and plays for the other eleven;* were they to work all together, the world would be burned up by the heat. The rest would perch on a tree: a Finnish motif variant is *A714.2. Sun and moon placed in top of tree.* This is a variant motif of *H725.1. Riddle: bird nests on top of one cypress in morning, on top of another in evening. (Bird is the sun.)* Their appearance at the same time caused terrible disasters to earthlings: *A761.1 several suns, moons in sky simultaneously.* Emperor of Heaven sent Hou Yi to help: *A185.16 God pities mortal.* Hou Yi shot down all but one suns: A Siberian motif variant is *A716.1. Four suns at first: culture hero shoots three down.* Later, for a fatal mistake, he and his wife Chang'e were banished to earth to live as mortals: *F252.4. Fairies banished from fairyland.* Fearing inevitable death, Hou Yi went to a goddess on a mountain for help: *A151.1. Home of gods on high mountain. H1324. Quest for marvelous remedy.* The goddess gave him elixir of life: *D1346.7. Pill of immortality.* Hou Yi asked Chang'e to guard the elixir while hunting: *H922. Departing husband assigns his wife tasks.* A subordinate of Hou Yi discovered the hideout and tried to steal the elixir: *F601.3. Extraordinary companions betray hero.* In a struggle, Chang'e took the elixir by mistake and ascended to the moon, where she met a man condemned to cut a self-healing tree: *D1531.2. Magic pill gives power of flying. A192.2.1.1. Deity departs for moon. Q512. Punishment: performing impossible task.* Hou Yi paid tribute to his wife, and hence started a moon-worshiping tradition: *V1. 4.3. Worship of moon. A545. Culture hero establishes customs.*

Appendix B: Motifs and Tale Sources

Source: *Guicang (Return to Storage)*, said to be written before 221 B.C.; Liu An (206 B.C.–A.D. 24), "Hou Yi she ri (Hou Yi Shoots the Suns)," *Huainanzi: lan ming xun (Huainanzi: Lecture on Viewing the Darkness)*; Gao Rong, *Zhongguo shenhua gushi daquan jingbian lianhuanhua (The Complete Collection of Chinese Marchen—a Picture Book Series)*, Zhejiang Shaonian Ertong Chubanshe, 1994; Li Lulu, *Zhongguo jie: Tu shuo minjin chuantong jieri (Chinese Festivals: an Illustrated Account of Chinese Traditional Festivals)*, Fujian: Fujian Renmin Chubanshe, 2004.

The Origin of Kitchen God and the *Jizao* Festival. A gambler sold his wives and became a beggar: *N9.1. Gambler loses everything*. One of his wives hid him in her kitchen when he came begging: *N741. Unexpected meeting of husband and wife*. A chicken bone choked him to death: *N330. Accidental killing or death*. His ex-wife hid him in the kitchen stove and mourned his death by burning incense and paper, a practice that has since become a tradition and given birth to the worship of Kitchen God: *A1530. Origin of social ceremonials. A1546.2. Origin of worship of particular god(s)*.

Source: The author collected this tale from an oral tradition from Zhang Caicai, farmer and storyteller of Geng Village, Gaocheng City, Hebei Province, China, on June 14, 2005.

A Steed Lost Is More Horses Gained. This tale is *Type 944A* "Losing a horse may be good fortune; getting a horse may be bad luck."* When a horse breeder's son fell from a horse and broke his legs, the horse breeder did not feel sad. Sure enough, the son survived a brutal war owing to his injury: This is a variant of *N178.1. Broken leg saves man from fatal fight*.

Source: Liu An (206 B.C.–A.D. 24), *Huainanzi: renjian xun (Huainanzi: Lecture on This World)*; Xu Zhensheng, ed., *Xinhua chengyu cidian (New Chinese Dictionary of Idioms)*, Shangwu Yinshuguan, 2002; Qi Yusheng, ed., *Zhonghua chengyu diangu (Chinese Dictionary of Literary Quotations)*, Jilin Sheying Chubanshe, 2002.

A Professed Dragon Lover. The tale is *Type AT 1321—Fools frightened*. A Mr. Ye boasted that he was a fan of dragons, and he acted out as if he were: *K2000. Hypocrites*. When a real dragon visited him, he was scared out of his wits: This motif is a variant of *Q267.1. Devil comes for hypocrite*. The motif is also a variant of *J261. Loudest mourners not greatest sorrowers*.

Source: Liu Xiang of Eastern Han (A.D. 25–220), ed., *Xinxu: zashi (New Order: Miscellaneous)*; Lin Zhiman, *Zhonghua diangu (Chinese Literary Quotations)*, Zhongguo Xiju Chubanshe, 2002; Xu Zhensheng, ed., *Xinhua chengyu cidian (New Chinese Dictionary of Idioms)*, Shangwu Yinshuguan, 2002.

Number Is Security. When an emperor paid pipers to play in an ensemble, an impostor took part in the performances: *L114.4 Cheater as hero*. When the emperor died, his son preferred to hear the pipers play solo: This motif is a variant of *H15.1. Identity tested by demanding that person say again what he said on former occasion*. The imposter had to flee from possible punishment: *K1200. Deception into humiliating position. K1600. Deceiver falls into own trap*.

Source: Han Fei (ca. 280 B.C.–233 B.C.), *Han feizi*; Qu Yang (retold), *Zhongguo chatu yuyan* (shijie yuyan congshu) (*Illustrated Chinese Fables* [World Classic Fables Series]), Beiyue Wenyi Chubanshe, 1996.

Forgot How to Walk Back Home. A man wanted to learn how people of another country walk. In the end, however, he not only failed to learn from others, but also forgot how he originally walked. As a result, he had to crawl back home: This motif is a variant of *J512.6. Crow tries to imitate partridge's walk. Only spoils his own. J2400. Foolish imitation*.

Source: Zhuang Zhou (ca. 369 B.C.–286 B.C.), *Zhuangzi: qiu shui (Zhuangzi: Autumn Water)*; Lin Zhiman, *Zhonghua diangu (Chinese Literary Quotations)*, Zhongguo Xiju Chubanshe, 2002; Xu

Zhensheng, ed., *Xinhua chengyu cidian* (*New Chinese Dictionary of Idioms*), Shangwu Yinshuguan, 2002.

Waiting for a Rabbit to Bump into a Tree. This tale is *Type AT1280* Waiting for Another Rabbit*. A rabbit ran into a tree stump and died: *N330. Accidental killing or death*. A farmer stopped farming to wait for more rabbits to do the same, but in vain: *J2066. Foolish waiting*. This motif is a variant of *J2066.3. Men (animals) wait in vain for nuts to fall from a tree*.

Source: Han Fei (ca. 280 B.C.–233 B.C.), *Han feizi: wu du* (*Han Feizi: Five Maladies*); Lin Zhiman, *Zhonghua diangu* (*Chinese Literary Quotations*), Zhongguo Xiju Chubanshe, 2002; Xu Zhensheng, ed., *Xinhua chengyu cidian* (*New Chinese Dictionary of Idioms*), Shangwu Yinshuguan, 2002.

Fishing for a Sword Dropped into a River from a Moving Boat. The tale is *Type 1278. Marking the place on the boat*. A man made a mark on the boat where he dropped his sword. Instead of fishing for it immediately, he tried to retrieve the sword when the boat reached shore, thinking that the mark would help him locate it: This motif is a variant of the Japanese *J1922.1. Marking the place on the boat. An object falls into the sea from a boat. Numskulls mark the place on the boat-rail to indicate where it fell*.

Source: Lü Buwei (ca. 280 B.C.–235 B.C.), *Lü Shi chun qiu: cha jin* (*Spring and Autumn of the Lü Family: Examining Today*); Lin Zhiman, *Zhonghua diangu* (*Chinese Literary Quotations*), Zhongguo Xiju Chubanshe, 2002; Xu Zhensheng, ed. *Xinhua chengyu cidian* (*New Chinese Dictionary of Idioms*), Shangwu Yinshuguan, 2002.

No Sycee Buried Here But Three Hundred *Liang*. This tale is *Type 1341B The Buried Silver and the Thief*. A fool buried his gold and put up a sign to discourage theft but instead encouraged it: This motif is a variant of *J2100. Remedies worse than the disease*.

Source: Xu Zhensheng, ed. *Xinhua chengyu cidian* (*New Chinese Dictionary of Idioms*), Shangwu Yinshuguan, 2002; Qi Yusheng, ed. *Zhonghua chengyu diangu* (*Chinese Dictionary of Literary Quotations*), Jilin Sheying Chubanshe, 2002; Guan Jiaqi, *Yuyan: guren de zhihui* (*Fables: Wisdom of Ancient People*) Taiwan, You Shi Chubanshe, 2003.

The Invincible Spear Versus the Impenetrable Shield. A man selling a spear and a shield said at one time that his spear was invincible, and at another, that his shield was invulnerable: *F834.4 All-conquering spear*. When asked to try his spear on his shield, he became speechless: This motif is a variant of *J1477. Demonstrate here. A man boasts of his jump on Rhodes and says that if he were in Rhodes he could prove his boast. Reply: "No need to go to Rhodes. Show us your jump here." K1200. Deception into humiliating position. K1600. Deceiver falls into own trap*.

Source: Han Fei (ca. 280 B.C.–233 B.C.), *Han feizi: nanshi pian*, (*Han Feizi: On Difficult Situations*); Xu Zhensheng, ed., *Xinhua chengyu cidian* (*New Chinese Dictionary of Idioms*), Shangwu Yinshuguan, 2002; Qi Yusheng, ed., *Zhonghua chengyu diangu* (*Chinese Dictionary of Literary Quotations*), Jilin Sheying Chubanshe, 2002.

A Smile Worth a Thousand Ounces of Gold. This tale is a variant of *Type AT125F* Crying Wolf or Raising False Alarm*. A dragon's saliva turned into a turtle, the sight of which impregnated a maidservant: *D812.7. Magic object received from dragon king. A1725.1. Animals from spittle of deity (saint). T533. Conception from spittle*. The child, when grown up, became a concubine of an emperor, who liked her so much that he neglected his duty: *P12.11. Uxorious king neglects duties*. The concubine never smiled: *F591. Person who never laughs*. The emperor would pay a thousand ounces of gold to have her smile: *H1194. Task: Making person laugh*. He ordered military beacons to be lit as if he were in danger: *J1705.4. Foolish king*. The folly made the concubine laugh, but later caused the emperor his life, as no one believed his call for help when real danger came: *J2050. Absurd short-sightedness. Q499.2.2. Humiliating death as punishment for taking concubine*. This tale is a variant motif of *J2172.1. The shepherd who called "Wolf!" too often.*

> **Source:** Cui Yin (?–A.D. 92), *Qi yi* (*Seven Reliances*); Cai Yuanfang of Qing dynasty (1644–1911), *Dongzhou lieguo zhi* (*Records of the Eastern Zhou States*), based on Feng Menglong (1574–1646) *Xin lieguo zhi* (*New Records of the Eastern Zhou States*), which was in turn based on Yu Shaoyu's *Lieguo zhizhuan* (*Records and Biographies of the Eastern Zhou States*) written between 1521 and 1572; Lin Zhiman, *Zhonghua diangu* (*Chinese Literary Quotations*), Zhongguo Xiju Chubanshe, 2002.

Reducing an Iron Rod to a Sewing Needle. An elderly woman, who was honing an iron rod to produce a sewing needle, taught a truant that perseverance would eventually lead to success: This motif is similar to *J67.1. Lazy pupil determines to be more diligent by watching man building home one wattle at a time, and seeing how water fills hole one drop at a time. Q81. Reward for perseverance*.

> **Source:** Zhu Mu of Southern Song dynasty (1127–1278), *Fangyu shenglan: meizhou: mozhen xi* (*Beautiful Scenes of Fangyu: Meizhou: Needle-grinding Brook*); Chen Renxi (1581–1636), *Qianqueju leishu* (*Book of Qianqueju*), chapter 60; Qi Yusheng, ed., *Zhonghua chengyu diangu* (*Chinese Dictionary of Literary Quotations*), Jilin Sheying Chubanshe, 2002.

An Unfolded Map Reveals a Dagger. A courageous man offered to kill the First Emperor of Qin: *W33 Heroism*. He tried to assassinate the king with a dagger he had hidden in the map, but in so doing, he lost his own life: *K910. Murder by strategy. W28 Self-sacrifice*.

> **Source:** Sima Qian (ca. 145, 135 B.C.–ca. 87 B.C.), *Shiji: cike liezhuan* (*Record of History: Biographies of Assassins*); Liu Xiang (ca. 77 B.C.–ca. 6, 7 B.C.), *Zhanguo ce: yance san* (*Stratagems of the Warring States: The 3rd of the Strategies of the State of Yan*); Lin Zhiman, *Zhonghua diangu* (*Chinese Literary Quotations*), Zhongguo Xiju Chubanshe, 2002.

A King Who "Eats Bitter." A captive King of Yue pretended to submit to the captor King of Wu and was released: *R74. Defeated warriors go into the conqueror's service. K500. Escape from death or danger by deception*. He vowed to avenge his humiliation: *M161.2. Vow to revenge (king, friends, father) or die*. He slept on straw and tasted bile when eating so as not to let good life dull his will: *H1502. Test: enduring hardship*. He sent pretty women to corrupt King of Wu and boiled seeds to sabotage Wu's economy: *K2350. Military strategy*. When King of Yue conquered the state of Wu, its king committed suicide: *M451.1. Death by suicide*.

> **Source:** Sima Qian (ca. 145, 135 B.C.–ca. 87 B.C.), *Shiji: yuewang goujian shijia* (*Record of History: Well-Known Family of King Gou Jian of Yue*); Chen Shousun, *Luo yusheng yanchang jingyundagu xuan* (*Selected Beijing Drum-storytelling Episodes Performed by Luo Yusheng*), Baihua Wenyi Chubanshe, 1983; Qi Yusheng, ed., *Zhonghua chengyu diangu* (*Chinese Dictionary of Literary Quotations*), Jilin Sheying Chubanshe, 2002.

GLOSSARY

Allegory: a symbolic representation

Asceticism: denial of material comfort

Avalokitesvara: Guanyin or Guanshiyin in Chinese—Goddess of Mercy

Baigujing: (1) name of character; (2) vicious person

Baoliandeng: Magic Lotus Lantern

Bao Zheng: legendary judge famed for his uprightness, insight, and courage

Baxian: Eight Immortals

Bian: stir-fry before stewing (v.)

Biao: watch (a timepiece)

Bodhisattva: pusa in Chinese—gods or goddesses next to Buddha

Caimiyu: to guess a riddle (v.)

Caiqiu: colored balls of silk used as souvenir

Caizijiaren: gifted scholars and pretty women

Cattail: a plant with which rural Chinese plait cushions

Cha: tea

Chang'e: the Moon Goddess

Chang-nian-zuo-da: types of performance in Chinese operas: singing, speaking, performing, and fighting

Chanjuan: (1) beautiful girl; (2) moon

Chao: stir-fry (v.)

Chen Shimei: (1) name of character; (2) unfaithful husband

Chengyu: proverb

Chiang Kai-shek: Chinese military and political leader who succeeded Sun Yat-sen as Chairman of the Nationalist Party until his death in 1975

Chiku: endure hardships (v.)

Chongyangjie: traditional Chinese festival on the ninth day of the ninth moon

Choreographed: of the art of creating and arranging dances

Chuan: Sichuan (or Szechuan) cuisine, noted for its bold spiciness

Ci: poem of uneven lines, popular during the Song dynasty

Conscription: forced enrollment

Couplet: two-line rhymed verse

Crevasse: crack

Daga: to hit a diamond-shaped twig tossed up in the air (v.)

Damask: rich patterned fabric of cotton, linen, silk, or wool

Dandanmian: Sichuan noodles

Danziqiu: children's game of marbles

Daqi: lacquer ware

Deity: god or goddess

Demigod: half-human, half-god

Deng Xiaoping: China's paramount leader from1978 to1997; initiated economic reform in 1998

Di: ground or earth

Dissipation: indulgence in excessive pursuit of pleasure

Diushoupa: handkerchief game

Dizhi: twelve earthly branches combined with *tiangan* to designate time

Dongguo xiansheng: (1) name of character; (2) a gullible softy

Dougong: nail-less brackets between crossbeams and columns

Doukongzhu: to play diabolo (v.)

Doushouqi: board game of animals

Douzhi: soybean milk

Drake: male duck

Duanwujie: Dragon Boat Festival

Dun: to stew (v.)

Ecliptic: imagined path of the sun's movement

Erhu: *urheen* or Chinese fiddle

Errenzhuan: song-and-dance duet, popular in Northeast China

Exorcist: one that gets rid of evil spirits

Feitian: flying angels or fairies

Feixingqi: board game of aerial battles
Fenghuolun: Nezha's magic wheels of wind and fire
Fu: cultural symbol of happiness
Fuma: emperor's son-in-law
Fusang: mythical tree where the sun perches during the night
Fuxishi: legendary founder of Chinese polity
Gang of Four: Mao Zedong's widow Jiang Qing and three other associates, who were blamed for the "Cultural Revolution" started by Mao
Gaoqiao: stilt
Ge: leather
Gongbi: way of painting characterized by preciseness
Gonggong: legendary god of water
Gongxi facai: Chinese New Year greeting
Goubuli baozi: steamed dumpling popular in Tianjin
Goutuizi: henchmen (literally "dog's leg")
Great Cultural Revolution: movement started by Mao Zedong in 1966 and ended by the arrest of the "Gang of Four" after Mao's death in 1976. The revolution is blamed for nearly bankrupting China economically and almost ruining it culturally and socially.
Great Leap Forward: movement designed to industrialize China in an unrealistically short time, started by Mao in 1958; it ended disastrously in 1962
Guan: Daoist temple
Guanyin: Avalokitesvara, Goddess of Mercy
Guifang: woman's private living quarters
Guiren: respectable person
Guonian: to celebrate the New Year (v.)
Guozi: deep-fried dough
Guqu: art forms of *quyi* characterized by the use of drums in storytelling
Han: the majority ethnic group in China
Hanchuan: "dry-boat": a folkdance genre
Hanren: Han Chinese
Hanyu Pinyin: Chinese phonetic alphabet
Hanzi: Chinese characters
Harem: a house for women members of a royal family
Hasp: metal fastener fitting over a *staple*
Hemiplegia: partial paralysis
Herbivore: animal that feeds on plants
Hongniang: (1) name of character; (2) matchmaker
Huaju: play
Huangdi: Yellow Emperor
Huapi: (1) demon in human skin; (2) evildoer's disguise
Huaqiao: Chinese residents abroad
Huaren: Chinese in general

Huaxia: ancient name for China
Hudan: great courage
Hui: (1) Hui ethnic minority; (2) Muslim
Hui: to braise (v.)
Hui: Anhui Cuisine
Hun: nomadic tribe, also known as Xiongnu
Implacable: impossible to satisfy
Incantations: verbal charm or spell
Indelible: impossible to remove
Jia: cangue—heavy wooden yoke for punishing petty criminals
Jiachangcai: home-cooked dishes
Jian: to fry in shallow oil (v.)
Jianbing: thin pancake
Jianbingguozi: thin pancake with deep-fried dough, popular in Tianjin
Jiang Qing (or Chiang Ch'ing): Mao Zedong's wife and one of the "Gang of Four." She committed suicide in prison in 1991.
Jianpu: numbered notation
Jianzhi: paper-cut
Jiaozi: dumplings
Jiashan: rock garden
Jieqi: solar terms
Jiguchuanhua: children's game assisted by drumming
Jin: (1) metal; (2) gold
Jingtailan: cloisonné
Jingubang: Monkey King's golden rod weapon
Jiri: lucky day
Joss paper: money for the dead
Juren: successful candidate in provincial imperial examination
Kang: sun-dried mud brick bed
Keju: imperial civil-service examination
Koxinga: Hakka for Zheng Chenggong, Ming general who freed Taiwan from Dutch occupation in 1662
Kuaiban: clapper talk
Kuaishu: clapper talk in Shandong accent
Laba zhou: porridge of various grains
Laoshouxing: God of Longevity
Laoying zhuo xiaoji: children's game of eagle catching chicks
Laozi: Lao Tzu, founder of Daoism
Laran: batik or wax printing
Lenggong: solitary palace for disfavored queens and concubines
Li: ½ kilometer (about ⅓ mile)
Liang: unit of weight (1/16 of *jin*)
Liannian youyu: cultural symbol (fish with lotus) of long-term affluence
Lichun: a solar term—beginning of spring

Lin Biao (or Lin Piao): second only to Mao Zedong in power, but discredited as a traitor after a planned military coup was exposed and he was found dead in a plane crash in Mongolia in 1991.

Lingwei: tablets to represent deceased family members

Lingzhi: glossy ganoderma—rare Chinese medicinal herb

Liu Shaoqi: Chinese president (1959–1968), died of persecution during the Cultural Revolution

Liudong renkou: migrant population

Loba: Loba ethnic minority in Tibet

Longgong: dragon palace

Longmen: gate of dragon palace

Longnü: dragon princess

Longzhu: dragon pearl

Louhua: ornamental engravings

Lu: official salary

Lucrative: money-making

Luzhanqi: board game of infantry warfare

Majiang: Chinese mah-jongg

Manchu: Manzu ethnic minority

Mao Zedong (or Mao Tse-tung): China's paramount leader between 1949 and 1976

Maodun: contradiction (literally "spear vs. shield")

Maopian: children's game of paper chips

Mazu: Goddess of the Sea

Meiji huaren: American Chinese

Meisheng changfa: bel canto

Mendang hudui: well-matched in social and economic status in marriage

Miao: (1) Miao ethnic minority; (2) Buddhist or Confucian temple

Mimicker: one who imitates

Minuscule: very small

Minjian gongyi: folk handicraft

Min yueqi: Chinese musical instruments

Minzu changfa: style of Chinese singing

Momo: kind of steamed bread

Monsoonal: of seasonal wind

Mt. Kunlun: residence of *Xiwangmu*, the mythical Queen Mother of the West

Mu: wood

Nalakuvara: *Nezha*—a boy god

Nian: (1) year; (2) mythical beast

Niangao: rice cake for Chinese New Year

Nianguan: end of the year

Nianyefan: dinner on New Year's Eve

Ning: cultural symbol of peace

Niren Zhang: brand name for clay figurines made by the famed Zhang Family in Tianjin

Nocturnal: of the night

Nongminhua: peasant painting

Nüwa: creator of humans

Nüzi shi-er yuefang: "Twelve Girls Band"

Omnipresent: present everywhere

Pangu: creator of the universe

Pao: gourd

Paofan: soup of cooked rice, popular for breakfast in Shanghai

Pedantry: of one that shows off his learning

Peng: to quick-stir-fry in hot oil (v.)

Phantasm: something apparently seen but having no physical reality

Pingmin: common people

Pingshu: storytelling with commentary

Pingtan: ballad singing in Suzhou dialect

Pipa: lute

Polygamy: practice of having more than one spouse at one time

Polytheistic: of a system of multiple gods and goddesses

Predilection: preference

Premonition: feeling that something in particular is going to happen

Pusa: Bodhisattva, particularly Guanyin

Putonghua: Common Speech of the Chinese Language, known as Mandarin to Westerners

Qian: bamboo slips used for divination

Qianliyan: farseeing, supernatural being

Qichu: seven reasons for divorcing a wife in feudal China—infertility, adultery, disobedience, quarrelsomeness, thievery, jealousy, and serious illness

Qin Shihuang: First Emperor of Qin

Qixi: the seventh evening of the seventh moon—Chinese Valentine's Day

Qixiannü: (1) seven heavenly daughters; (2) the seventh heavenly daughter

Queqiao: (1) bridge of magpies; (2) a chance for potential lovers to meet

Quyi: folk art forms of storytelling

Rattan: climbing palms having long, slender, and tough stems

Reincarnation: rebirth of soul in another body

Ren: human

Ren-yi-li-zhi-xin: Neo-Confucian doctrine of benevolence, righteousness, propriety, wisdom, and fidelity

Sangang-wuchang: Neo-Confucian doctrine with three cardinal guides (ruler guides subject; father, son; and husband, wife) and five constant virtues (*ren-yi,-li,-zhi-xin*)

Sangong liuyuan: emperor's harem

Sanhuang Wudi: three primordial sovereigns and five mythological emperors

Sanmenxia: a gorge at the Yellow River

Shanban: Chinese flat-bottomed boat

Shanghen wenxue: literary movement castigating Cultural Revolution

Shanshuihua: traditional Chinese painting of mountains and rivers

Shao: to grill (v.)

Shaoshu minzu: ethnic minority

Shegeng: snake soup, popular in Guangdong

Sheng-dan-jing-chou: roles in Chinese operas—men, women, men with painted faces, and clowns

Shengjian: Shanghai fried dumplings

Shi: (1) poetry; (2) poem; (3) stone

Shihuangdi: First Emperor of Qin dynasty

Shitou-jianzi-bu: "paper-rock-scissors"

Shou: cultural symbol of longevity

Shougongyi: handicraft

Shuaijiao: wrestling

Shuangmianxiu: double-sided embroidery

Shuchang: place for storytelling

Shunfeng'er: clairvoyant supernatural being

Shuochang: storytelling and ballad singing

Shuxiang: any Twelve Zodiac Animal

Si: (1) string; (2) silk

Sinicize: to make Chinese in character (v.)

Songzhong: to care for a dying relative (v.)

Staple: U-shaped metal driven into a door surface. Holding a **hasp**, it serves as a handle and a doorbell

Su: (1) Jiangsu cuisine; (2) vegetarian

Suanlatang: hot and sour soup

Suanrong lajiang: garlic red pepper sauce

Suirenshi: prehistoric mythical leader who first made fire

Sully: soil or stain

Sun Yat-sen: first president of the Republic of China (1912–1925)

Suyu: popular sayings, often unpolished

Sycee: *yinding*—lumps of pure silver

Tang: soup

Tanggua: maltose candy

Tangrenjie: Chinatown

Tangyuan: also *yuanxiao*, rice dumpling

Tao (or Dao): (1) Taoist doctrine; (2) the Way

Tezhong gongyi: special craft

Tian: (1) heaven; (2) sky

Tiangan: ten heavenly stems. See also **dizhi.**

Tiangong: Heavenly Palace

Tianmenzhen: invulnerable military array

Tiaofangzi: hopscotch

Tiaoma: leapfrog game

Tiaopijin: children's game using rubber bands

Tijianzi: to kick a shuttlecock (v.)

Tongsu changfa: a style of popular singing

Tonsure: to shave the head of (v.)

Touhu: ancient game of arrow throwing

Trellis: a structure with a crisscross pattern, for the support of vines

Tu: dirt

Tudiye: local god of land

Tui: legs

Tuitiehuan: to push an iron ring (v.)

Weiqi: board game of Go

Wenmiao: Confucian temple

Wubishuma: Chinese computer input method

Xi: cultural symbol of happy marriage

Xiabing xiejiang: mythical marine army

Xian: celestial being; immortal

Xiang: Hunan cuisine

Xiangqi: Chinese chess

Xiangsheng: comic dialogue

Xiaocheng: Hinayana sect of Buddhism

Xiaochi: snack

Xiaopin: skit

Xiehouyu: two-part allegorical sayings

Xieyi: freehand brushwork in painting

Xingseng: itinerant monk

Xionghuang: arsenic sulphide

Xiongnu: Hun

Xiqu: traditional operas

Xirang: magic earth

Xiu: to embroider (v.)

Xiwangmu: Queen Mother of the West

Xiyang yueqi: Western musical instruments

Xuanzhi: rice paper

Yangge: rural folk dance of North China

Yangliuqing nianhua: Chinese New Year paintings of Yangliuqing style

Yangrou paomo: bread with mutton soup, popular in Xi'an

Yanhuang zisun: a name for the Chinese

Yanyu: easily understood, familiar sayings

Yao: Yao ethnic minority

Yecha: Yaksa, malevolent spirit

Yinhe: Milky Way

Youchaoshi: prehistoric mythical leader who invented shelter

Youtiao: deep-fried dough. See also **guozi.**

Youzi sifu: traveling men and their women at home—a theme of Chinese literature

Yuanbao: shoe-shaped gold or silver ingots

Yuanlin: garden

Yuanxiao: rice dumpling. See also **tangyuan.**

Yuanyang: (1) mandarin ducks (cultural symbol of eternal love); (2) an affectionate couple

Yue: Guangdong cuisine

Yuebing: moon cake

Yuefu: official conservatory of Han dynasty

Yuhuang Dadi: Jade Emperor of Heaven

Zaju: poetic drama set to music

Zao Wangye: Kitchen God

Zha: (1) to construct with bamboo strips or metal wires (v.); (2) to deep-fry (v.)

Zhang: unit of length (about 10 feet)

Zharan: bandhnu or printing by tying part of cloth to create patterns

Zhe: Zhejiang cuisine

Zheng: to steam (v.)

Zhezhi: paper folding; origami

Zhi: to weave (v.)

Zhima shaobing: cakes with sesame seeds

Zhongguo: China

Zhongguoren: Chinese

Zhongqiujie: Mid-Autumn Festival

Zhongshanlang: (1) wolf character of a tale; (2) an ungrateful person

Zhu: (1) to boil (v.); (2) bamboo (n.)

Zhuang: Zhuang ethnic minority

Zhuangguai: game of knee-bumping

Zhuangyuan: The Scholar—first winner of the imperial examination at the national level

Zhushi: staple food, usually carbohydrates

Zongzi: rice dumpling in bamboo or reed leaves, a snack for *Duanwujie*

REFERENCES

Aarne, Antti Amatus. 1971. *The Types of the Folk-tale: A Classification and Bibliography*. Translated and enlarged by Stith Thompson. New York: Lenox Hill Publishing & Distributing Company.

An, Zhimin. 1984. "Qian lun zaoqi huabei de xin shiqi wenhua" ("On the Early Neolithic Cultures in North China"). (Translated by Elaine Wong and edited by Bryan Gordon.) *Kaogu* (*Archeology*) 10: 936–944.

Ashliman, D. L. 2002. "Folktales from China." In *Folklore and Mythology Electronic Texts*. Available at www.pitt.edu/~dash/folktexts.html. (Accessed May 2, 2005).)

Baoliandeng (*Magic Lotus Lantern*). 1999. Adapted by Wang Dawei, produced by Sheng Chongqing, and directed by Chang Guangxi. Shanghai meishu dianying zhipian chang (Shanghai Art Film Studio). Videodisc.

Birch, Cyril, ed. 1967. *Anthology of Chinese Literature: From Early Times to the Fourteenth Century*. New York: Grove Press.

Birch, Cyril, and Donald Keene, eds. 1987. *Anthology of Chinese Literature: From the Fourteenth Century to the Present Day*. New York: Grove/Atlantic.

Børdahl, Vibeke, ed. 1999. *The Eternal Storyteller: Oral Literature in Modern China.* (*Zhongguo shuochang wenxue*). Richmond, Surrey: Curzon Press.

Central Intelligence Agency (CIA). 2004. *The World Factbook.* Available at www.odci.gov/cia/publications/factbook/geos/ch.html. (Accessed March 22, 2005).

Chang, Jie, ed. 2004. "Zhongguo shi shijie shang zui zao faxian jilu yanhua guojia" ("China Was the Earliest to Discover and Record Cliff Paintings")." *Shenzhen News* Available at www.sznews.com/n1/ca1213510.htm. (Accessed January 16, 2005).

Chen, Guoying, ed. 1988. *Liaozhai zhiyi lianhuanhua gushi xuan* (*Picture Books of Selected "Strange Tales of a Make-do Studio"*). Tianjin: Tianjin renmin meishu chubanshe (Tianjin People's Art Publisher).

Chen, Puqing, et al., eds. 1993. *Li jing qian nian heng kua qun shu de 199 ge zhongguo jingdian tonghua* (*Classic Chinese Tales: 199 Classic Fairytales from Books Written in a Period of 1,000 Years*). Taipei: Sanyanshe (Three Words Press).

"China Welcomes 1.3 Billionth Citizen in Mixed Mood." 2005. *People's Daily Online* (January). Available at http://english.people.com.cn/200501/07/eng20050107_169895.html. (Accessed April 8, 2005).

Chinese Folk Art. 2003. "Chinese Huxian Peasant Paintings' Background." In *Chinese Peasant Paintings* Available at www.chinesefolkart.com/peasantpaintings/huxian/. (Accessed January 18, 2005).

Davis, Edward, ed. 2004. *The Encyclopedia of Contemporary Chinese Culture*. London: Routledge.

DeFrancis, John, ed. 2003. *ABC Chinese-English Comprehensive Dictionary*. Honolulu: University of Hawaii Press.

Duanqiao (*The Broken Bridge*). 2000. Produced by Sun Jiren. Tianjin wenhua yishu yinxiang chubanshe (Tianjin Culture and Art Audio and Video Publisher). Videodisc.

Eberhard, Wolfram. 1983. *A Dictionary of Chinese Symbols: Hidden Symbols in Chinese Life and Thought*. Translated by G. L. Campbell. London: Routledge.

Gan, Bao. 1995. *Sou shen ji tongsu huaben* (*Record of Searching for Supernatural Beings in Vernacular Chinese*). Edited by Hu Yinglin, 1551–1602. Translated by Wang Yigong and Tang Shuwen from classic Chinese. Shanghai: Shanghai guji chubanshe (Shanghai Classics Publishing House).

"Hong Kong in Figures." 2005. In *Census & Statistics*. Available at www.info.gov.hk/censtatd/eng/hkstat/hkinf/population_index.html. (Accessed May 2, 2005).

Hou, Hui, ed. 2003. *Zhongguo shenhua gushi jingxuan* (*Best Selected Chinese Tales*). Beijing: Zhongguo da baike quanshu chubanshe (The Great Chinese Encyclopedia Publisher).

"How Many Words Are There in the English Language?" 2004. In *AskOxford*. Available at www.askoxford.com/asktheexperts/faq/aboutwords/numberwords. (Accessed March 25, 2005).

Hu Qiaomu et al, eds. 2000. *Zhongguo da baike quanshu* (*The Great Chinese Encyclopedia*). Beijing: Zhongguo da baike quanshu chubanshe (The Great Chinese Encyclopedia Publisher).

Hua pi (*The Painted Skin*). 1966. Adapted and directed by Huang Buyi and Bao Fang. Hong Kong fenghuang changcheng (Hong Kong Phoenix and Great Wall Studio). Videodisc.

Hua zhong ren (*A Beauty in a Painting Scroll*). 1962. Directed by Wang Bin. Changchun dianying zhipianchang (Changchun Film Studio). Videodisc. 90 minutes.

Ji, Xiao-bin, ed. 2003. *Facts about China*. New York: H.W. Wilson.

Jing, Xuan, reteller. 1993. *Fengsu gushi* (*Tales of Social Customs*). Xi'an: Weilai chubanshe (Future Publishing House).

Latsch, Marie-Luise. 1984. *Chinese Traditional Festivals*. (China Spotlight Series). Beijing: New World Press.

Li, Lulu, ed. 2005. *Zhongguo jie, tushuo minjian chuantong jieri* (*Chinese Holidays: An Illustrated Account of Chinese Traditional Festivals*). Fuzhou: Fujian renmin chubanshe (Fujian People's Press).

Lin, Zhiman, and Yu Yongyu, eds. 2002. *Zhonghua diangu* (*Quotations of Classic Chinese Literature*). 4 vols. Beijing: Zhongguo xiju chubanshe (China Theater Publisher).

Liu, Qiulin, and Liu Jian, eds. 2000. *Zhonghua jixiangwutudian* (*Pictorial Dictionary of Chinese Symbols of Good Luck*). Tianjin: Baihua wenyi chubanshe (A Hundred Flowers Press).

Liu, Xiang. 2002. *Shan hai jing* (*Classics of Seas and Mountains*). 77 B.C.–6 B.C. Collated by Liu Xin (?–A.D. 23). Beijing: Hualing chubanshe (Hualing Publishing House).

Mu guiying da po tianmenzhen (*Mu Guiying Breaks the Heavenly Gate Formation*). 2000. Produced by Guo Jinglong. Guangdong changjin yingxiang youxian gongsi (Guangdong Changjin Audio and Video Company Ltd.). Videodisc.

Na, Ren, ed. 2005. *Shenhua gushi* (zhonghua ertong yuedu jingdian V) (*Fairy Tales*) (Reading Classics for Chinese Children No. 5). Tongliang, Inner Mongolia: Inner Mongolian shaonian ertong chubanshe (Inner Mongolian Young Adult and Children's Publishing House).

Nezha chuanqi (*The Legend of Nezha*). 2003. Adapted by Wu Nan, Meng Yao, and Bian Zhihong. Produced by Yu Peixia. Directed by Chen Jiaqi and Cai Zhijun. Zhongguo guoji dianshi zonggongsi (China International Film Corporation). Videodisc.

"Oregon Trail." 2004. In *ThinkQuest*. New York: Oracle Education Foundation. Available at http://library.thinkquest.org/CR0210182/games.html. (Accessed May 2, 2005).

Pearson, Emma, and Nirmala Rao. 2003. "Socialization Goals, Parenting Practices, and Peer Competence in Chinese and English Preschoolers." *Early Child Development and Care* 173(1): 131–46.

Perkins, Dorothy. 2000. *Encyclopedia of China: The Essential Reference to China, Its History and Culture*. New York: Facts on File.

The Permanent Mission of China to the United Nations. 2004. "About China." Available at http://un.fmprc.gov.cn/eng/c2802.html. (Accessed March 22, 2005).

Pu, Songling. 2000. *Liaozhaizhiyi* (*Strange Tales of a Make-do studio*). 1640–1715. Reprint. Jinan, Shangdong: Qi-lu Shushe (Shandong Publisher).

Qi, Yusheng, ed. 2002. *Zhonghua chengyu diangu* (*Literary Quotations of Chinese Proverbs*). 4 vols. Jilin: Sheying chubanshe (Photography Press).

Qin xianglian. 1955. Produced by Li Yan. Directed by Xu Suling. Changchun dianying zhipianchang (Changchun Film Studio). Videodisc.

Qu, Yang, reteller. 1996. *Chatu ben zhongguo yuyan: shijie zhuming yuyan zhencang xilie* (*Chinese Fables with Illustrations: World Classic Collectible Fables Series*). Taiyuan: Beiyue wenyi chubanshe (North Mountain Literary Press).

"Registered Population." 2005. In *National Statistics*. Available at www.chinapop.gov.cn/rkzh/zgrk/tjgb/t20040616_13700.htm. (Accessed May 2, 2005).

Rosenberg, Donna. 1994. *World Mythology: An Anthology of the Great Myths and Epics*. Lincolnwood, Ill.: NTC Publishing Group.

"Shenhua gushi" ("Tales"). 2004. In *Zhongguo ertong wenxue wang* (*Chinese Children's Literature Net*). Available at www.61w.cn/index.htm. (Accessed February 10, 2005).

Tian, Ye, ed. 2005. *Shentong zhishi leyuan* (minjian gushi kewai duwu) (*Folktales for Extracurricular Readings* (Knowledge Fairyland for Prodigies Series). Hohhot: Yuanfang chubanshe (Faraway Places Publishing House).

Tian xian pei (*A Fairy's Marriage to a Man*). 1955. Adapted by Sang Hong and directed by Shi Hui. Shanghai dianying zhipianchang (Shanghai Film Studio). Videodisc.

Ting, Nai-tung. 1978. *A Type Index of Chinese Folktales in the Oral Tradition and Major Works of Non-religious Classical Literature*. Edited by Lauri Honko. Helsinki: Acadamia Scientiarum Fennica.

"2004 Macao in Figures." 2005. In *Statistics and Census Service*. Available at www.dsec.gov.mo/english/indicator/e_mn_indicator.html. (Accessed May 2, 2005).

Wang, Yicheng, reteller. 1993. *Yuyan gushi* (*Chinese Fables*). Xi'an: Weilai chubanshe (Future Publishing House).

Wang, Yufen, Zhu Yunling, Liu Shuying, and Xu Chen. 2002. *Chuzhong wenyanwen quan jie yi dian tong, si-nian zhi.* (*Analysis of and Answers to the Questions Concerning Middle School Classic Chinese Texts from the Latest Textbooks for the 9-Year Compulsory Education Curriculum*). Edited by Zhang Guangluo. Shijiazhuang: Hebei jiaoyu chubanshe (Hebei Education Press).

Wu, Cheng'en. 1982. *Xi you ji* (*Journey to the West*). (1582). Reprint. Beijing: Foreign Languages Press.

Wu, Jingrong, ed. 1999. *A Chinese-English Dictionary*. Beijing: The Commercial Press.

Xi you ji (cartoon collectable edition). 2002. Based on Wu Cheng'en's *Journey to the West*. Directed by Fang Runnan. Zhongguo guoji dianshi zonggongsi (China International Television Corporation). Videodisc. 52 episodes.

Xing, Zhe. 2005. "Shenhua chuanshuo" ("Tales and Folklore"). In *Zhongguo shici wang* (*China Poem Net*). Available at http://poetic.ayinfo.cn/sccs/shenhua/000.htm. (Accessed May 2, 2005).

Xu, Zhensheng, ed. 2002. *Xinhua chengyu cidian* (*Xinhua Dictionary of Idioms*). Beijing: Shangwu yinshuguan (Commercial Press).

Yuan, Ke, ed. 1990. *Zhongguo shenhua gushi da quan jing bian lianhuanhua* (*Chinese Tales: A Fine Collection of Picture Books*). Vol. 4. Hangzhou: Zhejiang shaonian ertong chubanshe (Zhejiang Young Adult and Children Publisher).

Zhang, Chao, ed. 2004. *Zui xin ban chatu chengyu gushi* (*Proverbial Stories, Latest Edition with Illustrations*). Beijing: Zhaohua chubanshe (Morning Flower Publisher).

Zhang, Juzhong, et al. 1999. "Oldest Playable Musical Instruments Found at Jiahu Early Neolithic Site in China." *Nature* 401(6751). Available at *EBSCOhost* (online database), (http://search.epnet.com/login.aspx?direct=true&db=aph&an=2359173. (Accessed April 2, 2005).

Zhang, Wenjun, Zhao Zhimin, and Qu Guanhua. 2002. *Gaozhong wenyanwen quan jie yi dian tong* (*Analysis of and Answers to the Questions Concerning Classic Chinese in High School Textbooks*). Edited by Zhang Guangluo. Shijiazhuang: Hebei jiaoyu chubanshe (Heibei Education Press).

Zhang, Zengmu, ed. 2001. *Xi you ji lianhuanhua* (*Picture Books of "Journey to the West"*). Shijiazhuang: Hebei meishu chubanshe (Hebei Art Press).

"Zhongguo si da minjian chuanshuo gushi" ("Four Great Chinese Classic Folktales"). 2003. In *Zhongguo minjian gushi wang* (*Chinese Folktales Net*). Available at www.6mj.com. (Accessed May 2, 2005).

Zi, Niu, reteller. 1993. *Shenhua gushi* (*Chinese Tales*). Xi'an: Weilai chubanshe (Future Publishing House).

INDEX

Abbot, 116, 119
Analect, The, 27. *See also* Confucius
Ancestry, common. *See* Huaxia
Ang Lee, 22
Aquila, 107. *See also* Lyra
Architecture, 25. *See also Dougong*
Art, folk, 25
Art of War, 192. *See also* Sun Tzu
Assassin. *See* "Unfolded Map Reveals a Dagger, An," *See also Hero* (movie)
Atoning, for past misconduct, 153
Avalokitesvara. *See* Guanyin
Axe, magic, 85, 143

Baigujing, 153. *See also* "Monkey King Strikes the White-bone Demon Three Times"
Ballet, 22. *See also* Dance
Bamboo
    books, 147, 147illus.
    cover, 128, 129
    crafts, made of, 56
    flute, 81, 128
    Forest, 119, 121, 122
    leaves, 40, 172. *See also Zongzi*
    pipes, 180
    slips, for divination, 83
    sticks, burning, 168, 169. *See also* Firecrackers
    tube, 89, 143

Bao Zheng
    courage, seed of, 132
    magic mirror of, 132
    most upright official, 100
    strange encounter with fox, 132
"Bao Zheng and the Fox Fairy," 131–34
Bat, 17
Baxian, 127, 131illus. *See also* Immortal
    battle intervened by Guanyin, 130
    burning sea, 129
    crossing sea, 128
    killing dragon prince, 129
Beggar,
    filthy, in street, 152
    immortal as, 76
    immortal's spirit in body of lame, 127
    in red cloak, 168
Bean sprout salad, 45–46. *See also* Recipes
Beauty
    in conspiracy, 192
    on painting scroll. *See* "Beauty on a Painting Scroll, A"
    with poker face, 187
"Beauty on a Painting Scroll, A" 75–78
Beef, 48. *See also* Recipes
Birth
    after protracted pregnancy, 73, 123, 187
    from dead body, 142
    in egg-shaped space. *See* Pangu
    as flesh ball, 73, 131
    from gourd, 108

Dragon (*Cont.*)
    lover for. *See* "Professed Dragon Lover,
        A"
    marking land. *See* Yinglong
    palace. *See* Palace: Dragon
    pearl. *See Longzhu*
    saliva, 187. *See also* Phlegm; Spittle;
        Turtle, sight of
    totem, 165
Dragon Prince, 74, 74illus., 129–30
Dragon Princess, 80–83, 122, 200–02. *See
        also* "Gunyin, Goddess of Mercy"
    bringing rainfall with *longzhu*, 82. *See
        also Longzhu*
    with Guanyin, 122
    marriage with human, 83
    turning into fish, 121
"Dragon Princess," 80–83
Dreams
    of becoming a cricket, 91. *See also*
        "Cricket Boy, A"
    of becoming immortal, 175
    of child of nobility, 131
    of feeling strange in chest, 152
    fox fairy in, 134
    of giving birth to child with dark
        complexion, 131
    of Gunyin prior to pregnancy, 122
    of husband in extreme cold, 110
    of marriage. *See* "No Sycee Buried Here
        But Three Hundred *Liang*"
    of shackled mother, 84
    of Taoist priest, 73. *See also* Taoist
        priest
Drought, 12, 74–74, 80–81, 98
Drum
    dance. *See* Dance
    and Flower, 54. *See also* Games
Duanwu Festival, 40, 164. *See also* "Origin
        of the *Duanwu* Festival, The";
        Zongzi
Duilian, 169, 169illus. *See also* Chinese
        New Year

Eagle and Chicks, 52–53, 53illus. *See also*
        Games
Economic reform, 5, 29
"Eight Immortals Crossing the Sea,"
        127–30
Embroidery, 56, 77–78, 103, 179, photo
        insert
Emperor
    celestial. *See Yuhuang Dadi*
    dissipation of, 75–77
    drowned, 78
    humiliated, 111
    killing himself, 192
Eternity, elixir of, 111. *See also*
        Immortality, pills of
Ethnicity, 6. *See also Shaoshu minzu*
Exorciser, 123, 151. *See also* Sword: magic
        wooden

Fairy
    Field-snail. *See* "Field-snail Fairy, The"
    fox. *See* "Bao Zheng and the Fairy Fox"
    reviving mortals, 77, 117
    Seventh, the. *See Qixiannü*
Family planning, 5. *See also* Population
Famine, 12, 81, 98
Fan, magic palm, 86. *See also* "Monkey
        King and the Iron an Princess"
Female, dressed like male, 94–95, 136
"Field-snail Fairy, The" 78–80
Filial piety, 30, 97
Firecrackers, 164illus., 168. *See also*
        Chinese New Year; *Duilian*
First Emperor of Qin. *See Shihuangdi*
"Fishing for a Sword Dropped into a River
        from a Moving Boat," 184
Flesh ball, 73, 131–32. *See also* Birth
Flood. *See also* Deluge
    caused by dragons, 75, 80
    from leaking sky, 166. *See also* Nüwa
    used to drown opponents, 78, 117, 129
Food, Chinese, 35–36. *See also*
        Jiachangcai; Recipes
    in Chinese restaurants in America, 35
    major cuisines of, 35

"Foolish Old Man Tries to Remove Two Mountains, A," 157–58
"Forgot How to Walk Back Home," 182
Forms, transformation of, 28, 88, 153, 155, 156
"Forsaken Wife and Her Unfaithful Husband, A" 97–100
Four great classics, 27–28
Fox
  concubine. *See also* Concubine
  fairy, 132–34
  of nine tails, 143
  spirit, 86
  tricking tiger. *See* "Fox and a Tiger, A—Who Is the Real King of the Jungle?"
"Fox and a Tiger, A—Who Is the Real King of the Jungle?" 65–66
"Frog in a Well, A," 64
Fuma, 98. *See also* Chen Shimei
Fusang, 173. *See also* Hou Yi; Sun

Games, 51–55
Gang of Four, 12. *See also* Great Cultural Revolution; Jiang Qing; Mao Zedong
Garden, Chinese, 25
Ghee, 56. *See also Minjian gongyi*; Tibet
Giant, 75, 142, 143,158
God
  of creation. *See* Pangu
  of dragon head. *See* Pangu
  of fire. *See* Zhurong
  of fountain, 123
  of kitchen. *See Zao Wangye*
  of land. *See Tudiye*
  of river, 143
  of water. *See* Gonggong
  of well, 133, 133illus.
  of wind, thunder, lightning, or rain, 84, 132
Goddess
  of creation. *See* Nüwa
  of Death and Longevity. *See Xiwangmu*

of healing, 83–85, 123–24. *See also* San Shengmu
of Mercy. *See* Guanyin
of Moon. *See* Chang'e
of the sailors. *See* Mazu
who eliminated *nian. See* Ziwei
who married with mortal, 84. *See also* San Shengmu
of wind, thunder, lightning, and rain, 84
Gonggong, 142, 144, 166, 169. *See also* Great Yu; Gun; Nüwa
Gongxi facai, 169. *See also* Chinese New Year
Gourd, bottle
  baby girl in, 108
  of flames, 129–30
  sucking smoke of demon's spirit, 151
Goutuizi. See "Man with a Dog's Leg, A"
Great Cultural Revolution, 12–13, 28
Great Wall, 108, photo insert
  dead husband in. *See* "Meng Jiang Wails at the Great Wall"
  length of, 108
Great Yu. *See also* "Gun and Yu Conquer the Deluge"
  fighting flood, 142–44. *See also* Gonggong
  miraculous birth of, 142. *See also* Gun
  scaring wife into rock, 144
  transformation into bear, 143–44
Guan, 15. *See also Miao*; Taoism: church; *Wenmiao*
Guanshiyin. *See* Guanyin
Guanyin. *See also* "Guanyin, Goddess of Mercy"
  assigning disciples to Tang Seng, 153. *See also* Tang Seng
  bestowing children, 119illus., 122
  disciples of, 121. *See also* Dragon Princess
  giving Tang Seng magic ring hat. *See* Magic ring hat
  helping Monkey King conquer demon, 86
  intervention in battle. *See* "Eight Immortals Crossing the Sea"
  Sinicization of, 119

"Guanyin, Goddess of Mercy," 119–22

Guanyin Pusa. *See* Guanyin; Pusa

Gun. *See also* "Gun and Yu Conquer the Deluge"

 giving birth to son in death, 142. *See also* Great Yu

 stealing magic earth, 142. *See also* Magic earth

 vanishing as yellow dragon, 142

"Gun and Yu Conquer the Deluge," 142–44

Guqu, 30, photo insert. *See also* Quyi; Storytelling

Han (dynasty), 6, 191. *See also* Qin; *Yuefu*

Han (people). *See* Hanren

Handan-xuebu. See "Forgot How to Walk Back Home"

Handkerchief, Drop the, 54. *See also* Games

Hanren, 6. *See also* Han (dynasty); *Shaoshu minzu*

Hanzi, 8–9. *See also Hanyu Pinyin*; Homophone

 computer input of, 9

 most frequently used, 8

Hanyu Pinyin, 9. *See also Putonghua*

Herder. *See* Bao Zheng; "Cowherd and Weaving Girl"; Long Nü

Hero (movie), 191

Himalayas, the, 3

History, Chinese. *See also* Great Cultural Revolution; Great Leap Forward; North Expedition; People's Republic of China; Republic of China; *Xia-shang-zhou* Chronology Project

 civil wars, 11

 dynasties, 10. *See also* Han (dynasty); Ming; Qin; Qing; Tang

 invasion by coalition of foreign powers, 11

 legendary rulers. *See Sanhuang Wudi*

 prehistoric, 10

Homophone, 8, 17

Hong Kong

 ceding and reclaiming, 11

 resident population of, 5

Honglou meng, 27. *See also* Four great classics

Hongniang, 112, 115illus. *See also* "Romance of Zhang Gong and Cui Yingying, A"

Horse. *See also* Dragon: Horse; Zodiac animals, Chinese

 Jumping, 53. *See also Games*

 lost, blessing in disguise. *See* "Steed Lost Is More Horses Gained, A"

Hou Yi. *See also* Chang'e; Mid-Autumn Festival

 quest for immortality, 174. *See also* Mt. Kunlun; *Xiwangmu*

 shooting down suns, 173

Huapi, 149

Huaxia, 6. *See also Sanhuang Wudi*

Hun. *See* Xiongnu

Husband

 faithful, 105

 murderous. *See* Chen Shimei

 possessed, 150

 sailing to sky to join wife, 106

 unfaithful, 117

Immortal. *See also* Baxian

 as beggar. *See* "Dancing Crane, A"

 belief in, 14

 as deified human beings, 15

 dreaming of becoming. *See* Dreams

 gardener of magic flower. *See* "Twin Sisters and the Magic Flower, The"

 keeping monster at bay, 168

 teaching martial arts. *See* "Magic Lotus Lantern, The"

Immortality, pills of, 174. *See also* Eternity, elixir of

Imperial examination. *See Keju*

Incantation. *See also* Charm

 to enlarge and shrink magic fan, 87

 inscribed on tablets, 123

Inscription, 81, 123, 143

Love (*Cont.*)
  helped by
    animal, 107
    deity, 76–78, 84–85
    human. *See* Hongniang
    loyal friend, 84–85, 117
  platonic, 27
  symbol of, 95, 96illus., 101illus.
  trysts, 114
Lyra, 107. *See also* Aquila

Macao
  ceding and reclaiming, 11
  origin of city name, 122
  population of, 5
Magic earth, 143. *See also* Great Yu; Gun
"Magic Lotus Lantern, The," 83–85
Magic Lotus Lantern, The (opera), 22
Magic ring hat, 153. *See also* Gunyin;
    Monkey King
Magpie, 106, 107illus. *See also* Cultural
    symbols; *Queqiao*
Majiang, 51, 51illus.
Malan flower. *See* "Twin Sisters and the
    Magic Manlan Flower, The"
Male dominance, 94, 101, 103, 118, 187
"Man with a Dog's Leg, A," 161–62
Mandarin. *See Putonghua*
Mandarin ducks, 19, 75, 75illus., 84, 95,
    105. *See also* Cultural symbols
Maodun. See "Invincible Spear Versus
    Impenetrable Shield, The"
Mao Tse-tung. *See* Mao Zedong
Mao Zedong, 11, 28. *See also* Great
    Cultural Revolution; Jiang Qing
Mazu, 124illus.
  sightings of, 124
  worship of, 122, 124
"Mazu, Mother Goddess of the Sea,"
    122–24
Mencius, 14. *See also* Confucius
Mendanghudui, 96. *See also* Wedding:
    involuntary
"Meng Jiang Wails at the Great Wall,"
    108–11

Miao, 15. *See also Guan*; *Wenmiao*
Mid-Autumn Festival, 164. *See also*
    "Origin of the Mid-Autumn Festival,
    The"; *Yuebing*
Milky Way, 106–7. *See also* Aquila; Lyra
Min yueqi, 20. *See also Xiyangyueqi*
Ming, 24, 101,119
Minjian gongyi, 56. *See also Shougongyi*
Monkey. *See also* Zodiac animals, Chinese
  fishing moon. *See* "Monkeys Fishing the
    Moon"
  killed accidentally by tiger, 71
  king (animal), 63
  King (god), 15, 21, 28, 72, 119,
    156illus. *See also* "Monkey King
    and the Iron Fan Princess";
    "Monkey King Strikes the
    White-bone Demon Three Times"
"Monkey and a Tiger, A," 69–71
"Monkey King and the Iron Fan Princess,"
    86–88
"Monkey King Strikes the White-bone
    Demon Three Times," 152–56
"Monkeys Fishing the Moon," 62–64
Moon
  cake. *See Yuebing*
  Festival. *See* Mid-Autumn Festival
  Goddess. *See* Chang'e
  god's eye becoming, 165. *See also*
    Pangu
Mother
  cabbage turned into, 69
  domineering, 103
  eaten by wolf, 68
  Goddess. *See* Mazu
  Queen of the West. *See* Xiwangmu
  savage, 172–73
  saved by son. *See* San Shengmu
  sister-in-law. *See* Saoniang
Mountain. *See also* Mt. Qomolangma; Mt.
    Qunlun
  digging, 144, 157–58
  of Flames, 86–88. *See also* Fan, magic
    palm
  god's limbs turned into, 165

imprisonment in or beneath, 144, 153, 156

moved by deity, 130, 158

pillar of heaven, 166

rebel in. *See* Mu Guiying

Movies, Chinese, 21

Mt. Qomolangma, 3. *See also* Himalayas, the

Mt. Qunlun, 58, 174. *See also Xiwangmu*

Mu Guiying. *See* "Women Generals of the Yang Family and Commander-in-Chief Mu Guiying"

Mulan, 135illus.

"Mulan Fights in the Guise of a Male Soldier," 135–38

Music, 20. *See also* Instruments, musical; Vocals

Muslim enclaves, 15

Nationalists, 11. *See also* Chiang Kai-shek; Taiwan

coalition and united front with Communists, 11

retreat to Taiwan, 11

Nezha

born as ball of flesh, 73

self-sacrifice and reborn, 75

slaying dragon, 74, 74illus.

"Nezha Fights Sea Dragons," 72–75

Nian. See "Origin of Chinese New Year and Its Customs, The"

Niangao. See also Jiaozi

food south of Yangtze, 35

interpretation of, 38

recipe for, 38. *See also* Recipes

"No Sycee Buried Here But Three Hundred *Liang*," 185–86

North Expedition, 11. *See also* Sun Yat-sen

"Number Is Security," 180–81

Nun, 120, 123

Nüwa, 167illus. *See also* "Origin of Human Beings, The"

Opera

Beijing. *See Jingju*

concept of time and space, 21

and folktales, 21

performances and roles of, 21

schools of, 21

types of, 21

Origami, 59

"Origin of Chinese New Year and Its Customs, The,"167–69

"Origin of Human Beings, The," 165–66

"Origin of Kitchen God and the *Jizao* Festival, The," 175–76

"Origin of the *Duanwu* Festival, The," 171–73

"Origin of the Mid-Autumn Festival, The," 173–75

"Origin of the Twelve Zodiac Animals, The," 170–71

"Origin of the World, The," 164–65

"Painted Skin," 149–52

Painting, Chinese

elements of, 24, photo insert

styles of, 25

techniques of, 25

Palace

Dragon, 81–82, 120–21, 122, 128–30

Heavenly, 105–6, 153, 170–71, 174

imperial, 18, 77–78, 180, 192

Pangu. *See* "Origin of the World, The." *See also* Nüwa

Peaches

ripening every thousand years, 128

symbol of longevity, 18

Peacock, 101, 101illus. *See also* Cultural symbols

"Peacock Flying Southeast, A," 101–5

Peasant Painting, 25

People's Republic of China, 11. *See also* Republic of China; Taiwan

Perpetual torture, 175

Phlegm, turning into heart, 152

Pig. *See also* Zodiac animals, Chinese god reborn as, 153. *See also* Monkey King

Pingshu, 30. *See also Quyi*

Sister-in-law
    bent on killing, 133
    nursing brother-in-law. *See Saoniang*
"Smile Worth a Thousand Ounces of Gold,
        A," 187–88
Snake. *See also* Zodiac animals, Chinese
    goddess with lower body of. *See* Nüwa
    incarnation of. *See* "Xu Xuan and His
        White-snake Wife"
    soup, 35
Snob, 96, 103, 115
Soup, hot and sour, 45–47. *See also*
        Recipes
Spittle, 209
Spring and Autumn Period, 11, 27. *See
        also* Confucius; Laozi
"Steed Lost Is More Horses Gained, A,"
        178–79
Storytelling
    forms of. *See Quyi*
    profession of. *See shuochang*
    village, 27
Sun
    god's eye becoming, 165. *See also*
        Pangu
    riding on back of raven, 173. *See also*
        Fusang
    shot by god, 173. *See also* Hou Yi
    twelve divisions of ecliptic, 170. *See
        also* Zodiac animals, Chinese
Sun Tzu, 192
Sun Wu. *See* Sun Tzu
Sun Yat-sen, 11. *See also* Nationalists;
        North Expedition
Sword
    blood stained, as evidence, 100
    dragon slaying, 129
    fishing, dropped into river, 184
    magic wooden, 151

Taiwan, *See also* Chiang Kai-shek;
        Koxinga; Nationalists; Republic of
        China
    history of, 11

Mazu's popularity in, 122. *See also*
        Mazu
    population of, 5
Tang, 11. *See also Tangrenjie*
    monk of. *See* Tang Seng
    music of, 20
    painting of, 51
    poets in, 27, 75, 188–89. *See also* Li Bai
    storytelling in, 30. *See also Shuochang*
Tang (soup), 46–48. *See also* Soup, hot and
        sour
Tang Seng, 86–87, 152–56
    disciples of, 28, 86–88. *See also*
        Monkey King; Pig
Tangrenjie, 11
Tangyuan. See Yuanxiao
Tao Te Ching, 14, 27, 145. *See also
        Analect, The*
Taoism. *See also* Laozi
    church of, 14
        founder of. *See* Zhang Daoling
    secret societies of, 14
Taoist, priest, 84, 150
Tea
    mosquito plunging into, 87
    and name of China, 6
    served to immortal, 125
    serving, 18, photo insert
    terrifying princess, 121
Television, 22
Terra Cotta Soldiers and Horses, 25, photo
        insert
Thieves, animal and human. *See* "Monkey
        and a Tiger, A"
Tiananmen Square, 12
Tiangan and *dizhi*, 36, 170
Tianmenzhen, 139–40, 141. *See also* Mu
        Guiying
Tibet
    local language teaching, 8. *See also
        Putonghua*
    Qinghai-Tibet Plateau, 3
    religion. *See* Lamaism

Tiger. *See also* Zodiac animals, Chinese
  fearing donkey. *See* "Tiger That First
    Sees a Donkey, A"
  goddess with teeth of, 174. *See also*
    Xiwangmu
  nursing baby, 132. *See also* Bao Zheng
  running from fox, 66. *See also* Fox
  running with human thief on back, 70
  white, rescuing dying nun, 120. *See also*
    Guanyin
"Tiger That First Sees a Donkey, A,"
  66–67
Tomato, fried, with eggs, 49. *See also*
    Recipes
Tree
  self-healing. *See* Perpetual torture
  talking, 148, 159
Trysts, 114. *See also* Hongniang
Tudiye, 120, 158. *See also Yuhuang Dadi*
Tuitiehuan, 52, photo insert
Turtle
  giant, 143, 166
  from sea. *See* "Frog in a Well, A"
  sight of, leading to pregnancy, 187
Twelve Girls Band, 23
"Twin Sisters and the Magic Malan
  Flower, The," 158–61

"Unfolded Map Reveals a Dagger, A,"
  190–91
United front, Nationalist-Communist, 11
Urbanization, 5. *See also* Population

Valentine's Day, Chinese, 107
Vocals, 20. *See also* Instruments, musical;
  Music

"Waiting for a Rabbit to Bump into a
  Tree," 183
Weaving Girl. *See* "Cowherd and Weaving
  Girl"
Wedding. *See* Customs: of wedding
  involuntary, 97, 104, 111, 113, 140
Wenmiao, 14. *See also* Confucius; *Guan*;
  Miao

White-snake Wife, 117illus. *See also* "Xu
  Xuan and His White-snake Wife"
Wolf
  eating cat and transforming into its form,
    159
  mimicking mother's voice. *See* "Wolf
    'Mother' "
  ungrateful. *See Zhongshanlang*
"Wolf 'Mother'," 67–69
"Women Generals of the Yang Family and
  Commander-in-Chief Mu Guiying,"
  139–41

Xi Shi, 192
Xi you ji, 15, 27, 38. *See also* Four great
  classics; Monkey King
Xia-shang-zhou Chronology Project, 10
Xiabing xiejiang, 117, 117illus., 128–29
Xian. See Baxian; Immortal
Xiangsheng. 30. *See also Quyi*
Xiaocheng, 15. *See also* Buddhism
Xiaochi, 35
Xiaopin, 31. *See also Quyi*
Xiongnu, 135, 137, 139, 141, 178–79
Xirang. *See* Magic earth
Xiwangmu, 58, 118illus., 128, 174
Xiyangyueqi, 21. *See also Min yueqi*
"Xu Xuan and His White-snake Wife,"
  115–17
Xuan Zang. *See* Tang Seng

Yangliuqing nianhua, 25. *See also* Chinese
  New Year
Yangmen nüjiang, 139–141. *See also* Mu
  Guiying
Yangtze, 1illus., 3, 35, 56, 57, 108
Yecha, 74–75
Yellow River, 10, 143, 172–73. *See also*
  Sanmenxia
Yin and *yang*, 14, 80, 165, 166
Yinhe. See Milky Way
Yinglong, 142, 143. *See also* Great Yu;
  Magic earth
Youzi sifu, 97. *See also Keju*

Yu, 180, 181illus. *See also* "Number Is
    Security"
Yuanxiao, 42. *See also* Recipes
Yuanyang. See Mandarin ducks
Yuebing. See also Mid-Autumn Festival
    favorite snack of Chang'e, 175
    recipe for, 44–45, 44illus. *See also*
        Recipes
Yuefu, 27. *See also* Han (dynasty)
Yuhuang Dadi, 16illus. *See also Xiwangmu*
    daughter of. *See* Cowherd and Weaving
        Girl
    fear of, 122
    giving help, 120, 159, 170, 173
    meting out punishment, 119, 120

Zao Wangye, 175, 177illus.
Zhang Daoling, 14
Zheng Chenggong. *See* Koxinga
Zhezhi, 59. *See also* Origami
Zhongguo. See China, origin of term
Zhongqiujie. See Mid-Autumn Festival
Zhongshanlang, 146. *See also*
    "Compassionate Scholar and an
    Ungrateful Wolf, A"
Zhu Xi, 14. *See also* Confucius
Zhuangyuan, 99, 134. *See also Fuma*; *Keju*
Zhurong,142
Ziwei, 169
Zodiac animals, Chinese, 171illus. *See*
    "Origin of the Twelve Zodiac
    Animals, The"
Zongzi. See also Qu Yuan (cultural hero);
    Qu Yuan (poet)
    recipe for, 40, 40illus. *See also* Recipes

ABOUT THE AUTHOR

HAIWANG YUAN is Associate Professor, Department of Library Public Services and Web Site & Virtual Library Coordinator, Western Kentucky University. He is also Adjunct Instructor of Chinese, Department of Modern Languages and Multicultural Studies, Western Kentucky University. A native of China, Mr. Yuan maintains a Web site, a large portion of which is devoted to Chinese traditions and folktales. He has published widely in professional journals and is a contributor to *The Encyclopedia of Comtemporary Chinese Culture* (2004). He is also recipient of the 1999 Kentucky Libraries Award.